# THE COMPLETE
# HANDBOOK OF
# FRANCHISING

**David D. Seltz** President  •  Seltz Franchising Developments, Inc.

▲▼ **ADDISON-WESLEY PUBLISHING COMPANY**
Reading, Massachusetts • Menlo Park, California • London • Amsterdam • Don Mills, Ontario • Sydney

**Library of Congress Cataloging in Publication Data**

Seltz, David D.
    The complete handbook of franchising.

    1. Franchises (Retail trade)—United States—
Handbooks, manuals, etc. I. Title.
HF5429.235.U5S44        658.8'708        80-27544
ISBN 0-201-07136-3

ABCDEFGHIJ-AL-8987654321

# PREFACE

The objective of this book is to assist in the development of business expansion programs by presenting franchising guidelines and information. The information and data, as well as the various supporting agreements, forms, charts, and tabulations presented here, are believed to be reliable and accurate, but are not guaranteed and should be considered neither endorsement nor recommendation for any specific program or procedure. Anyone intending business use of such material should consult legal counsel.

*New Rochelle, New York*
*September 1981*

D.D.S.

# CONTENTS

Although franchising has been somewhat fettered by such provisions as state and federal regulations requiring "full disclosure," it remains a viable marketing and distributing method. Franchisees "pay their own way," thus providing the franchisor with an affordable means of accelerating expansion, and total efficiency is generally improved as well.

A franchisee submerges some personal identity in return for the greater advantages of large-company reputation and resources. A McDonald's enterprise has a decided edge over "Lee's Burgers," even if the product and service are essentially the same.

During the nationwide economic slowdown of the mid-seventies, less than two percent of franchised establishments were discontinued; this is one indication of the economic stability of franchised establishments.

For maximum effectiveness, a franchisor must observe a number of conditions. Among these are the following:

Careful selection of franchisees

Thorough training of franchisees

Enforcement of standard operating procedures

Utilization and protection of trademark

**SYSTEM—A FRANCHISING KEYWORD**

The essence and success-orientation of franchising—the factors that differentiate it from other business concepts—can be expressed in a single, all-inclusive word: SYSTEM. The "system" distinguishes the untidy, disorganized "greasy spoon" from the sparkling-clean, highly organized franchised hamburger emporium. System signifies discipline, structure, and standardization. System means a multiplicity of collateral services and benefits. It is not the identity of the product or service that distinguishes the franchise—it's the *quality* of the SYSTEM!

**FRANCHISING BENEFITS**

Franchising has enabled manufacturers to retain more control over the conditions of merchandising their product than they would have if they utilized a channel of distribution in which relations with agents or representatives were not as close.

As several writers have pointed out, franchising has provided the last refuge in which a small businessperson can gain a foothold. By merging local capital and energy with national reputation and supervision, and the proven products and techniques of running such a business, an amalgamation is created whereby both parties are equally interested in the success of the business. If local franchises are not successful, the franchisor's program cannot succeed. If the franchisor becomes lax or does not adapt to changing market conditions, the system of franchisees will falter. It is believed that this mutually dependent relationship is responsible for the record of fewer failures in franchising than in other forms of retailing.

Despite recent stringent regulations—both state and federal—the franchising concept is booming. For example, according to the Department of Commerce:

> Franchising sales of goods and services in more than 463,000 outlets are expected to exceed $376 billion in 1981, about 11 percent higher than 1979. Expansion of franchising in a broad range of retail and service industries—including auto products, cosmetics, fast food, lodging, rentals, real estate—is gradually changing the traditional marketing system for consumer goods and services and, at the same time, continues to offer opportunities for small, independent business operations. Over 2 million persons are employed in franchising activities.

Retailing continues to dominate franchising. Retail sales of all firms associated with the franchise system—franchisee owned and company owned—reached an estimated $247 billion in 1978 and accounted for almost 32 percent of all retail sales in the United States.

ONE EXAMPLE: FAST FOODS
The success and popularity of the franchised fast-food restaurant continues. Menu expansion and increasing diversification are aimed at generating more breakfast and dinner business, and expanding customer counts and check averages to offset the rising food, labor, energy, and rental costs.

Sales of franchised fast-food restaurants reached $28 billion in 1980, up 12 percent over the previous year. Such restaurants, which numbered 58,936 in 1979 and 63,001 in 1980, now number about 68,500 units. The increase is expected to continue.

## CURRENT TRENDS

Today's economy is kaleidoscopic—changing gradually and constantly. For a business to endure, its conformance with economic shifts is vital. To remain static is to retrogress. With this in mind, let's evaluate some important trends that may affect business progress.

Trend awareness is particularly important to franchising, and especially so to franchisors. There must be a constant grasp of business changes requiring rapid adaptation on a daily, or almost continuous, basis. Failure to adapt can mean the deterioration, and possibly the demise, of a franchise business and network.

The following descriptions of important current trends will be invaluable to franchisors, helping them to expedite growth and provide the innovativeness that enables franchisees to achieve optimum sales and earnings in their areas.

TREND 1—AREA CONTROLLERSHIP
An area controller is an individual or group that undertakes the acquisition and operation of *multiple units* of a franchise, usually encompassing a viable trading area covered by a single, dominant advertising medium. Area controllers are characteristically well-financed, success-oriented, and good managers. Their designated areas may include from as few as two to as many as forty potential units. The area controller's role is equivalent to that of a "subfranchisor."

Area controllerships have become particularly popular during these inflationary times. Servicing franchisees on a one-by-one basis has become very expensive. Only *one* contact with a single area controller may cover *many* in-effort; the franchisor contributes managerial expertise. Their association will prosper and endure according to the effectiveness of this arrangement.

## TREND 7— FINANCING FLEXIBILITIES

A number of new financing approaches provide leveraging potential to help finance unit expansion.

For example, the concept of leasing is now characterized by new flexibility and new opportunities. In the past only tangible, secured, recoverable assets such as heavy equipment qualified for leasing, and additional personal or corporate recourse was usually requested. Today enterprising leasing companies may go beyond these standards and extend leasing privileges for an entire turnkey operation, including nonsecured intangibles. In some instances, they may even function as collectors, receiving the full amount and remitting the client's portion of the fees.

Another example is an investment vehicle popularly known as MESBIC, developed by the federal government. MESBIC provides exceptionally high financial leverage, accelerated company expansion, and an opportunity to appoint and participate in entrepreneurial management. A number of today's franchisors are beneficiaries of this type of financing.

For a closer look at these and other financing possibilities, see Chapter 7.

## TREND 8— GROWTH OF FRANCHISE ASSOCIATIONS

In recent years, there has been an increase in the formation of franchisee associations and advisory councils, and in franchisee participation in these groups. Although these organizations are usually initiated by the franchisor in order to develop more efficient communication with franchisees, they may also be initiated by the franchisees themselves or by an external trade or industry. Some franchisees may have the opportunity to join and participate in the activities of several such groups.

## TREND 9—ADI IDENTIFICATION OF FRANCHISE AREA

ADI (Area Dominant Influence) is an advertising industry concept. The bottom-line figure sought under this method is the amount of advertising budget required to produce a selected flow of customer traffic and sales within a designated area. In keeping with recent trends, franchise areas are now being defined in terms of marketing and sales-promotion criteria. The response of the franchise industry has been the creation of the cluster concept.

Since one or two outlets can no longer afford the heavy outlays of advertising and promotion needed to saturate a trading area, several stores, or clusters, within a single *media* area will share these costs. The ADI approach has been embraced by a large number of industry giants seeking projected growth in sales. This keeps advertising budgets climbing. For example, McDonald's advertising outlay now exceeds $200 million annually.

## COMPANY OWNERSHIP VERSUS FRANCHISED OWNERSHIP

Often, the change to franchisee ownership, even without the benefit of other changes, can produce dramatic results. Basic to this is the motivation and personal concern that the franchisee brings into the situation. Company employees usually labor at a barely adequate level and are seldom motivated to work more than a 40-hour week, whereas franchisees are motivated by their ownership and potential for increasing profit. Understandably, they will devote more time and attention to the operation of their own business than an employee will devote to the business of an employer.

Company-owned operations typically suffer from a high labor turnover. On the average, these units "turn" 100 percent of their labor one time every six months, at an estimated retraining cost of $3000 to $5000 a person. The lost patronage that results from the subsequent loss of image is an additional and not insignificant cost. On the other hand, the franchisee is far more stable and might be said to be locked-in by the combination of investment and pride of ownership.

## TODAY'S CAPITAL— INTENSIVE NEED FOR ACCELERATED GROWTH

With chains, conglomerates, and discount stores all competing for the consumer dollar, today's competition is not merely dynamic—it's downright voracious! It can easily consume the small entrepreneur who fails to expand; neighborhood loyalty is a thing of the past. Despite the cost of gasoline, today's motorized consumers continue to gravitate toward shopping centers and large department stores where the greatest variety of inventory and merchandising sophistication offer them the opportunity to buy selectively.

Greater capital investment plus working capital are required to compete with these marketing giants. Penetration cannot be effected with minimum capital. Statistics show that the main cause of business failure is that of insufficient capital with which to reach the break-even point. Hence the self-financing factor characteristic of franchising has become a primary consideration.

A research project was recently undertaken for a prominent chain of five-and-ten type variety stores to determine whether local stores would be more profitable on an independently owned or company-owned status. Fourteen stores were selected for testing, each having previously reported annual *losses* ranging between $15,000 and $50,000. The test results showed that if each store had been independently owned and managed under a franchise-type arrangement, it could have become a corporate asset contributing an average of $25,000 a year to parent earnings, while producing satisfactory profits for the local operator.

### ADVANTAGES OF FRANCHISING

- Provides wider and more rapid distribution.
- Allows expansion with less capital.
- Requires fewer company personnel and lower payroll.
- Reduces operating expenses.
- Achieves selective distribution in each territory.
- Attracts dedicated local entrepreneurs who are "locked in," known, and respected in their communties.
- Results in sales- and cost-conscious franchisees who will probably perform better than salaried managers and will be more likely to suggest money-saving ideas and merchandising innovations.
- Improves company image, public relations, and publicity.
- Attracts capital.

**Fig. 1.2** Income statements and cash flow: Comparison of company-owned operation with franchisee ownership ($10^3$).

| | Company owned | Franchisee owned | | Company owned | Franchisee owned | | Company owned | Franchisee owned | |
| --- | --- | --- | --- | --- | --- | --- | --- | --- | --- |
| | | Company statement | Franchisee statement | | Company statement | Franchisee statement | | Company statement | Franchisee statement |
| **Income** | | | | | | | | | |
| Sales | 250.0 | | 250.0 | 400.0 | | 400.0 | 600.0 | | 600.0 |
| Base rent income | | 45.0 | | | 45.0 | | | 45.0 | |
| Rent overage income | | | | | 4.5 | | | 10.5 | |
| Royalty income | | 12.5 | | | 20.0 | | | 30.0 | |
| Total income | 250.0 | 57.5 | 250.0 | 400.0 | 69.5 | 400.0 | 600.0 | 85.5 | 600.0 |
| | | | | | | | | | |
| **Variable expense** | | | | | | | | | |
| Cost of sales | 90.0 | | 85.0 | 144.0 | | 136.0 | 216.0 | | 204.0 |
| Variable labor | 45.0 | | 40.0 | 72.0 | | 64.0 | 108.0 | | 96.0 |
| Payroll taxes and fringes | 7.9 | | 5.0 | 12.6 | | 8.0 | 18.9 | | 12.0 |
| Maintenance | 6.3 | | 5.0 | 10.0 | | 8.0 | 15.0 | | 12.0 |
| Sales promotion | 10.0 | | 7.5 | 16.0 | | 12.0 | 24.0 | | 18.0 |
| Rent overage expense | | | | | | 4.5 | | | 10.5 |
| Royalty expense | | | 12.5 | | | 20.0 | | | 30.00 |
| Total variable expense | 159.2 | | 155.0 | 254.6 | | 252.5 | 381.9 | | 382.5 |
| | | | | | | | | | |
| Contribution to overhead & profit | 90.8 | 57.5 | 95.0 | 145.4 | 69.5 | 147.5 | 218.1 | 85.5 | 217.5 |
| | | | | | | | | | |
| **Fixed expense** | | | | | | | | | |
| Base rent expense | | | 45.0 | | | 45.0 | | | 45.0 |
| Supervisory wages | 25.0 | | | 25.0 | | | 25.0 | | |
| Payroll taxes and fringes | 4.4 | | | 4.4 | | | 4.4 | | |
| Utilities | 25.0 | | 25.0 | 27.0 | | 27.0 | 30.0 | | 30.0 |
| Insurance | 1.0 | | 1.0 | 1.0 | | 1.0 | 1.0 | | 1.0 |
| Property taxes | 7.5 | 7.5 | | 7.5 | 7.5 | | 7.5 | 7.5 | |
| Real-estate depreciation | 15.0 | 15.0 | | 15.0 | 15.0 | | 15.0 | 15.0 | |
| Equipment depreciation | 22.5 | 22.5 | | 22.5 | 22.5 | | 22.5 | 22.5 | |
| Total fixed expense | 100.4 | 45.0 | 71.0 | 102.4 | 45.0 | 73.0 | 105.4 | 45.0 | 76.0 |
| | | | | | | | | | |
| Net profit before taxes | (9.6) | 12.5 | 24.0 | 43.0 | 24.5 | 74.5 | 112.7 | 40.5 | 141.5 |
| | | | | | | | | | |
| Plus depreciation | 37.5 | 37.5 | | 37.5 | 37.5 | | 37.5 | 37.5 | |
| | | | | | | | | | |
| Net cash flow before taxes | 27.9 | 50.0 | 24.0 | 80.5 | 62.0 | 74.5 | 150.2 | 78.0 | 141.5 |

taxes rises to $24,500 at sales of $400,000 and to $40,500 at sales of $600,000, with increases of 96 percent and 224 percent, from profitability at a sales level of $250,000. Cash flow is also increased, reaching $62,000 a year at sales of $400,000 and $78,000 a year at sales of $600,000, the respective increases being 24 percent and 56 percent.

Even more dramatic, however, is the increase in profit before taxes that is earned by the franchisee. At sales of $400,000 a year, net income before taxes increases to $74,500, an increase of 210 percent, and at sales of $600,000 net income before taxes increases to $141,500, an increase of 490 percent.

## BREAK-EVEN ANALYSIS

The break-even analysis illustrated in Figure 1.3 graphically depicts the data shown in Fig. 1.2. Utilizing these contributions to overhead and profit ratios and overhead burdens, it depicts a decrease in break-even point for the operation under franchisee ownership as opposed to company ownership from approximately $280,000 to $185,000 a year, a decrease of 34 percent. It is, of course, this decrease in break-even—a decrease that results from the combination of a contribution to overhead and profit slope increase and overhead decrease—that leads to improved financial performance of the operation under franchisee ownership. Of the two, the more significant is overhead decrease at the $250,000 sales level.

Referring again to Fig. 1.2, note that at each level of increased sales both net profit before taxes and net cash flow before taxes increase under a franchisee owner, but are significantly below levels that would be attainable if the company were able to generate those sales with its own employee-manager. For an operation with sales at or close to break-even, this consideration may be irrelevant. A transfer to franchisee ownership may be the only way in which profitability,

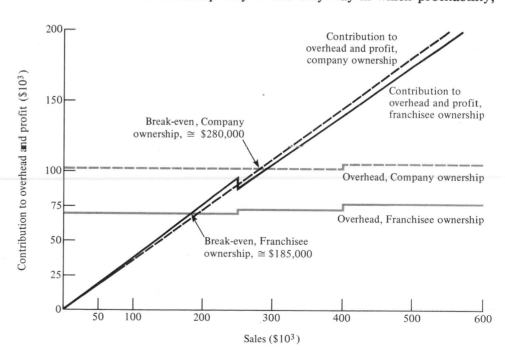

**Fig. 1.3** Break-even analysis: Comparison of company-owned operation (dashed line) with franchisee-owned operation (solid line).

ices. This expectation is often instrumental in an individual's decision to invest in a franchise rather than an independent business. Hence, even though a bargain was received, they require, and rightfully expect, the same services required and expected by a franchisee who pays a proper fee.

### FRANCHISEE FEE ESTABLISHED AT TOO HIGH A LEVEL

Our second franchisor overpriced its franchise. It charged the colossal fee of $100,000! Amazingly enough, seven franchisees were actually recruited, but they were absentee investors—so-called "coupon clippers," who sat at home awaiting dividend checks without becoming involved in the day-to-day operation of the franchise. They completely lacked qualifications for implementing the program.

**PROPER PLANNING AND STRUCTURING**

A franchise program should be designed and structured in the same manner as a high-rise building. Initial plans, carefully and expertly prepared, are needed. All component pieces of the construction—framing, cement, and beams—must be preplanned. Workers and supervisors to shape and mold these materials into their final form must be prescheduled. Arithmetic controls are necessary so that at every point each aspect of cost has been predefined. Projections of income potential based on the rate of occupancy should be at hand.

Most important, a solid foundation is required. Without it, the structure will topple. This foundation consists of two factors:

- Products and/or services that are salable, enduring, and capable of yielding proper earnings.

- In-depth organization that can effectively supervise and administer all aspects of the franchise program.

Initially the typical franchisee is just so much "raw material." The person must be shaped into an effective selling and operating entity. It is the manner in which this shaping takes place—generally during the franchisee's first 60 days of ownership—that often spells the difference between success and failure.

**PLANNING AND STRUCTURING PROCEDURE**

The establishment of a franchise program should be approached in two stages: the preparation of a business "blueprint," or detailed plan, and the preparation of a franchise package containing the "tools" necessary for franchisee recruitment and success. Each of these stages involves a number of vital steps.

**PREPARATION OF A BLUEPRINT**

A blueprint should be prepared and should treat every aspect of the planned program. This blueprint, or detailed plan, may be looked upon as a modus operandi and should contain, as a minimum, the following information:

1. *An assessment of the feasibility of the product or service that is the subject of the franchise program.* Specific questions should be formulated in assessing feasibility, and clear, explicit answers to each of them should be developed. Does the product and/or service exhibit a good potential for franchising on a nationwide basis? Does it have potential for producing

favorable earnings? Most important, is it the kind of product and/or service that is "teachable," or is it too complex to train a newcomer to the field?

2. *An evaluation of the type of franchisee sought.* What criteria represent appropriate selection standards for franchisee appointment? Is the franchisee to be a "working" franchisee or an absentee investor? If the former is the case, what qualifications are required to perform the job function? Must the franchisee exhibit any specific qualities on which training will be preconditioned? If the latter is the case, precisely how is the work to be performed and by whom?

3. *An evaluation of the type of franchise package required.* Of what should the franchise package consist? In answering this question, each aspect of the prospective franchisee's operation should be examined. Requirements for physical structure, equipment, inventory, and franchisor services must be defined. Total cost to the franchisor is a major determinant of franchise fee, so the quality and extent of the franchise package is a factor of critical importance. Establishing a franchise fee requires a measurement of value received by the franchisee—"big earnings" from the money received as a franchise fee should not be the objective. On the one hand, the franchisor should be reimbursed for every legitimate expense incurred in recruiting franchisees and establishing them in business successfully; in addition, a reasonable increment should be retained as an adequate reserve for unexpected emergencies. However, the franchisor should not look substantially beyond that. The anticipated big earnings should be sought as a result of royalties received from successful franchisees. In this light, measurement of value received by the franchisee is gauged with one instrument and one instrument alone: Total cost to the franchisor.

    The franchisee is the "infantry" of the franchise system. The successes of the franchisee can earn many millions of dollars for the franchisor, and the focus of concentration should be franchisee success—NOT the number of franchisees recruited and the franchise fees received or promised from them.

4. *A determination of territorial allotment.* Territorial allotment should be based on solid marketing criteria to ensure that every franchisee, no matter where located, has an equal and excellent chance to succeed. The territory allocated should contain a sufficient number of valid prospects to yield equitable franchisee earnings.

5. *A complete set of financial projections.* Every blueprint should contain a complete set of financial projections, not only for the franchisee but also for the franchisor. As an absolute minimum, these projections should consist of:

   • A statement of capital requirements for both franchisee and franchisor.
   • A series of pro-forma income statements for both franchisee and franchisor.

- A series of pro-forma cash-flow analyses for both operations' projected peak cash outflows.
- Graphic and mathematical break-even analyses for both franchisee and franchisor.

6. *Advertising and promotion plans.* An old adage says, "Build a better mousetrap and the world will beat a path to your door." Unfortunately this statement is no longer valid. Rather, today's economic and business environment calls for its restatement: "Build a better mousetrap, then go out and tell the people that it *is* a better mousetrap, and, while you're at it, show them *why* it is a better mousetrap; then tell them where your door is, and clear a path from your door to where the people are. Then, when you have done all of this, *perhaps* the people will come and buy your mousetrap—assuming, of course, that they are still interested in trapping mice." No blueprint can be considered complete in any sense unless it contains a set of directions and description of the tools that will be required to "tell the people that it is a better mousetrap" and to "clear a path from the door to where the people are." An integral part of the advertising and promotion plans that form these directions should be a variety of sales tools that literally surround the franchisee, ensuring customer flow. Sales tools should consist of two basic types of items, each of which has been tested and found to be successful by the franchisor: the kinds of things that are held in the hand, such as presentation books, and the kinds of things that are sent, such as direct-mail pieces.

7. *A training curriculum.* It is extremely important that a training curriculum be established. Adequate provision must be made for the schooling of the franchisee at the franchisor's facility and for followup training at the franchisee's facility, the franchisor's facility, or some combination of the two. Provision should be made for regularly scheduled field trips by the franchisor's training and field-support personnel. In many instances local, regional, and national sales clinics are conducted for the benefit of the franchisee. The critical point of training, with respect to the program's chronology—the time when the franchisee most vitally needs help—is during the first 60 days of operation. The franchisee has finished home-office training and is now in the territory, prepared to start in business. At this point, the franchisee is alone and "running scared." It is now that the cover of a hand-held "parental umbrella" is most urgently required to develop a winning momentum.

8. *PERT/CPM charts.* PERT/CPM charts are essential. They specify complete operating procedures on a step-by-step, day-by-day basis for both franchisor and franchisee. They define the specific functions that must be performed—the events that must occur—in advance of the franchise program's commencement and provide "road maps" for program implementation. We will discuss these charts further in Chapter 4.

PREPARATION OF A FRANCHISE PACKAGE

While many of the components of the franchise package and their relationship to each other derive from the blueprint, the package itself must always consist of two main categories of tools and directions:

- The tools required to ensure the franchisees' success, and
- The tools required to recruit franchisees.

**FRANCHISEE RECRUITMENT TOOLS**

In most instances the following tools and their proper use are necessary to mount a successful franchisee recruitment program:

1. *A franchisee recruitment presentation book.* To present the program properly and in a logical sequence, a book and/or an audio-visual presentation dramatizing and documenting the franchisee benefits will be required. This presentation should be utilized during the course of a personal meeting with a prospective franchisee.

2. *A franchisee recruitment brochure.* A franchisee recruitment brochure describes the program concisely and in less detail than the franchisee recruitment presentation book. Such a brochure is used as a part of the franchisor's response to inquiries resulting from media advertising.

3. *A franchise agreement.* The franchise agreement is the legal backbone of the franchise program and should be prepared in as compact a manner as possible. It must reflect all current legal considerations but be oriented towards "affirmatives," or what the franchisor will do for the franchisee, rather than "negatives," or what cannot be done. The franchise agreement specifies the precise nature of the relationship between the franchisor and the franchisee; consequently it is a legal document of critical importance. However, it is also a sales document, and a franchisor can be sure that anyone who would execute it and become committed to the provisions without a thorough understanding of its content would probably lack the qualifications of a successful franchisee. The simpler and clearer the agreement is, and the more it stresses positive rather than negative program aspects, the more useful and effective it will be for the franchisor.

4. *Disclosure.* Throughout the 1960s and into the 1970s a number of individuals and companies entered the field with the sole interest of collecting franchise fees in exchange for the expenditure of little or no effort. They measured their success in terms of franchise fees collected or promised versus sales commissions and recruitment advertising dollars expended, rather than in terms of system development or royalties collected from successful franchises.

    The natural consequence of this abuse was a growing number of extremely unhappy and quite vociferous franchisees, whose protests led to the eventual imposition of strict government regulations on franchisors and prospective franchisors. Among these are the full-disclosure requirements of many states and the recent federal full-disclosure requirement. Consequently, competent counsel must be retained to comply with all disclosure requirements for any geographical area in which a franchisor intends to operate. Compliance with these regulations must be considered a part of the franchise package, even though it is not directly related either to franchisee success or to the activity of recruiting franchisees; instead, it is a precondition to these activities.

5. *Recruitment control system.* Recruitment control and flow forms should provide a systematic method of recording prospect leads, their source, contacts and the results of these contacts.

## FRANCHISEE SUCCESS TOOLS

A well-developed franchise blueprint already contains many tools designed to ensure the success of franchises. But as the recruits prepare to launch their businesses, the following items are absolutely essential:

1. *An operating manual.* An operating manual is the bible of the program. It must be available in sufficient numbers and in such form as to encourage constant reference. A good manual describes in great detail every aspect of the franchisee's operation. It contains step-by-step review of each instruction given to the franchisee during training. The operating manual is so important a document that it must be part and parcel of the franchise agreement, defining and controlling the manner in which the franchisee will operate the business and specifying franchisee commitments to franchisor as well as franchisor commitments to franchisee.

2. *A sales manual.* In many instances the sales manual is contained within the operating manual and takes the form of one or a number of sections or chapters. In other instances the sales manual is a bible unto itself. Regardless of its format, however, it must provide the franchisee with the proven techniques and devices that the franchisor has implemented successfully to generate sales for the operation.

3. *A sales presentation book.* A sales presentation book (or audio-visual presentation) is an important tool that illustrates and describes the consumer benefits from the franchisee's goods and/or services. It is used by the franchisee in contacting potential customers.

4. *Ongoing advertising and promotion.* Methods of advertising and promotion vary greatly with the nature of products and/or services offered to the consumer. However, most programs should include the following:

   • A grand opening campaign.
   • Direct-mail pieces to be sent to potential customers in the franchisee's area.
   • Camera-ready advertising copy for local newspapers.
   • A public relations campaign or publicity writeups for local newspapers.

- A "leave-behind" brochure, describing the franchisee's products and/or services.

5. *A simplified bookkeeping system.* Use of a standardized simplified bookkeeping and recordkeeping system enables the franchisee to keep proper records with the expenditure of minimum time and effort. It also provides the franchisor immediate access to information regarding royalty payments.

6. *Franchisor support personnel.* The franchisor's organization must include personnel capable of supporting the program at each stage of its growth. At the outset a franchise director, who is the program's implementor, is necessary. As franchisees are recruited, other operating and administrative personnel should be added in accordance with a preplanned organization growth schedule. These individuals will provide the ongoing support and system-monitoring activities that are necessary for an effective franchise program.

# FRANCHISE FEASIBILITY DETERMINATION

**3**

**THE IMPORTANCE OF MUTUAL FEASIBILITY**

The determination of whether franchising is a viable method of marketing and distribution for a particular firm should be based on a thorough analysis. Unlike many other types of business analyses, however, an analysis of franchising feasibility must be multileveled. It must concern itself with the operations of both franchisee and franchisor. If master franchisee, area controller, or other levels of distribution are planned or under consideration, it must concern itself with these as well. Thus an analysis of franchising feasibility must consist of a minimum of two separate approaches: One from the viewpoint of the franchisee, and one from the viewpoint of the franchisor.

In most instances the franchisee will deal directly with the public. If an analysis of the planned, basic operation strongly indicates that (1) the public will be attracted to the franchisee's operation and motivated to purchase goods or services, and (2) the franchisee will be able to respond properly and profitably to the desires of the public, then utilization of franchising as a method of marketing and distribution is feasible for the prospective franchisee.

However, the prospective franchisor's position also must be analyzed. If this analysis indicates that (1) franchisees will benefit more from their inclusion in a system than from operating independently, and (2) the franchisor will be able to administer the franchise system and support franchisees properly and profitably, then feasibility of utilizing the franchise method of marketing and distribution exists from the viewpoint of the prospective franchisor.

Under any circumstances, mutual feasibility must exist. Both franchisee and franchisor must be considered. In actuality they are two separate and distinct entities, but their interlocking relationship is such that feasibility is totally destroyed by a failure of one or the other to withstand the analysis.

**FRANCHISEE FEASIBILITY**

In ascertaining franchisee feasibility, a number of areas should be examined and questions asked. Possibly an existing operation intended as a pilot unit might be modified to provide some critical indicators. In general, the questions

**25**

that must be answered positively can be grouped into four categories: production, finance, marketing, and personnel.

## PRODUCTION

1. Does the product or service have an *element of distinctiveness?* It is not necessary that the product or service be completely different from anything currently available on the market. Distinctiveness may lie in packaging, merchandising, servicing, structural format, or any number of additional characteristics. However, it should provide the consumer with a sense of "something different"—something that cannot be provided by competing products and services. Further, and of critical importance, this determination of uniqueness must be made objectively and from the viewpoint of the consumer.

2. Does the product or service have an *enduring consumer appeal?* Is there a fair degree of certainty that it is not a fad, or so highly stylized that it will be outdated before long? If not, can the franchise be structured in a manner that will allow the business to continue profitably and uninterrupted through the introduction of new products or services within its framework?

3. Does the product or service exhibit a *repeat factor?* While a lack of this characteristic does not necessarily rule out franchising, its existence is highly desirable. The "oil for the lamps of China" concept reveals the value of distributing free lamps in China: Obviously repeat oil sales are generated. Likewise, certain types of razor blades are sold repetitively when free razors are given. By building this concept into the business, the franchisee tends to ensure repeat patronage and create an annuity type of business, as opposed to that which depends on the single sale concept.

4. Have the franchisee's *inventory requirements been minimized?* Has adequate provision been made for controlling inventory so that it can be maintained at optimum levels: Neither so low as to have an adverse effect on sales, nor so high as to cause an unnecessary capital investment?

5. In the event that the basic operation under consideration as a franchise vehicle concerns itself with the sale of a product, and in the event that sale of the product is linked to an installation requirement, has *performance of the installation function been arranged carefully and economically?* Can it be "farmed out" to local tradespeople or technicians? Can it be accomplished at a reasonable, predetermined price?

6. In the sale of a product, *have freight costs been minimized?* Is the item in question heavy or bulky? If so, has everything possible been done to prevent the erosion of profit that results from excessive freight costs? Can regional warehousing with shipping on a minimum basis of full carloads solve the problem?

## FINANCE

1. Is the *success of the pilot operation fully documented,* or has provision been made for its recording and documentation? If so, the franchisee is buying a

proven success formula plus the franchisor's ability and commitment to extend that formula to a new market area.

2. Have projections been prepared for the franchisee, and *are the projections realistic?* Without price-cutting, does the firm have sufficient capital and management competence to penetrate a new market and experience the same margins that have been experienced in the past? Are projected rates of growth based on sound data? Has the pilot unit demonstrated that growth projections are within the realm of possibility?

3. Does the product or service under contemplation enjoy an *inherently good profit margin?* Is it sufficient to provide the franchisee with a reasonable standard of living, even at minimum sales projections? The quality of franchisees attracted to the program will probably vary in direct proportion to projected profitability—and to its believability.

4. Is a viable plan available for *franchisee financing?* Typically, franchisee financing is required for the following areas:

- Land
- Construction
- Equipment
- Inventory
- Modernization
- Working capital

Ordinarily this financing is obtained by utilizing one or a combination of the following sources:

a) The franchisor, who may provide capital directly by extending credit on inventory or by other means, or indirectly by guaranteeing a lease or by other means.

b) Local banks that know the franchisee and the potential of the franchise in his or her neighborhood.

c) The lessor, who may subordinate land or "build to suit." Builders and contractors will also "build to suit," recapturing their investment on the basis of a prescribed percentage of gross sales or a specified rental.

d) Government lending sources such as SBA, FHA, and HUD. These agencies can grant loans, but their activities in that area have been minimal lately. However, funding may become more easily available from these sources in the future.

e) Private investment sources, including SBICs (Small Business Investment Companies), insurance companies, private investors, and private syndicates. Syndicates are often composed of high-income professionals, such as physicians, dentists, and attorneys, who are receptive to absentee ownership and may enjoy certain tax advantages as a result of their participation. Syndicates have been used to finance relatively large investment franchisees, such as hotels, motels, and nursing homes.

f) MESBIC, a specialized SBIC assisting "disadvantaged persons" in the financing and operation of small businesses.

For an in-depth discussion of financing, see Chapter 7.

### MARKETING

1. Does the pilot unit occupy *a secure position in its market?* Does it have a reasonable share of its available market? Can a franchisee penetrate the available market to an equal or greater extent?

2. Can the product or service in question be projected to *a national market?* Has research confirmed that its consumer appeal is not only regional, but also national or international in scope? If so, are there supply sources of sufficient quality and quantity to furnish franchisees with their requirements?

3. Is the industry in which the franchisee will operate in *a growth position?* Is the potential market for the product or service largely unsaturated? Is the industry's annual growth rate increasing? An industry with minimal existing exploitation and consequent excellent potential for expansion is naturally more desirable for franchising.

4. Can the franchisee maintain a competitive position in a market that may be removed from that of the pilot unit and that may be dominated by a national operator? The pilot unit may be strong in its local area or region, but can that strength be duplicated in other markets? Can the franchisee compete effectively in them? How can this be accomplished?

5. Most important—does the pilot unit have *a good reputation* among its consumers? Is it "above average," as evidenced by minimal product returns or complaints and progressively higher sales?

### PERSONNEL

Will the product or service *accommodate a training program?* Can a franchisee with little or no experience in the field operate the business successfully or can the business be taught within a reasonable time frame? A business may seem simple to its creator or to someone who has been involved with it for years, but highly complex to a newcomer. An interesting statistic reveals that individuals experienced in nonrelated fields absorb training more easily and perform at higher levels than do those whose experience lies in the industry being taught.

**FRANCHISOR FEASIBILITY** Questions that a firm contemplating development of a franchise program must ask of itself may similarly be grouped into categories of production, finance, marketing, and personnel. But here a fifth category, that of research and development, must be added. Similarly, too, responses must be positive.

## PRODUCTION

1. If the business under consideration as a franchise vehicle will sell the product of the franchisor's firm, does the franchisor possess sufficient, unutilized *production capacity to satisfy the demands of a sudden, sharp increase in sales?* It is not unusual for a firm to be "killed by its own success." One franchisor, for example, was operating in the infrared-heating field. Its firms franchisee group produced over $1 million in sales in short order—a superb sales performance that had not been contemplated. The franchisor was not able to supply this demand, nor was it able to subcontract. The expected acquisition of a larger factory, with which it had hoped to increase production, fell through. The end result was failure due to success.

2. If the business under consideration as a franchise vehicle is a service business, can the franchisor *supply (or arrange the supply of) materials* that a group of franchisees will need to sell and perform their service? Can this be done economically and within acceptable time parameters?

## FINANCE

1. Does the firm have *a record of financial stability?* The firm will assume a "parental" role in relation to its franchisees, and a sound financial structure is necessary both to attract qualified franchisees and to support them. The franchisee requires assurance that the franchisor is an enduring factor in the industry, and that it will not fail because it is undercapitalized.

2. Is the firm *ready, willing, and able to commit the necessary funds* to plan, develop, and implement a franchise program properly? A well-constructed and well-executed franchise program represents the prior investment of time and cash by the franchisor, and in some cases this investment is quite substantial. A program that is constructed with a view toward spending as little as possible rather than obtaining the highest value and effectiveness for each dollar expended becomes a blight—more of a liability than an asset.

   If the firm contemplating development of a franchise program is not ready, or not willing, or not able to commit the funds necessary to develop a functional program prior to the sale of the first franchise, then that firm is better advised to continue its business under its current mode of operation than to contemplate franchising.

## MARKETING

1. Has the firm developed *an effective marketing program based on sound data,* and is this effectiveness demonstrable? In addition to providing a marketing program for its franchisees, is the firm prepared to develop a program for its own marketing of the actual franchises?

## PERSONNEL

1. Does the firm employ *sufficient, capable personnel* to administer a franchise network? What is the depth of present personnel? If present staff is

already burdened with day-to-day operations, it must be expanded to respond to new program requirements. A minimum requirement is addition of a franchise director and a personnel manager. In the areas of administration, field contact, operations, and control, personnel must be added as the franchise system grows.

2. Is present staff *philosophically and psychologically equipped to function* in the role of franchisor? This is of critical importance. In most instances a transition from a "hands-on" to a "hands-off" situation will occur concurrently with a transition from a material to a human orientation.

3. Is the firm willing to *forsake a portion of its own business independence* for the good of the franchise system? The rapid expansion inherent in adoption of the franchise method of marketing and distribution often results in decreased flexibility and tends to increase the time required for implementation of change.

4. In considering franchising, is the firm's objective *long-range rather than short-range?* Normally, a franchisor should not expect significant profits from its receipt of initial franchise fees, which serve to reimburse it for expenses incurred in recruiting, training, and establishing franchisees in business. The larger profits are long-term in nature, and are derived from the multiplicity of successful franchisees established by the franchisor.

5. Are the firm's principals and executives willing to *delegate responsibility and authority?* Unwillingness to delegate authority and failure to do so in the face of an expanding franchise system invariably lead to destructive inefficiencies and dissensions that can have the ultimate effect of endangering not only the system, but also the firm itself.

## RESEARCH AND DEVELOPMENT

1. Is the firm prepared to *plan and implement a research and development program* for the purpose of providing its franchisees with the updated products, services, tools, and materials they will need to compete effectively in their markets? Neither the market nor the total environment in which franchisees and franchisors function is static. Rather, it is dynamic and changing. Today's product may be replaced with another tomorrow, and any firm considering franchising as a method of marketing and distribution must be prepared to ensure the long-term as well as the short-term profitability of its franchisees.

# PERT/CPM CHARTS

Among the most effective planning and control tools available to modern business are PERT/CPM charts. Developed by the consulting firm of Booze, Allen and Hamilton, working in conjunction with the U.S. Department of the Navy during World War II, PERT was conceived as a method for planning, administering, and controlling the construction of naval vessels. Later it was expanded to include CPM.

PERT is an acronym for Project Evaluation Revue Technique, while CPM stands for Critical Path Method. PERT, CPM, and PERT/CPM refer to singularly and specifically defined methodologies. They should never be confused with other methods similar in appearance but requiring far less sophistication and offering limited scope and usefulness.

The ultimate goal of PERT/CPM is to chart the progress of a specific project from beginning to end in terms of time, and to define within the chart a "critical path"—that is, an identification of those events which, if they do *not* occur at or before specified dates, will delay completion of the overall project.

A PERT/CPM chart consists of a clear delineation of related events connected by lines that indicate their sequential nature and the time period required for whatever activity leads to each event's occurrence. In keeping with its primary use as a planning and control technique, PERT/CPM specifies events and times explicitly but indicates activities only implicitly.

CPM is involved in PERT analysis by defining in terms of time the longest "path" through which the events required for the project's completion must pass. This path includes all events of which a delayed completion will cause the entire project to be delayed. These are the events that are referred to as being "on the critical path" or "critical-path events." All other events are "off the critical path," or "noncritical events." From the viewpoints of planning and control, all other events are subsidiary to critical-path events.

Figure 4.1 shows the kind of PERT/CPM chart that might be developed by a business desiring to utilize its existing concept in a soundly developed franchise program.

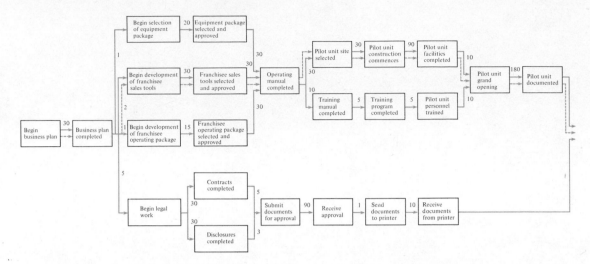

**Fig. 4.1** PERT/CPM: Franchise program development concept to opening of first franchiser unit.

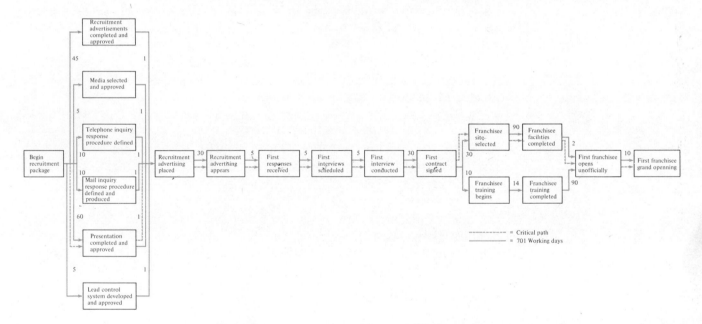

It specifies 43 separate and distinct events, all of which must occur prior to the opening of the prospective franchisor's first franchised unit. It also specifies the time that is allotted to completing the activity that leads to the occurrence of each event and the sequential dependence of each event upon the others. For realistic planning purposes, it states that 701 working days will be required by the franchisor to reach the goal of the first grand opening. Further, it defines the following events as being on the critical path:

1. Begin business plan
2. Business plan completed
3. Begin development of franchisee sales tools

4. Franchisee sales tools selected and completed
5. Operating manual completed
6. Pilot unit site selected
7. Pilot unit construction commenced
8. Pilot unit facilities completed
9. Pilot unit grand opening
10. Pilot unit documented
11. Begin recruitment package
12. Presentation completed and approved
13. Recruitment advertising placed
14. Recruitment advertising appears
15. First responses received
16. First interviews scheduled
17. First interview conducted
18. First contract signed
19. Franchisee site selected
20. Franchisee facilities completed
21. First franchisee opens unofficially
22. First franchisee grand opening

As an example of its many statements, the chart tells us that 90 working days from commencement of construction at the site, the pilot unit's facilities will be complete. It further states that the pilot unit's facilities will be completed 242 working days from the time that the franchisor commences work on developing the business plan that will control the overall project. If this event does not occur within 242 days of the business plan's commencement, the first franchisee's grand opening will not occur within the 701 working days projected but at some later time, which may be determined by adding to 701 the difference between 242 working days and the number of working days between actual commencement of the business plan and actual completion of the pilot unit's facilities.

The chart also specifies that all legal documents will be received from the printer, so that recruitment package development may commence 171 days from the project's beginning. If this event does not occur at the time specified, the first franchisee's grand opening will not necessarily be delayed, so long as the documents are received within 432 days of the project's commencement. However, receipt of the documents at any time later than 432 days from the project's commencement will alter the critical path, so that it must be traced through the legal-work branch, rather than through the pilot-unit branch.

Many of the time periods specified on this PERT/CPM chart represent projects in themselves and, as such, are subject to their own PERT/CPM planning and control. In fact, the most effective use of PERT/CPM requires that subsidiary charts be prepared and utilized by personnel whose line responsibility is the completion of those projects within a project, or by those personnel whose line responsibility is to direct or perform the activity that leads to the occurrence of an event within the specified time frame. Preparation of these ancillary PERT/CPM charts is particularly crucial for subsidiary projects lying on the critical path. Even for projects lying off the critical path, PERT/CPM charts are undeniably useful.

As an example of this, the time specified for completing and receiving approval of the presentation is 60 working days from commencement of the recruitment package. Performance of the functions that lead to this event are complex with respect to sequence, timing, and time required, and each may be prespecified in terms of the occurrence of events. As each of them is subsumed under the 60-day time period from "Begin recruitment package" to "Presentation completed and approved" on the critical path for the overall project, it is generally wise to prepare a PERT/CPM for that subproject and to utilize it in evaluating progress.

By the same token, although it is not on the critical path, the 45-day time period between "Begin recruitment package" and "Recruitment advertisements completed and approved" lies within 15 days of the critical path; delays in the occurrence of the latter event may well affect definition of the critical path, so preparation and utilization of PERT/CPM charts and techniques are warranted in this case, as well.

As has been noted, PERT/CPM technique is useful both as a control device and as a planning tool, and its utility in these areas is evident. In addition to utility, however, PERT/CPM technique accomplishes an additional and critically useful end. Its use literally *forces* logical thought during the planning process. This benefit of PERT/CPM technique utilization cannot be over-stressed! Because its proper utilization requires that a prospective franchisor define events of major importance in terms of sequence and in terms of time, it often raises questions and identifies areas of concern that would not otherwise be raised or identified. This often results in substantial, beneficial program modifications.

# BLUEPRINTING THE PROGRAM

**5**

When we hear the word "blueprint," we usually think of those white-on-blue drawings that detail every little aspect of an architect's plan. But *Webster's New Collegiate Dictionary* gives a second definition for the word: "A program of action." It is in this sense that we apply "blueprint" to our preparation of a sound franchising package. The prospective franchisor is the architect; the franchise blueprint must indeed detail every little aspect of the plan!

**IDENTIFYING PROGRAM OBJECTIVES**

To understand the procedures and blueprint a program for any corporate endeavor, it is first necessary to define the goals or objectives. A device for measuring the program's effectiveness must be created prior to initiation of the program, and flexibility must be built in to allow for changes, additions, deletions, and modifications that will improve the overall concept. But first, the objectives must be clearly understood.

The basic objectives of a franchise program should include the following:

1. To establish at least one successful franchisee prototype operation in accordance with the format presented here. The prototype will serve as

   a) a "proving ground" for the concepts, methods, and techniques established for the planned franchising program;

   b) a secondary training center for the development of corporate administration and operational personnel;

   c) an additional pilot operation to provide the necessary income, expense, and profit documentation required for every successful franchise offering;

   d) an additional research-and-development center for the testing of all concepts, promotional campaigns, and advertising programs.

When the prototype operations have achieved the desired success, and the image and format have been clearly established, the parent company will be in a position to proceed with the subsequent objectives of the franchise program:

2. To establish a nationwide network of franchisees as quickly as practicable in accordance with the dictates of sound-management practices.

3. To develop the executive staff and administrative procedures required for efficient control and operation of the franchise network.

4. To create methods for franchise sales, franchisee training, administration, and sales promotion that provide reasonable assurance of achieving initial and long-range success for both franchisee and franchisor.

5. To formulate the franchise program so that it will become self-sustaining within a minimum period.

6. To increase franchisor net profits not only from the sale of franchises but also (and mainly) from the increased business produced by successfully operating franchisees.

7. To research other possible sources of income—e.g., additional products and services that franchisees may offer to the public within their existing facilities and with minimum add-on overhead.

While this outline provides a practical set of objectives for executing a profitable growth program, a degree of flexibility should always be maintained. In fact, flexibility is the key to meeting the nonrecurring or special events that may lie in the company's future. Therefore, while whole objectives and directions remain essentially unchanged, the tactics required to meet them may be reconsidered from time to time. Methods must be subject to continuous review, and the program that allows room to maneuver can be revised quickly and effectively.

**DETAILING PROCEDURES**

An effective franchise blueprint must detail all aspects and procedures of the program. On the following pages is an outline of a blueprint prepared for a typical fast-food drive-in restaurant system featuring hamburgers. Think of it as a Table of Contents for what will obviously be a large volume containing many documents and much pertinent data.

*Section 1. Location*

General information
Trading area population trends
Determination of favorable sites
Basic site requirements explained
Location forms, general survey
Location evaluation form
Preliminary real-estate survey
Methods of acquiring hamburger drive-in locations
Structure analysis form
Site analysis form

Site certification form
Land-survey form
Location approval and securing form
Utility: gas form
Utility: water form
Utility: electric form
Utility: sewer form
General completion check
Construction check form

*Section 2. Legal*

Legal documents, general information
Transactions requiring legal documents
Preliminary franchise agreement
Preliminary franchise escrow agreement
Preliminary location agreement
Preliminary location escrow agreement
Preliminary agreement of territorial license
Preliminary license escrow agreement
Franchise agreement
License territorial agreement
Ground lease
Ground sublease
Building leaseback agreement
Improved sublease
Thirty additional legal documents used in fast-food drive-in transactions
Complete legal documents for closing a sale

*Section 3. Building*

General information
Plot plan layout data
Parking plan layout data
Turnkey construction methods
Ninety detailed drawings of hamburger building plans
Building specifications (over 50 pages)

*Section 4. Equipment*

General information
Complete lists of required hamburger drive-in equipment
List of griddle manufacturers
List of fryer manufacturers
List of shake-machine manufacturers
List of soft-drink dispenser manufacturers
List of ice-machine manufacturers
List of cooler manufacturers
List of freezer manufacturers
List of coffee-maker manufacturers

Itemized list of custom-fabricated stainless-steel equipment
Set of drawings of custom-fabricated stainless steel equipment
Specifications and price for a griddle
Specifications and prices for fryers
Specifications and prices for shake machines
Specifications and prices for freezers
Specifications and price for a soft-drink dispenser
Specifications and price for an ice machine
Specifications and price for a walk-in cooler
Several itemized wholesale price lists of hamburger drive-in equipment packages
Specifications and price for a coffee maker
Specifications and price for a potato peeler
Specifications and price for a cash register
Specifications and price for a shake-holding cabinet
Specifications and price for a sink
Specifications and prices from several alternative manufacturers of equipment in each of the above categories
Equipment-layout and utility hook-up drawings
Complete list of special "small equipment" package

*Section 5. Sign*

General information
General description and explanation of signs to be used
Dimensions and drawing of signs to be used
Interior menu signs
Sign manufacturers' names and addresses
Retail and wholesale prices from several manufacturers of signs

*Section 6. Operation*

General information
Complete operations manual, including the following sections:
- Hamburger drive-in food service prior to installation of equipment
- Duties of the owner and manager prior to opening date
- Equipment hook-up
- Additional construction projects, general equipment, and supplies needed prior to opening
- Miscellaneous supplies
- Food production
- Preparation of the food products
- Store opening
- Manager's responsibilities
- Opening procedures
- Closing procedures
- One week before opening, things to do
- Four days before opening, things to do
- Additional items for sale

- Operating procedure
- Cleaning procedure
- Ordering procedure
- Paper supplies
- Inventory control
- Damaged merchandise
- Advertising
- Safety procedures
- Cleaning and maintenance procedures
- Cleaning and maintenance schedule
- Uniforms
- Pilferage
- Spoilage and waste
- Profits

Sixteen operating forms (daily, weekly, and monthly)
Food and paper cost breakdown to the hundredths of a cent of all items
    sold (e.g., patty paper—0.0008)
Initial articles and supplies, general information
Complete list of food supplies
Complete list of paper supplies
Complete list of miscellaneous supplies
Complete list of office supplies
Complete list of cleaning supplies

*Section 7. Advertising and Promotion*

General information
Copy for advertising in local media
Advertising manual
Grand-opening program
Building local public acceptance
Obtaining local publicity
Continuing promotions

*Section 8. Bookkeeping, Financing, and Corporate Structure*

Bookkeeping, general information
Bookkeeping for a hamburger drive-in
Bookkeeping manual and forms
Financing, general information
Financing signs—all methods
Financing a licensee or franchisee
Financing equipment—all methods
Financing the building
Methods of financing used for a hamburger drive-in
The corporate setup for a hamburger drive-in
The corporate structure for a hamburger leasing and development corpora-
    tion
The corporate setup for a territorial franchise company

*Section 9. Miscellaneous*

Costs, general information
Total hamburger drive-in equipment costs, wholesale and retail
Total sign costs, wholesale and retail
Total supply costs
Total initial costs, wholesale and retail
Projected gross and net profit breakdown and methods of figuring
Actual gross and net profit breakdown figures
Complete literature of competitive hamburger drive-in chains
Image, decor, and theme—general information
Store name, colors, and atmosphere
The market, general information on customers, population, and trends
Money- and labor-saving methods, general information
Complete outline of territorial licensing methods and procedures
Complete outline of procedures for selling the franchise and license
Complete sales literature
History and development of the hamburger drive-in concept
Hamburger drive-in franchise companies

*Section 10. Franchisor's Organization and Objectives*

Present organization
The new organization
Franchisor organization chart
Manpower scheduling
Management employees and suggested starting salaries
Organizational job descriptions
Utilization of job descriptions
Corporate identification
Trademark—registration and design

*Section 11. Franchisor's Program*

General information
Store types
Local franchise sales
Table I, 3-year projection-sales of local franchises
Table II, sales of local franchises by month
Franchisee's projected revenue and cash flow
Table III, franchisee percentage income and expenses
Table IV, franchisee dollar income and expenses
Local franchisee package cost
Table V, local franchisee package cost breakdown
Table VI, local franchisee equipment and improvement package
Table VII, franchisee fee breakdown of franchisor cost
Franchisor income from franchise sales
Table VIII, franchisor income from local franchisee sales
Projected franchisor income from royalties
Table IX, 3-year projected franchise royalty income

Table XXVI, master franchisee's franchise fee
Table XXVII, master franchise package cost
Additional franchisor income
Table XXVIII, franchisor's income from franchise sales
Table XXIX, franchisor's income from royalties
Table XXX, franchisor's income from product sales
Table XXXI, franchisor's income from all sources
Table XXXII, franchisor projected income, integrating master-franchisee program

*Section 17. Implementation*

Program implementation checklist
Program phasing
Franchisee selling materials
Preparation and sales timetable
Consultant services
Creative cost budget analysis

# PERSONNEL: A TABLE OF ORGANIZATION

# 6

In the development of a new franchising program, personnel must be selected and hired chronologically, according to the program's Table of Organization. Initially, one designated person functions as Franchise Director, working in liaison with franchisees and franchisor executives. The Franchise Director's functions include the following:

- Consultation as required in the preparation of the franchise package.
- Accumulating data and material necessary to expedite the program.
- Consultation regarding franchisee recruitment procedures.
- Ordering and scheduling franchisee equipment included in the franchise package.
- Supervising training school.
- Supervising franchisee field-support operations.
- Representing the home office as a central communication source for both franchise salesforce and prospective franchisees.

As the program progresses, new people and offices are added to conform to the pace of franchisee recruitment. These include additional field representatives and administrative assistants, who will have the following responsibilities:

- Evaluating the organization plan and manpower planning on a regular, systematic, periodic basis, in light of corporate objectives as they relate to goal accomplishment.
- Evaluating and modifying budget plans and controls.
- Performing special assignments.
- Serving on special or regular committees according to the organization's needs and the individual's talents.

Figure 6.1 is a summary of manpower scheduling organized in terms of the venture's Table of Organization. Figure 6.2 presents the same information

**43**

chronologically, and Figure 6.3 projects initial salaries for each of the required personnel.

|  | Hired during phase no. |
| --- | --- |
| Franchise Director | 2 |
| Franchise Sales Manager | 2 |
| Training Director | 1 |
| Accounting, legal, and statistical functions | 1* |
| Purchasing Director | 1 |
| Pilot Unit Manager | 1 |
| Professional Liaison Director | 3 |
| Advertising and Promotion Director | 3 |
| Field personnel | 2† |
| Pilot Unit personnel | 1 |
| Secretarial and clerical personnel | 1‡ |

**Fig. 6.1** Personnel scheduling summary for suggested table of organization.

\*  Supplied to the Franchisor on a fee basis
†  Hired singly as required by scheduled grand openings and total Franchisees in operation
‡  To be hired as required

|  | Hired during phase no. |
| --- | --- |
| Accounting, legal, and statistical functions | 1* |
| Purchasing Director | 1 |
| Pilot Unit Manager | 1 |
| Pilot Unit personnel |  |
| Training Director | 1 |
| Secretarial and clerical personnel | 1† |
| Franchise Director | 2 |
| Field personnel | 2‡ |
| Franchise Sales Manager | 2 |
| Professional Liaison Director | 3 |
| Advertising and Promotion Director | 3 |

**Fig. 6.2** Manpower scheduling summary in chronological terms.

\*  Supplied to the franchisor on a fee basis
†  Hired as required, not only in Phase 1, but throughout the development of the program and administration of the franchise system
‡  Hired singly as required by scheduled grand openings and total franchisees in operation

|  | Annual Compensation |
|---|---|
| Accounting, legal, and statistical functions | As required |
| Purchasing Director | $24,000* |
| Pilot Unit Manager | $24,000* |
| Pilot Unit personnel | As required |
| Training Director | $18,000* |
| Secretarial personnel | $ 9,600† |
| Clerical personnel | $ 8,400† |
| Franchise Director | $48,000* |
| Field personnel | $21,600* |
| Franchise Sales Manager | $21,600‡ |
| Professional Liaison Manager | $36,000* |
| Advertising and Promotion Manager | $16,900* |

**Fig. 6.3** Starting salary guidelines.

\* Plus bonus and/or planned increases based on performance
† Depending upon and as required by local custom, but it is suggested that the top portion of the local scale be considered and that these personnel be included in a bonus based on performance plan
‡ Plus commission. Any franchise salespeople required are assumed to share in this commission and be totally compensated on that basis

The theoretical example of preplanning additions to a franchisor's staff that follows assumes that:

1. The franchisor company is a new venture.
2. The franchisor company will be established as a wholly owned subsidiary of an existing, larger corporation that will make available its accounting, legal, and analytical staffs, including computer facilities.
3. The franchise itself is a business the sales of which depend in large part, albeit not solely, on the cooperation of banks, other financial institutions, attorneys, and generally sophisticated organizations and individuals.
4. The purchasing function has been defined as that which is most critical to the success of the franchisor and to the pilot unit.
5. The existing, larger corporation's staff is adequate to perform all of the functions that must be performed to plan and initiate the franchisor company and the pilot unit, and it will not be necessary to begin staffing the franchisor company or the pilot unit until approximately a month to a week prior to the opening of the pilot unit.

Figure 6.4 is a depiction of the table of organization required by a venture during its first phase of operations and while primary concentration is devoted to the pilot unit and establishing its success.

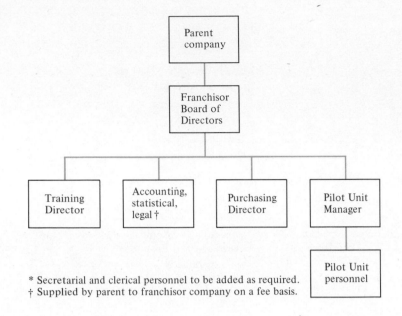

**Fig. 6.4** Table of organization for Phase 1* (approximately one month to one week prior to opening of pilot unit).

* Secretarial and clerical personnel to be added as required.
† Supplied by parent to franchisor company on a fee basis.

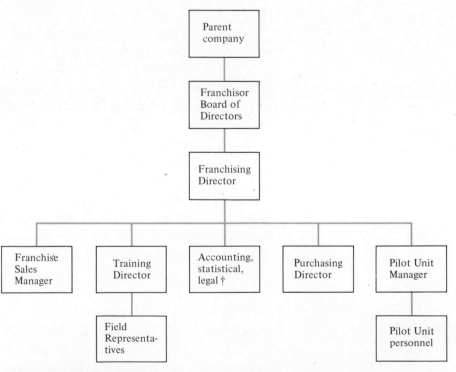

**Fig. 6.5** Table of organization for Phase 2* (one month to one week prior to the sale of the first franchise).

* Secretarial and clerical personnel to be added as required.
† Supplied by parent to franchisor company on a fee basis.

Figure 6.6 depicts the venture's organization at full development, when the franchisor company is operating its pilot unit, recruiting and training franchisees, establishing franchisees in business, and servicing the franchise system.

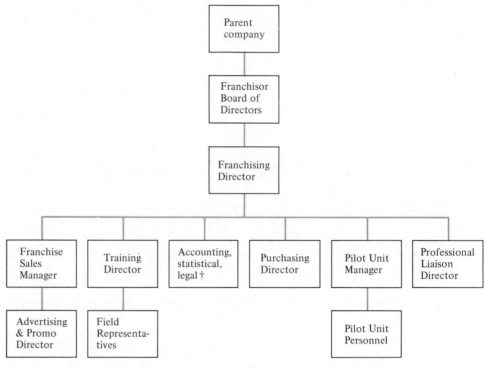

**Fig. 6.6** Table of organization for Phase 3* (end of first year of operation).

*Secretarial and clerical personnel to be added as required.
†Supplied by parent to franchisor company on a fee basis.

## JOB DESCRIPTIONS

Specific job descriptions for each of the personnel indicated in Figs. 6.4 through 6.6 have been written and are shown in the following sections.

### FRANCHISE DIRECTOR

REPORTING RESPONSIBILITY

Directly to the franchisor's Board of Directors.

AUTHORITY

Complete authority for all phases of the franchisor's operations, limited only by policy statements and directives of the Board of Directors.

SPECIFIC RESPONSIBILITIES

Overall, line responsibility for all phases of the franchisor's operations, including but not limited to:

- All aspects of franchise recruitment and sales, supervising and directing the activities of the franchise Sales Manager.

- Advertising, sales promotion, public relations, marketing research, and all programs related to sales, working with and directing the activities of the franchisor's advertising agency and/or public-relations firm.

- All aspects of purchasing, merchandise distribution, and storage, supervising and directing the activities of the Purchasing Director.
- All aspects of franchisee training, both initially and on a continuing basis, supervising and directing the activities of the Purchasing Director.
- All aspects of franchisee training, both initially and on a continuing basis, supervising and directing the activities of the Training Director.
- All aspects of Pilot Unit operations, supervising and directing the activities of the Pilot Unit Manager.
- All aspects of financial and statistical reporting and information retrieval.
- All legal requirements, working with outside counsel.
- All aspects of professional liaison, supervising and directing the activities of the Professional Liaison Director.
- Coordination of all activities within the franchisee organization, supervising and directing the activities of appropriate personnel.
- Continuing development and implementation of programs to improve methods of providing services and assistance to franchisees.
- Preparation and delivery of regular, systematic financial and operating reports to the Board of Directors.
- Receipt and analysis of regular systematic financial and operating reports from each franchisee.
- Collection of all royalties.
- Ascertainment of the correctness of all royalties.
- Collection of all franchise fees.
- Maintenance of personal contact with franchisees.
- Acting as principal spokesperson for the franchisor, promoting and advancing the most favorable image possible to all business sources.
- Developing and maintaining sound, meaningful relationships with members of the local, regional, and national financial communities for the purpose of acquiring additional sources of franchisor and franchisee funding.

## FRANCHISE SALES MANAGER

### REPORTING RESPONSIBILITY
Directly to the Franchise Director.

### AUTHORITY
Complete authority for all franchise sales activities, limited by the policy statements, directives, and directions of the Franchise Director.

### SPECIFIC RESPONSIBILITIES
Line responsibility for all aspects of franchise sales, including but not limited to:

- Establishment and administration of franchisee qualification procedures consistent with the franchisor's stated policies.
- All aspects of franchise advertising and promotion, supervising and directing the activities of the Advertising and Promotion Director.

- Making presentations to prospective franchisees, employing the skill of negative selling—a highly specialized technique generally required to sell franchises.
- Negotiating all franchisor-franchisee contracts presenting executed documents and downpayment monies to the Franchise Director for review and approval.

## TRAINING DIRECTOR

### REPORTING RESPONSIBILITY

Directly to the Franchise Director.

### AUTHORITY

Complete authority for all franchisee training, both initially and on a continuing basis, limited by the policy statements, directives, and directions of the Franchise Director.

### SPECIFIC RESPONSIBILITIES

Line responsibility for all aspects of franchisee training and continued education and franchisor personnel functions, including, but not limited to:

- Supervision of all activities of the franchisor's training center.
- Teaching classes, conducting seminars, and examining franchisees.
- Continually refining and developing training methods, subject matter, and material presentation.
- All aspects of franchisee field assistance, supervising and directing the activities of all field personnel.
- Assisting franchisees in the selection and training of their staffs and providing adequate training materials for their use.
- Visiting franchisees periodically to ascertain the effectiveness of training received and field-personnel assistance, as well as employee morale, knowledge, and effectiveness.
- Developing techniques and systems for the indoctrination of franchisees into new programs created by the franchisor.
- Coordinating the development of training materials and methods with the Franchise Sales Manager, so that the Franchise Sales Manager may utilize their existence to best advantage in franchise recruitment activities and public-relations activities.
- All aspects of the franchisor's personnel functions, including the establishment and administration of procedures for hiring personnel, developing manpower planning programs, administering the franchisor's home office, and defining new job descriptions in accordance with the franchisor's requirements as dictated by the expanding franchisee network.

## PURCHASING DIRECTOR

### REPORTING RESPONSIBILITY

Directly to the Franchise Director.

## AUTHORITY

Complete authority for all purchasing, storage, transportation and distribution of merchandise, limited by the policy statements, directives, and directions of the Franchise Director.

## SPECIFIC RESPONSIBILITIES

Line responsibility for all aspects of merchandise purchasing and distribution, including storage, and including but not limited to:

- Establishing and maintaining high product quality specifications.
- Locating several alternative sources of supply for each product in order to ensure the proper service of franchisees and the pilot unit.
- Inspecting all materials and products as they are received from vendors.
- Establishing warehousing facilities as required.
- Evaluating, as a result of critical analysis, product quality, price, source availability, delivery schedules, warehousing discount arrangements, product damage, and other factors and items connected with the purchasing function.
- All aspects of product distribution.
- Establishing franchisee purchasing procedures for purchases from vendors and from the franchisor.
- Evaluating vendors with whom franchisees deal directly to ensure product quality, competitive price, and adherence to delivery schedules.
- Purchasing all equipment and supply requirements of the franchisor.

## PILOT UNIT MANAGER

### REPORTING RESPONSIBILITY

Directly to the Franchise Director.

### AUTHORITY

Complete authority for all aspects of the pilot unit's operation, limited by the policy statements, directives, and directions of the Franchise Director.

### SPECIFIC RESPONSIBILITIES

Line responsibility for all aspects of pilot unit management, including, but not limited to:

- Conducting the business of the pilot unit.
- Arranging and conducting off-premises business.
- Hiring, training, and administering pilot-unit personnel.
- Remitting all due royalties and advertising funds to the franchisor.
- Establishing and administering effective local advertising and public-relations programs.
- Submitting all reports required of a franchisee to the franchisor.
- Advising the Franchise Director of significant developments and/or improvements in management of the business that may come to his or her attention as a result of "on-line" experience.

## PROFESSIONAL LIAISON DIRECTOR

### REPORTING RESPONSIBILITY

Directly to the Franchise Director.

### AUTHORITY

Complete authority for all aspects of professional liaison activity, limited by the policy statements, directives, and directions of the Franchising Director.

### SPECIFIC RESPONSIBILITIES

Line responsibility for all professional contact, liaison, and staff responsibility to the Franchising Director for activities in this area, including, but not limited to:

- Establishing and maintaining relationships with local, regional, and national professional utilizers of the business services, such as bankers, attorneys, representatives of the courts, insurance companies, manufacturing companies, and government officials.
- Addressing professional groups as a public speaker with respect to franchisor and franchisee services.
- Conducting seminars on franchisee services.
- Entertaining professional heavy utilizers of franchisee services on formal and informal bases.

This position requires an articulate, congenial, and well-educated person, probably a professional executive who is willing to travel extensively. The emphasis of this work will be on assisting ongoing franchises to build disciplined harmonious systems.

## ADVERTISING AND PROMOTION DIRECTOR

### REPORTING RESPONSIBILITY

Directly to the Franchise Sales Manager.

### AUTHORITY

Complete authority for all aspects of advertising, promotion, and public relations, as delegated by the Franchise Sales Manager.

### SPECIFIC RESPONSIBILITIES

Line responsibility for implementation of advertising, promotion, and public relations programs, including, but not limited to:

- Acting as liaison with the franchisor's advertising and/or public-relations agency.
- Coordination and liaison with respect to the franchisee recruitment program.
- Developing advertising, promotion, and public-relations programs for use by franchisees.
- Coordinating all advertising, promotion, and public-relations functions with respect to each franchisee grand opening.
- Assisting and advising franchisees and field personnel in the areas of advertising, promotion, and public relations.

- Assisting the Franchise Director in developing and administering national advertising budgets and plans.
- Developing and administering various methods for franchisee-franchisor communications, such as a house newsletter.
- Participating, perhaps as a lecturer, in franchisee training.

## FIELD PERSONNEL

### REPORTING RESPONSIBILITY

Directly to the Training Director.

### AUTHORITY

Complete authority for franchisee field relations, as delegated by the Training Director.

### SPECIFIC RESPONSIBILITIES

Line responsibility for maintaining personal contact with franchisees on a periodic but irregular and unannounced basis, including, but not limited to:

- Advising and helping franchisees with specific problems that they may express, including obtaining advice and help from appropriate franchisor personnel where applicable.
- Checking franchisee books and records in order to lend more meaningful assistance and, incidentally, to verify the correctness of royalty and advertising fund remittances.
- Acting as general, personal liaison between franchisee and franchisor.

### FIELD REPRESENTATIVE

The first few months of operation are critical to most, if not all, franchisees. It is during this period of time that the recruit must "go over the hurdles" and build the business into a profitable entity. In the vast majority of cases it is unrealistic to assume that a new unit, regardless of the impact of its grand opening, will operate at sales and cost efficiency levels resulting in satisfactory profit status. Any business, including a franchised one, usually experiences sorting-out problems during its initial operating period. Such problems generally lead directly to cost structures of greater magnitude than those experienced by more mature operators, and sales tend to taper off after grand opening until the business catches on and sales rise. In most instances, in fact, it is realistic to predict an initial period of time during which the franchisee's operation will exhibit a net loss rather than any net profit at all.

It is during this period of time that the franchisee is most likely to become discouraged and stands most in need of franchisor support. Typically, this support is provided to the franchisee by the franchisor's Field Representative, an individual who must be qualified by training and temperament to function as a "hand-holder." A Field Representative must be capable of retracing all the steps of initial training in the field, demonstrating that adherence to them will enable the franchisee to do well. The Field Representative must be able to re-inspire the franchisee and replace what may be lagging morale with renewed drive and spirit.

During these first critical months, the franchisor's Field Representative should plan at least one weekly visit and/or telephone call to the franchisee. He or she should strive to further solidify the base that was created during initial training and on which future franchisee-franchisor relationships will stand. It is at this time that the franchisor, through the activities of the Field Representative, can help assure retention of a loyal and productive franchisee for years to come by offering wisdom, kindness, and sympathy, as well as direct sales assistance.

Of course, the role and function of the Field Representative do not cease as soon as the franchisee attains acceptable profitability. The Field Representative should continue to schedule periodic visits and maintain telephone and written contact with the franchisee. By this means, a personal link between franchisee and franchisor is established and questions of control and the implementation of program modifications are more expediently addressed. Thus is a highly effective, unofficial, informal two-way communications link created.

## PILOT UNIT PERSONNEL

### REPORTING RESPONSIBILITY

Directly or indirectly to the Pilot Unit Manager, as specified by the Pilot Unit Manager and the operating manual.

### AUTHORITY

As specified by the Pilot Unit Manager and the operating manual.

### SPECIFIC RESPONSIBILITIES

As specified by the Pilot Unit Manager and the operating manual.

# FINANCING

**7**

## Capital Requirements of the Franchisor

Despite the fact that every prospective franchisor faces a unique situation, certain general approaches apply to the franchising of virtually every product or service imaginable. All franchisor capital investment can be divided into five categories, each of which must be considered a distinct but related variable, regardless of the product or service under consideration.

**THE CHRONOLOGICAL PROCESS**

As a franchise program is developed, key areas of investment occur in the following order:

1. Capital requirements for blueprint development, including research.
2. Capital requirements for prototype development.
3. Capital requirements for franchise package development and production, including legal preparation.
4. Working capital requirements, including initial recruitment advertising expenditures.
5. Reserve capital.

The total capital required to embark confidently on development and implementation of a franchise program is, of course, equal to the sum of these individual components. We strongly advise prospective franchisors to consider these categories chronologically, so that capital requirements can be matched with capital availability. The essential purpose of chronological grouping is to define franchise program development and implementation in terms of function completion and to relate function completion to capital availability. This leads us to emphasize the importance of having both the money and the ability to finish the job before you become involved in it.

In Chapter 5, we examined the process of blueprinting a new franchise program. Chronologically, this will be the initial area of capital requirement.

Upon completion of a blueprint, capital will be required to develop a prototype operation. As we have mentioned, this will probably be necessary whether a program is evolving from an existing operation or merely from a concept. The major difference between an existing operation and a concept in this context is that prototype development from an existing operation is usually cheaper and involves less risk than prototype development from a concept.

Like the blueprint, the prototype may be used as a tool to attract additional capital to the project. In addition, the prototype operation should represent an earnings center, repaying its capital investment together with an adequate profit even if no further franchise program development is undertaken. Consequently, logic dictates that a prospective franchisor must never, under any circumstances, embark on development of a prototype operation unless he or she is absolutely certain that funds are available to finish the project. These funds must include working capital in an amount sufficient to sustain the operation until it becomes self-sustaining and profit-generating.

## CAPITAL REQUIREMENTS FOR PROTOTYPE DEVELOPMENT

Capital requirements for prototype development cannot be quantified in a general sense. The dollar amount of this expense is totally dependent on the specific operation being considered as a franchise vehicle, on what financing may be available, and on a number of other critical factors.

Qualitatively, however, we may make the general statement that total investment in a prototype should not be recaptured through the receipt of franchise fees or royalties. Rather, the prototype should be looked upon as an investment in its own right, with returns derived from its own profits.

There is one exception to this rule: That is when one or a number of prototype units are operated by a franchisor *solely for the purposes of testing* new products, services, marketing approaches, and other innovations, *and/or for the training and retraining* franchisees. Even then, the prototype should be managed so that it at least breaks even; In the rare instance that a franchisor's prototype is viewed as a true "loss operation," costs associated with its maintenance should be considered part of the franchisor's operating overhead—allocable to research-and-development or training expense, or some combination of the two.

This exception usually occurs in a well-established franchise chain. Beginning networks can seldom afford the luxury of loss-operation prototype units. In fact, most find that profitable prototype operations are a necessary factor in franchisee recruitment and establishment. Documentation of a profitable prototype operation is a major inducement for potential franchisees to become actual franchisees.

Under any circumstances, a prototype operation should be capitalized conservatively. Only on very rare occasions will a new venture attain sales at a level sufficient to break even immediately. Rather, a "building time" is usually required, and the operation must be capitalized with sufficient monies to carry it through this initial period of net losses and net cash outflows.

CAPITAL REQUIREMENTS FOR FRANCHISE PACKAGE DEVELOPMENT

Like costs incurred in blueprint development, the expense of developing and producing a franchise package should be considered a capital investment amortizable over a carefully chosen number of franchises. For tax purposes, a prospective franchisor may choose to treat these costs in various ways. Reimbursement should be gained from receipt of franchise fees.

Here, too, precise quantification of capital requirements is difficult because they tend to vary with factors related to the specific business in question. As a general rule, however, a total of $25,000 to $35,000 can be considered the minimum capital required to develop and produce an acceptable franchise package, but this figure does not include initial media advertising allowance. Such an investment usually produces a franchise package that will "do the job," but remain highly dependent on the personal talents and capabilities of the personnel who utilize it as a tool in the recruitment of franchisees.

With respect to time, a minimum of two to three months should be allocated for creation and production of a proper franchise package; it is unlikely that any franchise package will require more than 15 months.

WORKING-CAPITAL REQUIREMENTS

During the course of blueprint development, a prospective franchisor should define working-capital requirements both theoretically and practically. One of the major blueprint items is a series of pro-forma cash flows for the franchisor, and working-capital requirements may be equated with the operational peak cash outflow identified by these statements. However, a general rule in the venture-capital industry is to double this amount, and a safety factor of "plus 50 percent" is considered a minimum.

Adequate working capital is particularly crucial to the success of a franchise program whose basis is conceptual. Where a successful operation already exists, it is conceivable that all or a portion of its profits may be diverted to franchise program development. In the case of a program evolving solely from concept, this possibility does not exist.

RESERVE-CAPITAL REQUIREMENTS

It may seem that the prospective franchisor is providing reserve capital when that safety factor is added to the projected working capital requirements. However, the federal government and many individual states require that the franchisor show evidence of financial stability through possession of adequate funds to fulfill all commitments to franchisees. In many states this reserve-capital requirement is $100,000. These funds should be included in franchisor capital requirements *in addition to* the excess working capital provided by the minimum fifty-percent safety factor. Reserve capital represents a legal requirement for the financial protection of the franchisee, whereas working capital represents a practical requirement for the financial protection of the franchisor. Reserve capital is dictated by a third party—a government body of one form or another—for the stated purpose of protecting a "consumer class." Working capital is dictated internally, for the purpose of ensuring both franchisor and franchisee viability and success.

**SUMMARY OF FRANCHISOR CAPITAL REQUIREMENTS**

We have shown that franchisor capital requirements can be divided into five general categories:

1. Capital requirements for blueprint development, including research.
2. Capital requirements for prototype development.
3. Capital requirements for franchise package development and production, including legal preparation.
4. Working-capital requirements, including initial recruitment advertising expenditures.
5. Reserve capital.

Further, we have shown why precise quantification of capital requirements in any category is highly dependent upon the specifics of the prospective franchisor's capabilities, strengths, and weaknesses. However, subject to those qualifications and the results of the analyses to which they lead, franchising experience allows identification of some very broad ranges of capital requirements in each area:

| Capital Requirement | Estimated minimum | Estimated maximum |
|---|---|---|
| Blueprint development | $ 5,000 | $ 40,000 |
| Franchise package development | 25,000 | 125,000 |
| Working capital | 100,000 | 500,000 |
| Reserve capital | 50,000 | 250,000 |
| Total capital required before prototype development | $180,000 | $915,000 |

As a general rule, then, franchisor initial capital requirements will fall into the range of $150,000 to $1,000,000, *plus* a properly capitalized, functioning prototype operation.

## Capital Requirements of the Franchisee

A prospective franchisee will require varying amounts of capital, depending upon the magnitude of the franchise sought. Franchisees anticipating a number of units may require as much capital as a regional franchisor. In fact, the problems and opportunities faced by multiunit franchisees parallel those of the franchisor, with the added limitation of the franchise contract.

While a franchisor may view the setting up of a franchise chain as a fast, inexpensive method of expansion, there are certain basic initial outlays that can prove substantial. These include acquisition of real estate, creation of a recruiting division, construction of a selection and training program and hiring of associated personnel, hiring of field-supervision personnel, plus advertising and public-relations budgets. In fact, these initial costs may very nearly equal the costs of establishing a fully owned company chain. It is only in later stages that the profit advantages of franchising become apparent.

On a smaller scale, comparable costs are incurred by the franchisee, including the initial franchisee fee, real-estate rental, equipment costs, start-up inventories and expenses, and working capital.

One key to franchisor success is the development of a program that does not require large-scale financing. If the franchise operation is sound, bankers may seriously consider the franchisee's membership in the system favorable to granting a loan. Loans from banks will be intermediate-term. A good location will also be instrumental in obtaining a bank loan. If the loan is to finance equipment, a repurchase agreement from the franchisor will be helpful. In recognition of this problem, some equipment manufacturers offer their own financing arrangements.

## FRANCHISEE FINANCING SOURCES

Depending upon the quality of sponsorship and current financial needs, the franchisee may employ a number of the following financing techniques:

- Short-term financing
- Intermediate-term financing
- Long-term senior financing
- Current-assets financing
- Small Business Investment Companies (SBICs)
- Various venture-capital organizations
- Government sources
- Sale of equity

## SHORT-TERM FINANCING

Short-term financing generally consists of *unsecured bank loans* as lines of credit designed to meet seasonal demand. Usually a bank will require that the borrower project the ability to repay such a loan from earnings or inventory reductions. Such funds enable the franchisor to accumulate real-estate sites, and construct and equip the units, after which a blanket mortgage or an institutional sale and leaseback of the properties will be arranged.

Another short-term financing method is *revolving credit* that consists of a definite principal loan, any amount of which can be drawn at any time, not to exceed the agreed principal amount. These agreements usually run for a period of from three to four years, and interest is due only on the outstanding amount drawn.

## INTERMEDIATE-TERM FINANCING

Intermediate-term financing involves secured loans requiring monthly or quarterly amortization. The entire principal amount of the loan is taken down immediately. Since the loan term is longer, the bank may require more detailed information in order to judge relative risk. Such information may include a statement of the purpose of the loan and documentation of how the loan will be secured. Frequently the borrower will be asked to agree to a number of the following restrictions:

- Maintenance of stated minimum capital.
- Limits on dividends and stock acquisitions.

- Limits on borrowing other than from current lender.
- Maintenance of security free of liens.
- Limits on loans and guarantees of obligations of third parties.
- Prohibition of mergers, acquisitions, or consolidation with other corporations.
- Prohibition of sale or loss of all or substantially all of the borrower's assets.
- Agreement to furnish lender with interim financial statements, annual audited financial statements, and allied information.

Further, the borrower must make a commitment to the interest rate, the schedule of repayment, and a prepayment schedule.

LONG-TERM FINANCING

Long-term financing is a term used to describe loans that run for a period of five to twenty years. These may include unsecured term loans, mortgage loans, and lease agreements.

Long-term loans are generally provided by such institutions as insurance companies and pension funds, and are written at interest rates above high-grade bond rates.

CURRENT-ASSETS FINANCING

Current-assets financing is usually a loan secured by receivables, by inventories, or—in unusual cases—by equipment.

SBICs AND VENTURE-CAPITAL ORGANIZATIONS

Small-business investment companies and venture-capital organizations make certain loans available providing they receive a higher-than-prevailing interest rate supplemented with a significant equity bonus. Despite general opinion, these concerns are more interested in secondary financing than "start-up" financing. Essentially they are secured lenders rather than venture capitalists. This type of financing is usually of minimal use to franchisees—especially beginning franchisees.

GOVERNMENT FINANCING

There are many doors to knock on for possible government financial assistance. A partial list is shown below. The agency's name usually provides a clue as to its possible financing relevancy. To obtain more detailed information, write to the agencies that are pertinent to your business.

- Commercial, industrial, and financial loans

  Small-Business Administration
  Treasury Department
  Federal-Reserve System
  Federal Home Loan Bank
  Maritime Administration
  Department of Commerce Office of Economic Assistance

- Agricultural loans

  Farm Credit Administration
  Rural Electrification Administration
  Farmers Home Administration
  Commodity Credit Corporation

- Housing and community development loans
  Office of Transportation
  Community Facilities Administration
  Public Housing Administration
  Urban Renewal Administration
  Federal Housing Administration

- Veterans' loans
  Veterans Administration

- Natural-resources loans
  Department of Interior
  Bureau of Reclamation
  National Marine Fisheries Service
  Bureau of Indian Affairs

- International loans
  Export-Import Bank
  Agency for International Development

SALE OF
EQUITY

The sale of equity or part of the ownership interest in the corporation may be accomplished in a variety of ways:

- By sale of a minority equity interest.
- By acquisition of a controlling interest in a public corporation.
- By merging with a public company.
- By public acquisition of the corporation.
- By sale for cash or convertible debt.
- By public offering of stock.

Here are some of the definite advantages in becoming a public corporation:

- Cash is obtained.
- Net worth is increased.
- Borrowing is made easier.
- Stock-option plans can be inaugurated.
- Franchisees will have more confidence.
- Stock may be traded for acquisitions.
- Liquidity is improved.

However, there are pertinent questions to answer before making the final decision to become a public corporation. Consider these:

- Are the costs of public financing excessive?
- Is the company large enough for a public issue?
- Can operations be effective if they include "outside" directors?
- Can the maximum price be obtained for the shares offered?

Before approaching a good quality investment banker, the company should have the following:

- A five-year series of audited financial statements
- A stock-option plan
- A profit-sharing or pension plan
- Adjusted executive salaries and benefits
- A restructured board of directors.
- Arrangements for registrar and transfer agents.

Becoming a public corporation is very nearly irrevocable and the costs involved can be very high. Costly items include these:

- Legal fees,
- Auditing expenses,
- Printing expenses,
- Underwriting commissions.

The investment industry cites the following sound reasons for becoming a public entity:

- To create a public market for the company's stock.
- To provide valuation and liquidity for estate-planning purposes.
- To diversify the portfolios of the selling stockholders.
- To facilitate acquisition of other businesses.
- To acquire additional franchisees.
- To expand existing divisions.
- To permit franchisees to acquire franchisor shares.
- To encourage use of company services by customers.
- To improve the industry's image.
- To modernize operations more.
- To provide key-employee stock options.
- To acquire high-calibre personnel through options.
- To obtain publicity.

## PREPARING A FINANCIAL PROSPECTUS

When a franchisor considers financing through such institutions as banks and insurance companies, it is wise to construct a "banker's report." This report should include the usual information required by a lending officer. It will make that individual's task easier, improve chances for a favorable decision, and often result in earlier action. This report should cover the following points:

- The background and history of each management member, including education and pertinent personal data.
- The expected share of the regional and national market.

- The background and competence rating of each franchisee.
- The quality of relationship between franchisor and franchisee, including the status of any legal actions.
- The economic potential of the various trading areas.
- Current expansion plans and justification thereof.
- Financial operations of franchisor:
  - Are notes accepted in partial payment of franchise fees?
  - Do earnings exclude nonrecurring income?
  - Are cost controls sound?
  - Does company require long-term financing prior to commencement of real estate development and construction?
  - Are lease liabilities excessive?
  - Are audit procedures satisfactory to verify royalty payments?
  - Is a return on investment a criteria in considering expansion?
- The franchisor's financing relationships:
  - The long-term debt to equity should not exceed 1:1; otherwise it may be top heavy and restrict bank borrowing.
  - Lease financing indicated in balance-sheet footnotes should be consolidated with long-term debt to provide an accurate ratio.
  - A current ratio of 3:1 is most desirable; 2:1 is a minimum.
  - The franchisor should keep in mind that high debt produces high volatility in earnings as a result of capital structure leverage.

During the early days of the franchise industry, certain doubtful accounting practices were common. These should be scrupulously avoided. They are:

- Recognition of initial franchise fees as revenue at the time the franchise agreement is signed, even through the franchisor is committed to provide substantial services to the franchisee.
- Inadequate provision for collection and cancellation of losses.
- Inadequate interest charged on notes received for initial franchise fees, inventories, and equipment.
- Financial interests in franchisee operations through stock ownership, options, or obligations to purchase the franchisee's business.

## The MESBIC Program

MESBIC is a government-sponsored, private-sector program that provides a potential for leveraged financing and accelerated expansion for businesses—and unique *equity* growth potential for so-called "disadvantaged" individuals. Through MESBIC the federal government encourages private industry and private investors to assist "disadvantaged" Americans in the development and ownership of their own business enterprises.

Let's pose a problem. Suppose we told you of a country with almost 40 million population—a country contiguous to the United States, with U.S. laws and regulations, buying patterns, living standards, educational facilities, and sharing U.S. newspaper and television media. Suppose this country's gross national product, average income, and discretionary income were increasing at a rate more rapid than that of the U.S. economy. Yet suppose this urban country had only one percent of the number of businesses in the United States and had only a limited, though growing, business heritage. Now suppose the United States signed a mutual assistance treaty allowing free two-way access for businesspeople to develop these markets.

Would there be opportunity? Would there be dynamism? Would there be a potential for mutual benefit and gain?

This is the marketplace of the "disadvantaged" American businessperson! It's a marketplace of broad horizons, freedom of entry, stern competition—and opportunity to succeed. This is the market for the MESBIC investor, the "advantaged" individual or company that is willing to provide the needed financial and managerial assistance, be it for personal gain, strategic marketing purposes, or social responsibility.

To encourage such investors, the federal government has developed a specialized investment vehicle, blending private initiative and expertise with government incentives. It's known as the MESBIC program.

## WHAT IS A MESBIC?

Just what is a MESBIC? What can it do? How do you start one? How long does it take? In the following pages we'll try to answer some of the most frequently asked questions.

Actually, there is no such thing as a MESBIC. Originally, Small Business Investment Companies that specialized in minority-owned ventures were called Minority Enterprise Small Business Investment Companies, or MESBICs. However, the 1972 amendments to the Small Business Investment Act broadened the term from "minorities" to "disadvantaged Americans," and the official title of a MESBIC is now a Section 301(d) SBIC. Rather than stumble over that awkward designation, most people continue to use the term MESBIC. We will, too.

A MESBIC is a privately owned, privately managed venture-capital corporation. Incorporated in the state of your choice, it is licensed to do business anywhere in the United States by the U.S. Small Business Administration (SBA) under authority of the Small Business Investment Act of 1958, as amended.

MESBICs can be organized by anyone, or any group of individuals or corporations, including foreign citizens and foreign corporations. A minimum of $300,000 in capital funds must normally be paid into the MESBIC in order for it to be licensed; however, there is no upper limit on the amount of capital a MESBIC may have. Most MESBICs are now organized at $500,000 or more due to the added leveraging of funds available to MESBICs of this size. A recent change in the law permits banks to own 100 percent of a MESBIC.

MESBICs are subsidized by the federal government as an incentive to attract private investors to place their funds into businesses owned by disadvantaged Americans. The simple intent of the MESBIC legislation is to encourage profitable investments by the MESBIC in profitable businesses operated by disadvantaged Americans, providing a desirable return on investment for all parties and therefore stimulating the economic development of the nation.

ELIGIBILITY For MESBIC purposes, disadvantaged Americans fall into three categories:

1. Ethnic minorities—Black Americans, American Eskimos and Aleuts, American Indians, Asiatic-Americans, Spanish-American citizens, including persons of Puerto-Rican, Mexican, and Cuban extraction.

2. U.S. citizens who have served honorably on active duty (other than training) in the U.S. armed forces anywhere in the world for at least one day on or after August 5, 1964, regardless of rank or grade.

3. U.S. citizens whose participation in the free enterprise system is hampered by social, economic, or physical considerations beyond their personal control. Lack of formal education, limited financial capacity, geographic or regional economic distress, and physical or mental handicaps are some of the conditions that restrict individuals from full participation in our economic system.

   A MESBIC may invest in or assist any business that is owned at least 50 percent by the disadvantaged American(s) at the time the investment/assistance package is accepted by both parties—MESBIC management for the investor and business management for the business firm. The federal government does not enter into the analysis, negotiation, funds transfer, or any follow-on management or technical assistance rendered. The decision to invest or not to invest remains solely with the MESBIC. Voting control is the paramount issue; although 50 percent of the business must be owned by disadvantaged persons, there is no requirement that these persons participate in active day-to-day management.

**RANGE OF SERVICES** The range of services a MESBIC can provide to a business owned at least 50 percent by disadvantaged Americans involves four areas:

1. *A direct investment in either a preferred or common stock,* or an investment as a limited partner. Since the MESBIC negotiates and determines its own investments, the terms and conditions may include any stipulations mutually acceptable to the parties involved. For instance, the stock might be voting or nonvoting, fixed or variable dividend, participating or nonparticipating, with or without "rights," class A or class B, callable or noncallable, convertible or nonconvertible. The only limitation is that the disadvantaged businessperson(s) must own a minimum of 50 percent of the voting stock of the corporation at the time the transaction is closed (including exercise of warrants/options).

2. *A direct loan to the business,* either in the form of a convertible debenture, or as an ordinary loan. Such loans may be for periods of up to 20 years; however, most MESBIC loans mature in the three-to-seven-year range.

Again, the actual terms of the loan depend upon negotiations between the MESBIC lender and the borrower. Loan agreements may provide for monthly payment, annual payment, or interest only for a given period; they may be convertible into stock, may carry restrictive legends regarding dividends and investments, and may require personal guarantees, collateral, reserves or other specific operating limitations. Forward commitments are also authorized.

MESBIC interest rates are limited to the state usury rate applicable or 15 percent simple interest, whichever is lower. In determining the interest rate charged, SBA includes such items as placement fees, bonuses, and "points" paid to the MESBIC. However, SBA does not so consider the intrinsic value of warrants or options to purchase stock in the business. Warrants or options may therefore be obtained so long as the exercise of the warrants/options will not cause the disadvantaged owners to hold less than 50 percent of the voting shares.

3. *MESBICs may guarantee 100 percent of a loan from any third party* to a business concern owned at least 50 percent by a disadvantaged person(s). The guarantee may provide specific coverage or be general in nature and may stipulate terms and conditions similar to loans (i.e., personal guarantee, collateral, reserves). A guarantee fee may be charged for this assistance, including the issuance of warrants or options.

4. *MESBICs can provide management and technical assistance for a fee.* Such assistance may include but is not limited to financial consulting, bookkeeping or accounting, legal assistance, marketing and advertising, and inventory control and procurement. Such services can be provided on a direct or indirect basis, and MESBICs may set up a wholly owned subsidiary to provide such services.

**MESBIC INCENTIVES**

All we've really indicated so far is that the MESBIC program is simply designed and rather broad in scope; that MESBICs may be owned by anyone, U.S. citizen or not, and can provide investment funds to a sizable "disadvantaged" segment of our population—perhaps one out of every four American citizens. Now, what about incentives?

MESBIC incentives fit into five readily defined categories: ease of entry, immediate leveraging of funds, low money costs, tax advantages and management assistance.

1. *MESBICs are readily licensed.* The licensing process is relatively simple and uncomplicated. Select your corporate name, its directors and officers, and incorporate. Complete the license application and mail the application and supporting documents to the SBA in Washington. (Suggested wording and examples will be provided by the SBA.) Within a short time you will receive a comment letter outlining any requirements that have been overlooked and authorizing the publication of notification of the license application in a

local newspaper. Following this action, the SBA will process the license—usually within 60 to 90 days from receipt of the initial application.

2. *Leveraging is something special.* Once licensed, and before one cent of MESBIC's own funds are invested, application may be made for a first 100-percent matching sum of money from the SBA. Later, application may be made for additional matching sums. . .up to four dollars for each dollar you invest.

It works like this. If you start with less than $500,000, *three* times the capital in matching sums may be obtained from the SBA. If there is $500,000 or more, *four* times the capital in matching sums may be obtained. If this fund is started at $300,000 and then increased to $500,000 or more, there is no penalty; everything is handled on a retroactive basis and leverage to four times on your full paid-in capital and paid-in surplus base can be obtained.

Note that the first matching sums come before the fund had used one cent of private capital. Then, when the fund has committed approximately two-thirds of the first matching sum (i.e., a total investment or commitment to invest of $665,000 of the $1,000,000 in assets for a $500,000 capital MESBIC), application may be made for a second matching sum; and the third and fourth matching sums may be received when funds have been invested or committed.

3. *Money costs are a distinct advantage.* MESBICs under $500,000 in capital may obtain their three matching sums as 10-year debentures. The SBA purchases these debentures from the MESBIC on the following basis:

a) The MESBIC is liable for repayment; no personal endorsements or guarantees are required.

b) The 10-year debenture requires *interest only* every six months; the principal is payable at the end of the 10-year term.

c) No reserved or sinking funds are required.

d) No collateral is required.

e) The interest rate on the debentures is the cost of money on a 15-year government bond, usually well below commercial rates and/or the bank prime rate.

f) The debentures may be "rolled over," or renewed for an additional 10-year term at normal expiration; or they may be paid off by the MESBIC or any interest anniversary date if so desired.

g) If requested, the SBA will defer payment of three percent of the interest rate during the first five years of the 10-year term. For instance, if the interest rate is six percent for 10 years, the MESBIC may delay three-percent payment during years one through five, pay six percent years six through nine, and then pay the arrearages (3 percent × 5 years) plus the normal six percent in the tenth year. No interest is charged on the interest deferred; however, all deferrals must be brought up to date at the time dividends are paid to stockholders.

**MESBICS OF $500,000 OR MORE**

As we stated earlier, MESBICs with $500,000 or more in private paid-in capital may receive four matching sums. All four sums may be in debentures similar to those outlined above—low interest, no personal endorsement or guarantee, no reserves or sinking funds, interest-only until maturity. However, should the MESBIC prefer, one matching sum may be purchased by SBA in the form of a three-percent cumulative preferred stock, eliminating the interest charge and providing for no-cost funding if your MESBIC does not earn a profit. The preferred may be sold to the SBA at first matching or at subsequent matching in increments of $50,000 up to the total of a one-time capital match.

Of course, most MESBICs do not provide the total funds required for a business. In fact, most MESBICs provide perhaps 20 percent of the funds required, subordinating their loan or stock position to other funding sources. For instance, an illustrative situation might be as follows:

| | | |
|---|---:|---:|
| Funds required | $100,000 | $500,000 |
| Disadvantaged person has: | $ 5,000 | $ 10,000 |
| MESBIC provides: (As loan with options) | 15,000 | 150,000 |
| Capital and subordinated debt | $ 20,000 | $160,000 |
| From others (i.e., 90-percent SBA guaranteed bank loan) | 80,000 | 340,000 |
| TOTAL | $100,000 | $500,000 |

Because of these leveraging opportunities we believe that a MESBIC, when fully leveraged and invested, may provide up to 25 times its capital in funds for disadvantaged businesses. For example, a $500,000 MESBIC might be able to provide funds as follows:

| | |
|---|---:|
| Base capital | $ 500,000 |
| SBA funds to MESBIC | 2,000,000 |
| | $ 2,500,000 |
| Four times from other sources (including SBA guaranteed bank loans) | 10,000,000 |
| TOTAL FUNDS PROVIDED | $12,500,000 |

In addition to these low money costs, MESBICs have certain special tax advantages:

1. Gains on the sale of stock in a MESBIC are always long-term capital gains.
2. Loss on the sale of stock in a MESBIC is always a short-term capital (ordinary) loss, regardless of the term held.
3. Dividends received by the MESBIC from portfolio companies are 100-percent tax excludable.
4. MESBIC profits on sale of equity interests in portfolio companies are long-term gains to the MESBIC.
5. MESBICs may create loss reserves on outstanding balances.
6. MESBICs may create unlimited contingency reserves from profits.
7. MESBICs may register as an investment company and receive pass-through authority under the Investment Act of 1940.

Of course, the key to MESBIC success includes locating viable business opportunities. Some MESBICs, such as those owned by franchisors, may specialize in a given business area, while others will be general in purpose and will use banks, attorneys, and accountants as a source of ventures. All MESBICs may utilize the services of the federal government for this purpose. For instance, the Commerce Department's Office of Minority Business Enterprise (OMBE) has almost 300 contract agencies across the country that locate and assist disadvantaged businesspersons in developing feasibility studies, marketing plans, and financial packages. These business-development organizations will welcome a new source of badly needed capital funding. In addition, the SBA and the Office of Economic Opportunity have offices that will refer viable business clients to a MESBIC. The rest is up to the MESBIC loan committee or board of directors.

MESBIC sponsors include such giants as General Motors, Bank of America, ITT, Rockwell International, Exxon, Sun Oil and Chase Manhattan Bank. Others include franchise companies, religious groups, universities, foundations, groups of individuals, and in six cases, single individuals.

MESBICs today have financed businesses in many categories. MESBICs have assisted radio and television stations, newspapers, auto dealerships, builders, minority-owned banks, mortgage bankers, finance companies, import/export companies, restaurants, groceries, barber shops, airline maintenance, manufacturers, wholesalers, distributors, and retailers. There are few investment limitations—other than your imagination!

And now a word of caution! MESBICs are *not* for everyone. MESBICs are businesses, too, and they must be operated like businesses if they are to succeed. They need capital, income to cover their overhead, sound analysis of opportunities, good negotiating capacity, and the ability to provide mature management and technical assistance when required by their portfolio companies.

MESBICs are *not* a get-rich-quick scheme. With the incentives now provided, with patience and diligence in operations, MESBICs may provide you, your company, your organization, or your associates with the opportunity to help others earn a profit while you also earn a profit.

We hope so!

The Office of Minority Business Enterprise, which has marketing responsibility for MESBICs, will readily assist any organizing group in the development of a MESBIC. Assistance can be obtained by writing to:

The MESBIC Staff
Capital Development
Office of Minority Business Enterprise
U.S. Department of Commerce
Washington, D.C. 20230

# AREA ALLOTMENT

**EVALUATION OF THE TRADING AREA**

A prospective franchisee must study the market in which selling is expected to take place. Answers should be sought to the following questions:

1. Does the proposed territory have enough potential for the product or service? In other words, does it have sufficient ability to buy? Among the factors to consider are total population, population per square mile, by age, by ethnic origin, and general population trends; number and size of families; birth, marriage, and death rates; number of single homes and number of apartments; income levels, retail spending habits, and bank deposits; ownership of telephones, cars, and major appliances; number of employed and unemployed; education levels and school enrollment.

2. Is the potential sufficient to produce a level of profit commensurate with the franchisee's needs?

3. What are the present buying habits for this kind of product or service?

4. Does there seem to be a need and desire for the proposed brand of product or service? If necessary, a consumer study should be conducted.

5. Does the proposed territory constitute a logical whole trading market, or are some parts excluded?

The franchisee may have an exclusive territory. If not, the franchisor must maintain the confidence and cooperation of the franchisees by not over-saturating a particular market.

**SITE SELECTION**

For many franchise businesses, especially those dependent upon a walk-in or drive-in public, site selection is one of the most crucial operating decisions. Site selection refers not to the *territory* within which the franchisee is entitled to operate, but to the *location*, or address, where the business will be established. While franchisees usually select their own sites, franchisors often reserve the right to approve them. Aggressive franchisors have been known to purchase a site and then begin looking for a franchisee to build on it.

A number of important factors must be evaluated when considering a potential site. Among them are the following:

- Cost
- Automobile traffic density
- Safe and convenient entry and exit
- Pedestrian traffic density
- Parking facilities
- Neighborhood
- Taxes
- Utilities
- Zoning regulations
- Protective services (police and fire).

## SITE SELECTION CRITERIA

Site criteria factors are basically intended to list important site parameters inclusive of:

- Vehicular traffic in the area, entry and exit from the site, and accessibility to a main highway.
- Availability of additional parking in the area.
- The size and shape of the available site, the amount of space needed for on-site parking, and the grade of the land.
- Sign visibility, possible obstructions, and potential obstructions from future buildings.
- Identifying landmarks in the area (for directions) and nearby tourist attractions.
- Availability of utilities and services—water, gas, electricity, sewer, garbage and refuse removal (private or municipal).
- Zoning of property.
- Considerations of general area and accessibility to most of the upper-middle-class residential section.
- Long-term evaluation of general area; area growth or regression as it relates to the total metropolitan area; residential property values; belt highway and passenger highway systems.
- Competition from other businesses; suburban development situations—shopping malls, office buildings, industrial areas.
- Travel patterns in the area.
- Local market details.

## A SUGGESTED GUIDELINE

The following material is excerpted from SBA Small Markets Aid No. 152, *Using a Traffic Study to Select a Retail Site.*

**Factors to be Considered**

Three factors confront an owner-manager in choosing a location: selection of a city; choice of an area or type of location within a city; and identification of a specific site.

If you are going to select a new *city*, naturally you consider the following factors:

- *Size of the city's trading area.*
- *Population and population trends in the trading area.*
- *Total purchasing power and the distribution of the purchasing power.*
- *Total retail trade potential for different lines of trade.*
- *Number, size, and quality of competition.*
- *Progressiveness of competition.*

In choosing an *area or type of location* within a city you evaluate factors such as:

- *Customer attraction power of the particular store and the shopping district.*
- *Quantitative and qualitative nature of competitive stores.*
- *Availability of access routes to the stores.*
- *Nature of zoning regulations.*
- *Direction of the area expansion.*
- *General appearance of the area.*

Pinpointing the *specific site* is, as you know, particularly important. In central and secondary business districts, small stores depend upon the traffic created by large stores. Large stores in turn depend upon attracting customers from the existing flow of traffic. (However, where sales depend upon nearby residents, selecting the trading area is more important than picking specific site.) Obviously, you want to know about the following factors when choosing a specific site:

- *Adequacy and potential of traffic passing the site.*
- *Ability of the site to intercept traffic en route from one place to another.*
- *Complementary nature of the adjacent stores.*
- *Type of goods sold.*
- *Adequacy of parking.*
- *Vulnerability of the site to unfriendly competition.*
- *Cost of the site.*

NECESSARY
DOCUMENTS

- Letter from realtor stating why site meets requirements.
- Completed checklist.
- Neighborhood map.
- Plan or survey of the property.
- Photographs—eight shots of site, land on each side, area across the street.
- Lease offer.
- Aerial photo, with site marked and two-mile radius noted.
- City map showing site, a two-mile radius circle, and all other committed locations.
- Census tract study—two-mile radius.

USING CENSUS
DATA

The following material is excerpted from SBA Small Markets Aid No. 154, *Using Census Data to Select a Store Site.*

**Geographical Breakdowns**

The *Standard Metropolitan Statistical Area* (SMSA) geographical designation includes a county (or counties) containing a central city of at least 50,000 inhabitants, plus contiguous counties which are socially and economically integrated with the central county. In some cases, there may be twin cities with a total population of 50,000 or more (the smaller of the two cities with at least 15,000 people). There are 267 tracted standard SMSAs in the United States and Puerto Rico.

*Census tracts* are subdivisions of SMSAs. Large cities and adjacent areas have been divided for the purpose of showing comparable small area statistics. The average tract has about 4,000 to 5,000 residents. One report is published for each SMSA. It includes statistical information about each and also includes a map for reference. The information is based on the 1970 Census of Population and Housing. Altogether this amounts to some 34,000 tracts.

The census tract usually constitutes a geographic unit small enough for a retail store location analysis. *Block statistics* within a census tract are also available for urbanized areas.

**AN EXAMPLE: ONE FRANCHISOR'S SITE-SELECTION CRITERIA**

On the following pages you will find an example of the in-depth information required by some franchisors in the selection of a business site.

## LOCATION REPORT

1. Submit THREE OR MORE reports at ONE time to the home office.

2. DO NOT MAKE ANY LEASE COMMITMENT UNTIL YOU RECEIVE WRITTEN APPROVAL FROM THE HOME OFFICE.

**ADDRESS OF PROPERTY:**

Street _____

City                County                State                Zip Code

**TRAFFIC COUNT:**

**POPULATION DENSITY AND AREA IMAGE:**

| Population | Description of area | | | | Total |
|---|---|---|---|---|---|
| | % Residential | % Commercial | % Industrial | % Undeveloped | |
| 1-mile radius _____ | _____ | _____ | _____ | _____ | 100% |
| 3-mile radius _____ | _____ | _____ | _____ | _____ | 100% |
| 5-mile radius _____ | _____ | _____ | _____ | _____ | 100% |
| Average income: | Low _____% | Middle _____% | High _____% | | |

**VISIBILITY AND ACCESSIBILITY:**

Site is on corner: Yes ____ No ____ (If on corner, include information on both streets or highways where applicable.)

If not on corner, how far is the site from nearest intersection? _____ feet

Is site on a metropolitan city street? Yes _____ No _____

Is site in a shopping mall? Yes _____ No _____ (If yes, enclose their literature and indicate which stores are available to you.)

Is site on a highway?               Yes _____          No _____

The highway is:                     Major _____        Secondary _____

If corner:                          Major _____        Secondary _____

Speed limit: _____ mph

Approach visibility is (poor, fair, good, excellent):

|              | By car | By foot |
|--------------|--------|---------|
| From north:  | _____ | _____ |
| From east:   | _____ | _____ |
| From south:  | _____ | _____ |
| From west:   | _____ | _____ |

Visibility is poor or fair *because* (specify curve, rise or dip in road, obstructing trestle, sign, trees, etc.):

_____

_____

Number of lanes in *EACH* direction:          _____

                    If corner:                _____

Is there a center mall or other divider: Yes _____ No _____

Is traffic permitted and able to make a lefthand turn onto the site? Yes _____ No _____

Is traffic congested? Yes _____ No _____

How many curb cuts are there? _____

Where are they located on the property? _____

_____

How wide are they? _____

Describe on-premises parking facilities (number of cars, type of paving, size of slots, sufficient backout space, ramps, obstructions, etc.): _____

_____

_____

Describe off-premises parking facilities (street, metered, municipal, lots, garages, price, etc.): _____

_____

_____

Future street or highway plans, if any, and when scheduled (widening, repair, center divider, by-pass, etc.): _____

_____

Is the site paved and curbed? Yes _____ No _____

COMPETITION:  State names, addresses, distances, and your comments about similar businesses:

1. _____
_____
_____
_____
_____

2. _____
_____
_____
_____
_____

(use separate sheet if more space required)

NEIGHBORING BUSINESSES:  List *ALL* businesses within two blocks in every direction, whether competitive or not.

ZONING AND PERMITS:  Is site zoned for restaurant use? Yes ____ No ____

Source of information (Specify Certificate of Occupancy, Building Department, other):

_____

Will signs be permitted, by landlord and zoning rules, on
- Front of building (flush mounted)                    Yes ____ No ____
- Sides of building (flush mounted)                    Yes ____ No ____
- Roof of building (structure mounted)                 Yes ____ No ____
- Projecting from building (swinging)                  Yes ____ No ____
- Parking lot (free-standing)                          Yes ____ No ____

Restrictions, if any, on overall height of signs: _____

_____

Limitations on size, area, type, and number of signs: _____

_____

_____

(use separate sheet if more space required)

Source of information on signs: _____

_____

_____

STRUCTURE DIMENSIONS:  Measurements (inside)
- Frontage _____ ft.     Depth _____ ft.
- Square feet (frontage × depth) _____

Clear ceiling height: _____ ft.

Nature of previous occupant's business (if any): _____

_____

**STRUCTURE SPECIFICATIONS:**

Describe front: _____

_____

Number of entrances: _____ Where located: _____

_____

Size of each entrance: _____

_____

Type of roof (if 1-story building): _____

Electric service: _____amps.

Water availability:
  Cold:  Yes _____ No _____        Hot:  Yes _____ No _____

Natural gas availability:  Yes_____ No _____

Type of Heat: _____

Air conditioned:  Yes _____ No _____        Central:  Yes _____ No _____

Number and size of all windows: _____

_____

Number of bathrooms (indicate which have toilet facilities, washing facilities, or both):

_____

Describe type and condition of:

- Floor: _____
- Walls: _____
- Ceiling: _____

What is landlord offering to do to prepare the premises for your occupancy? _____

_____

_____

**LAND AREA:**

Measurements:
- Frontage _____ft.    Depth_____ft.
- Square feet (frontage × depth) _____

**RENTAL:**

How much is the rental for the initial term? $_____monthly

Will you be responsible for increases in any of landlord's costs, such as taxes, insurance, utilities, cost-of-living, etc.? Yes _____ No _____

If yes, describe: _____

_____

_____

Is amount of rental tied to sales volume? Yes _____ No _____

If yes, describe: _____

_____

How much rent-free time for setup? _____

What services will landlord provide (sanitation, cleaning, maintenance, etc.? _____

_____

_____

## THE BPI CRITERIA FOR FRANCHISEE AREA ALLOCATION

In the 1979 Survey of Buying Power published by S&MM (Sales & Marketing Management) the Buying Power Index (BPI) is defined as:

A weighted index that converts three basic elements—population, Effective Buying Income, and retail sales—into a measurement of a market's ability to buy, and expresses it as a percentage of the U.S./Canada potential. It is calculated by giving a weight of 5 to the market's percent of U.S./Canada Effective Buying Income, 3 to its percent of U.S./Canada retail sales, and 2 to its percent of U.S./Canada population. The total of those weighted percents is then divided by 10 to arrive at the BPI.

The BPI principle can prove important to franchisors in planning franchise area allotment and site selection, since it provides a measuring stick of the area's potential marketing eligibility.

To illustrate the use of the BPI concept in gauging marketing viability, we use as an example the state of Ohio. The criteria used for this state exemplifies procedures that can be utilized for other states.

It is initially assumed that a BPI of .25 is required to support one franchisee at an acceptable profit level that has been predetermined on the basis of pro-forma analysis. To determine the BPI of projected Ohio area, proceed as follows:

1. Locate Ohio in Sales & Marketing Management's *Survey of Buying Power*.

2. Obtain maps of Ohio that define county lines.

3. See the relation of the numbers stated by SBP in relation to geography. This has been done on the map shown in Fig. 8.1 by making each metropolitan area light gray. You'll note that some metropolitan areas consist of regions, or counties, located in adjacent states. Utilize only those portions of the metropolitan areas in the State under consideration, in this case, the State of Ohio. The reason for this is that our ultimate goal is to define operating franchise areas and it is generally unwise to define franchise areas that cross state lines, unless the franchise in question is a large master franchise or area controllership. This, however, is not our goal at the moment. Rather, it is to define *single* franchise areas, each with a BPI of approximately .25. Later, these predefined areas can be combined into master franchises and area distributorships, if this is our desire.

4. Divide the metropolitan areas into three categories:

   - Those with a BPI of approximately .25
   - Those with a BPI of greater than .25
   - Those with a BPI of less than .25

**Fig. 8.1** The relation of the numbers stated by SBP in relation to geography for the state of Ohio. Metropolitan areas are light gray. Areas with a BPI greater than .25 are outlined with a dotted line; those with a BPI less than .25 are outlined with a dashed line. Youngstown, with a BPI of .25, is outlined with a dash-dot line. (©1979 S&MM Survey of Buying Power)

This has also been done on Fig. 8.1 of the map series. Areas with a BPI greater than .25 are outlined with a dotted line; those with a BPI less than .25 are outlined with a dashed line. Only one, Youngstown, has been found to have a BPI of approximately .25 and is outlined with a dash–dot line. All white areas do not fall into the category of metropolitan areas.

5. Now *reduce* or *increase* those areas outlined with dotted lines to areas that exhibit a BPI of approximately .25 or some even multiple of .25, and *increase* those areas outlined with dashed lines to areas that exhibit a BPI of approximately .25 or some even multiple of .25. The area exhibiting a BPI of approximately .25 may be defined as an area suitable for the establishment of one franchise, so that at this stage and in this case the first franchise areas has been defined: the Youngstown area, consisting of the counties of Trumbull and Mahoning.

6. The next concentration will be on those areas exhibiting a BPI of *greater* than .25. These areas—Toledo, Cleveland, Akron, Columbus, Dayton,

and Cincinnati—are presented in Fig. 8.2 together with the Youngstown franchise area.

**Fig. 8.2** The areas with a BPI greater than .25. (©1979 S&MM Survey of Buying Power)

7. Reference to SBP indicates that the Akron area, consisting of the counties of Portage and Summit, has a BPI of .3002, and that the county of Summit alone has a BPI of .2464. This is very close to .25. Thus the next franchise area has been defined: the Akron franchise area, consisting of the county of Summit.

8. The Cincinnati area exhibits a BPI of .6450, but care must be exercised in this case, as areas in Kentucky and Indiana are defined by SBP as falling within the Cincinnati area. Eliminating those areas, Cincinnati has a BPI of .6450 − .0120 − .0181 − .0349 − .0573 = .5227. This number is very close to an even multiple of .25, as (2) (.25) = .50, but if Warren County were eliminated from the Cincinnati area a number of .5227 − .0386 = .4841 can be achieved, which is even closer to .50. Thus is defined the next

franchise area: the Cincinnati franchise area, consisting of the counties of Hamilton and Clermont, and capable of supporting *two* franchises.

9. The Cleveland area consists of the counties of Cuyahoga, Geauga, Lake, and Medina. In toto, this area exhibits a BPI of .9683, but examination of the area's data reveals that Cuyahoga County alone exhibits a BPI of .7895, a number very close to (3) (.25) = .75, so that the next franchise area is defined as the Cleveland franchise area, consisting of the county of Cuyahoga, and capable of supporting *three* franchises.

10. The Columbus area exhibits a BPI of .5310 and consists of the counties of Delaware, Fairfield, Franklin, Madison, and Pickaway. Eliminating Madison and Pickaway, the remaining counties exhibit a BPI of .5310 − .0128 − .0181 = .5001, a number that is very close to (2) (.25) = .50, so that the next franchise area has been defined: the Columbus franchise area, consisting of the counties of Delaware, Franklin, and Fairfield, and capable of supporting *two* franchises.

11. The Dayton area consists of the counties of Greene, Miami, Montgomery, and Preble. Its BPI is .3901, but if the contiguous counties of Butler, Darke, and Mercer are added to it, the entire area under consideration exhibits a BPI of .3901 + .1113 + .0210 + .0152 = .4810, a number very close to (2) (.25) = .50, so that another franchise area has been defined: the Dayton franchise area, consisting of the counties of Miami, Montgomery, Preble, Butler, Darke, and Mercer, and capable of supporting *two* franchises.

12. The Toledo area consists of the counties of Fulton, Lucas, Ottawa, and Wood, and exhibits a BPI of .0163 + .2470 + .0179 + .0508 = .3320. However, Lucas County alone exhibits a BPI of .2470 and is definable as a franchise area capable of supporting *one* franchise.

13. The process that has been described is depicted graphically in Fig. 8.3. Those counties included by SBP in specified metropolitan areas but deleted from the defined franchise areas have been cross-hatched. Butler, Darke, and Mercer counties, which were not included by SBP in any specified metropolitan area but were added to the Dayton franchise area, are *outlined* with a dashed line. You will recall that we found it necessary to add these counties in order to fulfill the criterion of an area exhibiting a BPI of .25 or some multiple thereof, or a BPI very close to one or the other.

14. Fig. 8.4 shows the end result of the work thus far. On it, seven franchise areas are defined as follows:

   - The Youngstown franchise area, capable of supporting one franchise.
   - The Columbus franchise area, capable of supporting two franchises.
   - The Cincinnati franchise area, capable of supporting two franchises.
   - The Dayton franchise area, capable of supporting two franchises.
   - The Toledo franchise area, capable of supporting one franchise.
   - The Cleveland franchise area, capable of supporting three franchises.
   - The Akron franchise area, capable of supporting one franchise.

**Fig. 8.3** Counties that are included by SBP in specified metropolitan areas but that are deleted from the franchise areas. (©1979 S&MM Survey of Buying Power)

15. The next step is to superimpose the remaining metropolitan areas in the State of Ohio onto the map containing the franchise areas that have been defined in steps 1 through 14. Each of these areas exhibits a BPI of less than .25, and to them must be added counties, taking care not to consider a county already allocated to an already defined franchise area, until the entire area defined exhibits a BPI of approximately .25. A graphic depiction of this step is shown in Fig. 8.5.

16. Using contiguous counties as building blocks, each of the metropolitan areas exhibiting a BPI of less than .25 is increased, till each of them forms the "core" of an area exhibiting a BPI of approximately .25. This process is graphically depicted in Fig. 8.6. Predefined franchise areas *and* metropolitan areas are depicted in gray. The gray metropolitan and franchise areas, along with the counties added to them, are outlined to show 13 major franchise areas.

**Fig. 8.4** The seven franchise areas. (©1979 S&MM Survey of Buying Power)

17. The result of step 16 shows that, in addition to the franchise areas defined in steps 1 through 14, there is now defined additional, single franchise areas as follows:

   • The Canton franchise area, consisting of the counties of Carroll, Stark, and Portage.

   • The Newark franchise area, consisting of the counties of Licking, Knox, Conshocton, Muskingum, Wayne, Holmes, Tuscarawas, and Richland.

   • The Steubenville franchise area, consisting of the counties of Jefferson, Columbiana, Harrison, Belmont, Monroe, Guernsey, Noble, Washington, Athens, Meigs, Gallia, Lawrence, and Jackson.

   • The Springfield franchise area, consisting of the counties of Champaign, Clark, Madison, Union, Fayette, Clinton, Highland, Brown, Marion, Greene, and Peckaway.

**Fig. 8.5** The franchise and metropolitan areas. (©1979 S&MM Survey of Buying Power)

- The Lima franchise area, consisting of the counties of Allen, Auglaize, Putnam, Van Wert, Williams, Fulton, Defiance, Henry, Paulding, Hancock, and Hardin.

- The Lorain franchise area, consisting of the counties of Lorain, Medina, Erie, Huron, and Ashland.

18. In the process of defining these franchise areas, a number of counties were not allocated to specific franchise areas. These unallocated areas are the white spaces in Fig. 8.6. It is interesting to note that there are *no* defined franchise areas that are not contiguous with one or more unallocated areas. Further, the geometry of the division of the State into franchise areas is such that each unallocated area may be added to one of *at least* two defined franchise areas. These unallocated areas should remain unallocated. They will be useful in the future; as the franchise program develops, they may be added to a franchise area that proves to be weak in relation to the total system.

**Fig. 8.6** The extended metropolitan areas. (©1979 S&MM Survey of Buying Power)

19. The task of dividing the State of Ohio into franchise areas is now complete. It has been divided into four multiple franchise areas—Cleveland, Columbus, Cincinnati, and Dayton—as depicted in gray on Fig. 8.7, and nine single franchise areas—Youngstown, Steubenville, Newark, Springfield, Lima, Toledo, Lorain, Akron, and Canton—which are cross-hatched in Fig. 8.7.

20. Fig. 8.8 depicts the total franchise area allotment of the State of Ohio. Defined franchise areas are gray and unallocated areas have been left white.

21. Refer again to Fig. 8.7 to see the total franchise area with four multiple franchise areas, shown in gray, and nine single franchise areas that are cross-hatched. The unallocated areas are left white.

22. Multiple-franchise areas may be further refined and divided into single-franchise areas by referring to maps and data concerning the area but presented in geographical units smaller than counties. On the other hand, it

**Fig. 8.7** Multiple and single franchise areas. (©1979 S&MM Survey of Buying Power)

may be (and often is) more convenient to appoint one or more franchisees in the multiple area with the clear and contractual understanding that the number of franchises to be established within the area will be that which has been defined.

The following list shows the mathematics of the area allocation process and specifys the BPIs for each of the defined areas and for the unallocated areas.

| Franchise Area | County | BPI | BPI/.25 | Franchises |
|---|---|---|---|---|
| Cleveland | Cuyahoga | .7895 | 3.16 | 3 |
| Akron | Summit | .2464 | .99 | 1 |
| Youngstown | Mahoning | .1315 | | |
| | Trumbull | .1127 | | |
| | Total | .2442 | .98 | 1 |

**Fig. 8.8** The total franchise area allotment of the State of Ohio. (©1979 S&MM Survey of Buying Power)

| Franchise Area | County | BPI | BPI/.25 | Franchises |
|---|---|---|---|---|
| Columbus | Delaware | .0202 | | |
| | Fairfield | .0354 | | |
| | Franklin | .4445 | | |
| | Total | .5001 | 2.00 | 2 |
| Cincinnati | Clermont | .0499 | | |
| | Hamilton | .4342 | | |
| | Total | .4841 | 1.94 | 2 |
| Dayton | Miami | .0363 | | |
| | Montgomery | .2823 | | |
| | Preble | .0149 | | |
| | Butler | .1113 | | |
| | Darke | .0210 | | |
| | Mercer | .0152 | | |
| | Total | .4810 | 1.92 | 2 |

| Franchise Area | County | BPI | BPI/.25 | Franchises |
|---|---|---|---|---|
| Toledo | Lucas | .2470 | .99 | 1 |
| Canton | Carroll | .0099 | | |
| | Stark | .1836 | | |
| | Portage | .0538 | | |
| | Total | .2473 | .99 | 1 |
| Newark | Licking | .0460 | | |
| | Knox | .0108 | | |
| | Conshocton | .0138 | | |
| | Muskingum | .0334 | | |
| | Wayne | .0413 | | |
| | Holmes | .0096 | | |
| | Tuscarawas | .0339 | | |
| | Richland | .0612 | | |
| | Total | .2500 | 1.00 | 1 |
| Steubenville | Jefferson | .0419 | | |
| | Columbiana | .0484 | | |
| | Harrison | .0067 | | |
| | Belmont | .0352 | | |
| | Monroe | .0052 | | |
| | Guernsey | .0149 | | |
| | Noble | .0039 | | |
| | Washington | .0266 | | |
| | Athens | .0197 | | |
| | Meigs | .0074 | | |
| | Gallia | .0107 | | |
| | Lawrence | .0229 | | |
| | Jackson | .0108 | | |
| | Total | .2504 | 1.00 | 1 |
| Springfield | Champaign | .0122 | | |
| | Clark | .0634 | | |
| | Madison | .0128 | | |
| | Union | .0106 | | |
| | Fayette | .0105 | | |
| | Clinton | .0142 | | |
| | Highland | .0110 | | |
| | Brown | .0105 | | |
| | Marion | .0299 | | |
| | Greene | .0566 | | |
| | Pickaway | .0181 | | |
| | Total | .2498 | 1.00 | 1 |
| Lima | Allen | .0502 | | |
| | Auglaize | .0179 | | |
| | Putman | .0114 | | |
| | Van Wert | .0125 | | |
| | Williams | .0157 | | |
| | Fulton | .0163 | | |
| | Defiance | .0192 | | |
| | Henry | .0115 | | |
| | Paulding | .0065 | | |
| | Hancock | .0301 | | |
| | Hardin | .0119 | | |
| | Total | .2485 | .99 | 1 |
| Lorain | Lorain | .1233 | | |
| | Medina | .0453 | | |

| Franchise Area | County | BPI | BPI/.25 | Franchises |
|---|---|---|---|---|
| | Erie | .0377 | | |
| | Huron | .0237 | | |
| | Ashland | .0181 | | |
| | Total | .2481 | .99 | 1 |
| | Total | 4.4864 | 17.95 | 18 |
| Unallocated Northwest | Wood | .0508 | | |
| | Ottawa | .0179 | | |
| | Sandusky | .0292 | | |
| | Seneca | .0257 | | |
| | Wyandot | .0085 | | |
| | Crawford | .0213 | | |
| | Morrow | .0089 | | |
| | Total | .1613 | .65 | |
| Unallocated Northeast | Lake | .1024 | | |
| | Geauga | .0311 | | |
| | Ashtabula | .0402 | | |
| | Total | .1737 | .69 | |
| Unallocated South | Perry | .0094 | | |
| | Morgan | .0043 | | |
| | Hucking | .0083 | | |
| | Vinton | .0029 | | |
| | Ross | .0264 | | |
| | Pike | .0072 | | |
| | Adams | .0079 | | |
| | Scioto | .0316 | | |
| | Total | .0980 | .39 | |
| Unallocated Southwest | Total | .0386 | .15 | |
| Total Unallocated | | .4716 | 1.88 | |

## THE CONCEPT OF AREA DOMINANT INFLUENCE (ADI)

As we pointed out earlier in this book, ADI stands for Area Dominant Influence and is used to determine the amount of advertising money required to produce a selected flow of customer traffic within a designated area. When the nature and size of an area is known to produce a certain traffic flow, the projected income and capital investment required can also be calculated. With accurate projections of these figures, the franchise fee can be readily calculated.

Any one or combination of factors can be used to develop an "index" that permits an existing or potential franchisor to allocate territories on a consistent, equitable basis, thereby providing franchisees with an approximately equal and predefined potential for success. These factors may include such readily identifiable statistical data as retail sales, number of households, population, and average disposable income. Information that requires more research, such as number of students, population transiency, number and average age of automobiles, and average level of education, may also be used.

One criterion that has become recognized as a major determinant of franchise area allotment is the existence and definition of an ADI. In fact, the ADI has been selected by some franchisors as the *sole* criterion for franchise area allotment, and is of such critical importance that the general rule of "consistency of franchise fee, variability of geographical area" has been disregarded and replaced with the general rule of "geographical area consistently defined by ADI, variability of franchise fee." In these cases, franchise area is determined by ADI, and franchise fee—or, in a broader sense, franchise capital requirement—is thus determined by the geographical extent and marketing viability of the franchise.

Allocation of franchise areas by ADI is often found to be more suited to recruiting and establishing master franchisees or area controllers than it is to allocating areas to individual franchisees, unless those individual franchisees are established in a manner that allows them to be considered as a "franchise cluster" with "pooled" advertising resources. In this light, a separate discussion of ADI as a concept and as a criterion for use in determining franchise area allotment is warranted.

Since ADI is an Area of Dominant Influence, it refers specifically to areas defined by advertising media coverage. Its development and increasing use are a direct response to the business community's recognition of advertising saturation and effectiveness of advertising dollar expenditure as critical factors in determining business success in general, and franchisee success in particular. Central to the concept of ADI definition and use is the conformity of unit development within an area to optimum utilization of that area's dominant advertising medium or media.

As a specific example of this general statement, a particular franchisor may have found through experience that the sales volume of the franchises is particularly sensitive to local television advertising exposure. Further, the franchisee may be interested in defining an area containing a specific city as a franchise area. Examination of readily available data concerning television viewer numbers and characteristics in the area combined with advertising costs will serve to identify that station or those stations with which advertising should be placed. This is made possible by quantification of prospective customers on the basis of cost per thousand per minute, or another defined parameter based on the franchisor's experience and/or analysis.

In other words, utilization of an ADI as one of a number of area allocation criteria, or as a sole area allocation criterion, may well require that development of a predefined number of franchised units be a part of the original agreement under the terms of which the franchisor grants franchise rights to the franchisee.

If the area's dominant medium extends over twenty counties, for example, and if the franchisor's index is such that its application to those counties exhibits a total area capability, including an adequate safety margin, of supporting ten franchises, it follows that maximization of advertising expenditure effectiveness will not occur until such time as there are ten franchises in operation within the area.

In fact, in some instances, an analysis of specific situations indicates that the medium or media market coverage that determined ADI and, consequently, the franchise area should not be utilized at all, initially, and that use of it should commence only when a minimum number of franchises have been established within the area. In these cases both franchisor and franchisee find themselves in the seemingly anomalous position of having defined an area of operations because of the existence within that area of a characteristic, the use of which would serve to increase the probability of franchisee success.

Utilization of the ADI concept in these instances is usually warranted, all other things being equal, but the franchisor should require that the franchisee be committed to establishing a specific number of franchises within the area, within a specified time period. In most instances this requirement does not result from the franchisor's desire to maximize franchise fee income and in no instance *should* it result from that desire. Rather, it results and should result from the franchisor's desire to maximize advertising expenditure effectiveness within the area, thereby favorably affecting the probability of franchisee success.

As we have mentioned, an ADI can be utilized as one of a number of criteria in the development of an index for use in a franchisor's area allocation procedure, or it can be utilized as a sole criterion for area allocation. Further, utilization of ADI as a sole area allocation criterion does not necessarily imply that a franchisor is limited to one franchise or one master franchise, or one area controllership per ADI. Rather, the concept's flexibility is such that a number of franchisees can be appointed and established within an ADI.

The Arbitron Company of New York, Atlanta, Chicago, Los Angeles, Dallas, and Washington—a research service of Control Data Corporation—first introduced the ADI as a geographic market design in its *1966–1967 Arbitron Television Market Report.* Since then, the ADI has gained almost universal acceptance as a basic structure for the development of marketing and distribution areas. Each county in the United States, with some minor exceptions including Hawaii and portions of Alaska, is allocated exclusively to one ADI, and there is no overlap of ADIs as they are defined by Arbitron. ADIs are updated annually, and Arbitron publishes an array of statistical information concerning them each year in its *ADI Book, Arbitron Television Population Book,* a series of ADI maps, and other publications. The *1979–1980 ADI Book* lists and defines 231 ADIs, ranging from "New York" with 8.44 percent of the television households in the United States and consisting of the counties of Fairfield in Connecticut; Bergen, Essex, Hudson, Hunterdon, Middlesex, Monmouth, Morris, Ocean, Passaic, Somerset, Sussex, and Union in New Jersey; and Pike in Pennsylvania; as well as the New York Counties of Bronx, Dutchess, Kings, Nassau, New York, Orange, Putnam, Queens, Richmond, Rockland, Suffolk, Sullivan, Ulster, and Westchester; to "Miles City—Glendive," with .01 percent of the television households in the United States, and consisting of the Montana counties of Custer, Dawson, Fallon, and Prairie.

Arbitron's definition of ADIs in the United States leads readily to an identical division of the geography of the United States into franchise areas.

In Arbitron's *ADI Book,* counties are ranked as A, B, C, or D according to location and population as follows:

1. A—all counties located within the 25 largest metropolitan rating areas.
2. B—all counties not included under A, with a population over 150,000 or located within a metropolitan rating area with a population over 150,000.

3. C—all counties not included under A or B with a population over 35,000, or located within a metropolitan rating area with a population over 35,000.

4. D—all counties not included under A, B, or C.

Arbitron's *Television Population Book* is divided into three sections, essentially, as follows:

1. Section I—ADI Market Population Summary, including 21 demographic categories for each ADI.

2. Section II—alphabetical market listings for each individual demographic category.

3. Section III—ranking market listings for each individual category.

Arbitron's market division begins with electronic media and specifically television. The concept of applying an ADI to the development of franchise area definition does not, however, rely solely on electronic media. It may be found that the sales of franchisees within some franchise programs are particularly sensitive to print media advertising, such as magazines or local newspapers. In these instances, division of the country into ADIs based on magazine or local newspaper coverage is warranted.

The following article illustrates how Tastee-Freez International has applied ADI to its program. It is reprinted by permission of *Restaurant Business* and Tastee-Freez.

### Tastee-Freez puts ADI markets up for sale  /  *by Pete Berlinski*

Tastee-Freez International, Des Plaines, Ill., has introduced a new licensing concept designed to build clusters of its third generation Tastee-Freez stores, called Big T Family Restaurants, in those markets in which it franchises directly to store operators.

While the new program, unveiled early last year, was initially developed for multi-unit operators only, this year the national franchisor opened up selected company markets for development by single-unit operators as well.

Under the program, qualified multi-unit operators are being granted exclusive rights to specific ADI markets (area of dominant influence for a TV signal) in order to concentrate  advertising dollars in local and regional markets and thus compete more effectively with the huge national advertising budgets of the fast food industry giants.

In ADI markets where single-unit franchises are granted, the company will concentrate on clustering single-unit operators together in order to enable them to pool their resources and form advertising cooperatives.

"We want to create circles of success instead of the vicious circle faced by the small operator standing by himself," explains Tastee-Freez president George Mitros.

"McDonald's has shown us how a franchise chain can use mass media advertising to build traffic. We can't compete with them on a national scale, but the real fight is won and lost on the local level.

"By clustering our stores we will be able to attack the competition on a street-by-street and town-by-town basis, supported by regional advertising."

Founded in 1950 by Leo Maranz (still active in the company, Maranz serves on the board of directors of the parent company, TFI Companies Inc.), Tastee-Freez has historically concentrated its growth in "one-store" towns with populations between 1,500 and 10,000. Now, however, with its new cluster program, it hopes to penetrate metropolitan areas with populations between 25,000 and 100,000.

Tastee-Freez International franchised its first multi-unit market under the new licensing format this April to Robert Barron, an ex-Dunkin' Donuts franchisee. Under the terms of the agreement, Barron has the exclusive rights to the 10 counties comprising the greater Milwaukee area. Within this market, he has agreed to build and operate in excess of 50 Big T Family Restaurants within the next 10 years.

Under the Big T Family Restaurant franchise agreement, multi-unit operators pay an initial technical assistance fee of $10,000 per unit for the first two stores they open and $7,500 for each additional opening. The ongoing royalty fee is four percent of gross sales, paid weekly, for the first two units and three percent for succeeding units. The agreement is for 20 years, and it can be renewed for two consecutive five-year periods.

Franchisees, under the new license agreement, also agree to contribute four percent of gross sales for advertising and sales promotion. One percent of gross is budgeted for national, two percent for regional (within the ADI market) and one percent for local advertising efforts.

While Tastee-Freez has run spot commercials on network TV for the past three years, this is the first year it is advertising on prime time TV. In the past, its commercials were aired on children's programming.

This summer it aired seven 30-second spot commercials on Monday Night Baseball and the All-Star Game. The theme of the national ad program, "It's more than a meal, it's a treat," is designed to promote the varied menu—burgers, chicken, hot dogs and French fries, as well as Tastee-Freez soft-serve desserts—that's available at Big T Family Restaurants.

To get maximum mileage out of this limited national ad program, Tastee-Freez International has developed a series of local promotions—all built around its baseball advertising vehicle. Among the traffic-building promotional materials provided franchisees (at cost) are baseball score cards, a set of 26 baseball star trading cards, super star posters, and a rub-off World Series game, which will run this month.

Until last year, Tastee-Freez International had not actively promoted the development of franchise units in its state and regional licensing areas. Instead, for the prior four years, it devoted its energies to developing support systems for its 50 territorial franchise holders who have the exclusive rights to sub-franchise the Tastee-Freez format in 24 states and parts of 13 others.

Of the 2,000-plus units in the Tastee-Freez system, only about 80 stores—four of which are Big T Family restaurants—are licensed to operators directly from the national company, which operates no stores itself.

Thus, the vast majority of stores are sub-franchised by the territorial franchisors, 20 of whom are actively supporting the development of the new generation Big T Family Restaurants, which currently account for 10 percent of the total units in the Tastee-Freez system.

Available in three sizes—40-, 60- and 90-seat models, these new generation restaurants, debuted in 1974, are currently grossing from $250,000 to $500,000 in average annual sales.

The original Tastee-Freez soft serve stores still account for half of the systemwide units and currently average $70,000 in annual gross sales. And the second generation Big Tee Burger stores, introduced in 1968, account for the remaining 40 percent of systemwide stores and average $125,000 in yearly sales.

By the end of this year, Mitros expects the franchise holders as a group to have added over 90 new Big T Family Restaurants in their respective territories. Most of the units will come from new store constructions, and 10 percent from remodeling old line stores.

The Big T Family restaurant caters to an older and more affluent clientele than its predecessors. Its varied menu includes Big Tee and Quarter Pound burgers, Tastee Crisp chicken (with five portion variations), Tastee hot dogs, and Sea-Tee fish (available as a sandwich, snack or dinner).

In addition, many franchise operators are testing salad bars and a breakfast menu. While each restaurant offers a complete line of soft serve desserts, over 80 percent of store sales come from the other food items on the menu. Most Big T Family Restaurants now have drive-through windows which account for 25 to 35 percent of total store sales.

In addition to the standard menu items noted above, restaurant operators are permitted to feature regional items that appeal to local tastes. For instance, western units serve such Mexican items as tacos and burritos and southern based stores offer Tastee Dogs southern style—with chili and cole slaw added.

There are seven standard interior decor themes available for the new Big T's—early American, nautical, Spanish, contemporary, western, Victorian and French Cafe. Franchise operators are also permitted to develop their own distinctive themes with professional design assistance.

According to Mitros, the Big T concept is still in evolution. While all the restaurants are presently self-service, he has developed plans for Big T restaurants that include dining areas where table service will be provided. He also foresees the next generation Big T's offering beer and wine on a selected basis, while featuring an expanded salad bar as a standard item.

# FRANCHISEE RECRUITMENT

The recruitment of franchisees is usually planned in "clusters." The initial recruitment cluster thrust is in areas adjacent and accessible to the franchisor's home office. Recruitment of further areas is planned in similar clusters. This provides the opportunity to handle personnel and commissary requirements on an economical and efficient basis and offers the collateral economy of regional group advertising.

**GENERATING LEADS**

A number of accepted methods are utilized to generate leads for franchise salespersons. Through advertising, the franchisor attracts the interest of specific individuals who are motivated to contact the franchise salesperson for additional information about the program. Many go on to explore the possibility of becoming a franchisee.

## MEDIA ADVERTISING

Advertisements offering the franchise and describing the major facets of the program are inserted in newspapers, magazines, and other print media. The foremost print medium in the United States for this purpose is *The Wall Street Journal*, with its three separate sections for different parts of the country. Franchisee prospects read this newspaper; its "The Mart" section is replete with recruitment ads. In specific areas where franchisees are sought, local newspapers have also proved their efficacy as a medium for recruitment advertisements. Metropolitan newspapers are particularly effective.

## DIRECT MAIL

Some franchisors utilize direct mail to appeal to prospective franchisees, obtaining names from a variety of sources. In one instance a local franchisee wrote a letter attesting to "how well I am doing with the franchise, and how well you can do," and copies of it were sent to prospects.

## INVESTOR SEMINARS

Individuals seeking to establish their own businesses are invited to attend a seminar on business ownership. Attendees are advised that the seminar will be educational and noncommercial, and that the sponsors will present their program only at the seminar's end. It is emphasized that attendees are welcome to leave prior to this presentation. Full disclosure of the name of the sponsor is made, both in the advertisement announcing the seminar and throughout the seminar itself.

As one franchisor conducted its seminar, the first hour was completely educational, providing attendees with precisely the sort of own-your-own-business information they sought. Following this informative hour, they were invited into a nearby hospitality room for a presentation of slides, charts, and other material concerning the sponsor's franchise program. The sponsor's sales representatives were present to provide additional information and answer questions.

## LOCAL REFERRALS

Leads may be generated within a given locality by establishing personal dialogue with existing organizations and businesspersons. In addition to chambers of commerce and business and professional groups, bank executives, real-estate brokers, newspaper editors, and contractors are among those who may provide valuable local referrals.

## RECRUITMENT TECHNIQUES

Conventional techniques applied in selling most goods and services are not used in selling franchises. In fact, a franchise is never "sold"; rather, a *franchisee* is "appointed." Whereas most salespersons rely on a positive approach, sellers of franchises find that a negative approach is more effective. The conversations between a franchise salesperson and a prospective franchisee never lead to the question, "Will you buy the franchise?" Rather, they ask, "Are you eligible to be appointed as a franchisee?" It is up to potential franchisees to prove that they are eligible.

One of the country's foremost franchisee recruiters, a gentlemen responsible for millions of recruitment dollars, cites this credo: "Learn to qualify the propect, thereby saving yourself a lot of time and aggravation."

This basic philosophy holds that the more qualified a prospect is at the outset, the greater the odds against later misunderstanding and breakdown in negotiations. Our master recruiter call his sales approach "funnel recruitment"; it allows him to participate and interact *with* prospective franchisees rather than react *to* them. Prospects are given every opportunity to make a solidly based decision.

His sales procedure is divided into six essential stages, each of which might be called a sales "impact":

## THE FIRST IMPACT

During the first interview, discussion focuses on the prospect, not on the franchisor. The prospect's background, interests, and objectives are determined, along with an assessment of his or her mental and physical ability to perform the work required. At this point it is more important that the franchise salesperson be a good listener than a good talker. This is the practice of "reverse selling." The salesperson asks, "Why do you want to get into this business?" "Are you qualified for this type of work?"

### THE SECOND IMPACT

The prospect completes the application form, including the name of the attorney who will be present at the contract signing. The franchise salesperson reviews the application with the prospective franchisee.

### THE THIRD IMPACT

The franchise salesperson explains the complete program, stressing the negative as well as the positive factors involved in "owning" one's own business.

### THE FOURTH IMPACT

After a "good faith" deposit is received from the applicant, a thorough background check must be conducted. It is important that the applicant is advised of this requirement and of the fact that it is mandatory procedure.

### THE FIFTH IMPACT

An appointment is made for the reading of the contract. The franchise salesperson should review the document thoroughly with the prospect. It is important that *the prospect* understands it and its provisions. Then the prospect should have his or her attorney read the contract.

### THE SIXTH IMPACT

The salesperson schedules an appointment with the attorneys of both prospective franchisee and franchisor to meet at the office of the former. In this setting the contract is signed.

## SYSTEMS AND PROCEDURES

A well-organized system for maintaining prospect leads serves a number of purposes:

- It simplifies the search for records and correspondence.
- It provides cross-reference access to various types of prospect information.
- It enables the salesperson to log inquiries according to the advertising medium that generated them, thus providing clear comparisons from which to determine best per-dollar ad value.
- It helps establish follow-up procedures.
- It provides a means of registering phone calls and checking sales activities and progress.

### FILING SYSTEM

In addition to the numerical master file that contains the original inquiry plus all correspondence and forms, two cross-files will be needed.

1. Copies of prospect correspondence filed alphabetically.
2. Prospects filed by state with cities alphabetically within state sections.

A follow-up file is also necessary. This may be either a multi-sectioned accordion envelope numbered 1-31, or hanging files similarly numbered. For follow-up purposes, a third copy of the inner address portion of the letter will be made on a specially prepared form. This form will be kept with the master file except when it is removed and placed into the follow-up file and will have space to enter such information as first phone contact, interview date, remarks, follow-up, and remarks.

## RECOMMENDED MATERIALS

There are two means of conveniently handling the problem of making the simultaneous carbon copies:

- Carbon interleaved snap-apart sets (three-part or four-part with third and fourth parts partially carbonized).
- NCR (no carbon required) paper.

Either or both should be available from local supply sources.

## REFERENCE NUMBERS

As each inquiry is logged, assign it a reference number. This number provides a numerical sequence to the files, making retrieval faster and filing more accurate and dependable. By incorporating a key number system, the reference number can instantly identify media sources and date of ad placement. In order to perform these functions the following system is recommended:

| Letter before hyphen indicates inquiry source. | First two digits indicate month of ad. | Second two digits indicate date of ad. | Fifth digit indicates last digit of year. | Digits after hyphen indicate order of receipt. |
|---|---|---|---|---|
| W (Wall St. Journal) | 08 (August) | 06 (6) | 2 (1982) | 100 (One hundredth inquiry received) |

In other words, the first inquiry received from the ad that ran on January 6, 1982, would bear the reference number W-01062-1. The twentieth answer received would read W-01062-20. The last digits can run on from one ad to the next to provide a numerical sequence and identification for all inquiries. These last digits can then be the numerical sequence for the master file.

## RECORDING ADVERTISING RESULTS

A looseleaf book is recommended for evaluating advertising results. Each ad has its own page (or pages) with space for a proof of the actual ad to be attached. Figure 9.1 shows an example of how such a page should look.

**FRANCHISE ADVERTISING EVALUATION FORM**

(Attach ad here)

Box No. _____

Date of ad _____

Publication _____

Ref. no. prefix _____

Size _____

Per line rate $ _____

Total cost $ _____

No. of inquiries _____

Cost per inquiry $ _____

No. of interviews _____

Cost per interview $ _____

No. of franchises sold _____

Cost per franchise sold $ _____

| | Date recd. | Ref. no. | Last name | First name | City | State | Phone date | Interview date |
|---|---|---|---|---|---|---|---|---|
| 1 | | | | | | | | |
| 2 | | | | | | | | |
| 3 | | | | | | | | |
| 4 | | | | | | | | |
| 5 | | | | | | | | |
| 6 | | | | | | | | |
| 7 | | | | | | | | |
| 8 | | | | | | | | |
| 9 | | | | | | | | |
| 10 | | | | | | | | |
| 11 | | | | | | | | |
| 12 | | | | | | | | |

**Fig. 9.1** Franchise advertising evaluation form.

A supply of "second sheets" is recommended for this logging procedure so that you may note just the ad's box number and reference prefix and continue recording inquiries.

## TELEPHONE RECORD SHEETS

In designing an effective telephone-call record system there are two important considerations: First, it is necessary to record calls day by day and in the sequence made. Second, it is necessary to include a record of each conversation in the prospect's master file.

For this purpose a two-part carbon form is recommended, as shown in Fig. 9.2. The original is kept bound in a book as a permanent day-by-day record, and the copy is sectionally perforated so that each call can be separated from the others and placed in the prospect's master file.

## SALES ACTIVITY SHEETS

Sales activities can be recorded in much the same manner as telephone calls. Here it will be necessary to design a three-part form—one copy for headquarters, one for salesperson's file, and one for the master file. Figure 9.3 illustrates this form. All personal sales contacts, whether field calls or office interviews, should be recorded on this form. It is especially important that the names of *all parties* present at each meeting be recorded.

**FRANCHISEE CRITERIA**

1. *Status and Education*
   - Stable individual with substantial fixed personal overhead.
   - Age approximately 26-60.
   - High-school diploma or equivalent.

2. *Financial Background*
   - History of annual income in $18-30,000 range.
   - Financial ability to make franchise investment from own funds or from easily obtainable source.
   - Ability to finance leasehold improvements, inventory, and working capital requirements. (Some company assistance may be offered here if individual is qualified.)

3. *Skills*
   - Ability to communicate verbally.
   - Sensitivity to the reactions and desires of others.
   - Flexibility in dealing with all kinds of people.
   - Awareness of business and money concepts.

4. *Demeanor*
   - Acceptable physical appearance.
   - Acceptable dress and cleanliness.
   - Nonaggressive manner.

# PHONECALL RECORD

USE BALL POINT PEN
DETACH PERFORATED MESSAGES AND PLACE IN PROSPECT'S MASTER FILE

| PHONECALL RECORD | DATE | TIME |
|---|---|---|
| PROSPECT'S NAME | | |
| REF. NO. | | |
| PHONE NO. AND CITY | | ☐ INCOMING |
| | | |
| | | |
| | | |
| SIGNATURE | CALLED FROM | ☐ HOME ☐ OFFICE ☐ OTHER |

| PHONECALL RECORD | DATE | TIME |
|---|---|---|
| PROSPECT'S NAME | | |
| REF. NO. | | |
| PHONE NO. AND CITY | | ☐ INCOMING |
| | | |
| | | |
| | | |
| SIGNATURE | CALLED FROM | ☐ HOME ☐ OFFICE ☐ OTHER |

| PHONECALL RECORD | DATE | TIME |
|---|---|---|
| PROSPECT'S NAME | | |
| REF. NO. | | |
| PHONE NO. AND CITY | | |
| | | |
| | | |
| | | |
| SIGNATURE | CALLED FROM | |

| PHONECALL RECORD | DATE | TIME |
|---|---|---|
| NAME | | |
| | | |
| CITY | | ☐ INCOMING |
| | | |
| | | |
| | | |
| | CALLED FROM | ☐ HOME ☐ OFFICE ☐ OTHER |

> **PHONE CALL RECORD**
>
> In duplicate
>
> Top sheet—perforated message detached and placed in prospect file.
>
> Duplicate sheet not perforated.
>
> Stays in employee's or departmental record book.

| PHONECALL RECORD | DATE | TIME |
|---|---|---|
| PROSPECT'S NAME | | |
| REF. NO. | | |
| PHONE NO. AND CITY | | ☐ INCOMING |
| | | |
| | | |
| | | |
| SIGNATURE | CALLED FROM | ☐ HOME ☐ OFFICE ☐ OTHER |

| PHONECALL RECORD | DATE | TIME |
|---|---|---|
| PROSPECT'S NAME | | |
| REF. NO. | | |
| PHONE NO. AND CITY | | ☐ INCOMING |
| | | |
| | | |
| | | |
| SIGNATURE | CALLED FROM | ☐ HOME ☐ OFFICE ☐ OTHER |

**Fig. 9.2** Sample telephone-call record.

# PERSONAL CONTACT RECORD

USE BALL POINT PEN
DISPOSITION OF PERFORATED SECTIONS: 1. TOP SHEET TO PROSPECT'S MASTER FILE
2. SECOND SHEET TO HEADQUARTERS      ENTIRE THIRD SHEET TO BE RETAINED IN EMPLOYEE'S RECORD BOOK

## PERSONAL CONTACT RECORD

REF. NO.          DATE          TIME

PROSPECT'S NAME

WHERE ☐FIELD ☐OFFICE   OTHER:
RESULTS

SIGNATURE

## PERSONAL CONTACT RECORD

REF. NO.          DATE          TIME

PROSPECT'S NAME

WHERE ☐FIELD ☐OFFICE   OTHER:
RESULTS

SIGNATURE

## PERSONAL CONTACT RECORD

REF. NO.          DATE          TIME

PROSPECT'S NAME

WHERE ☐FIELD ☐OFFICE   OTHER:
RESULTS

SIGNATURE

## PERSONAL CONTACT RECORD

REF. NO.          DATE          TIME

PROSPECT'S NAME

WHERE ☐FIELD ☐OFFICE   OTHER:
RESULTS

SIGNATURE

**Fig. 9.3** Sample of a personal contact record.

**PROSPECT LEAD CONTROL**

Substantial time, effort, and money are spent in attracting and meeting with prospective franchisees. Proper controls provide an awareness of advertising and sales effectiveness. They also generate an awareness of lead costs to help determine media effectiveness. Figure 9.4 illustrates the type of form that is useful in maintaining this control.

**A SAMPLE CHRONOLOGY**

There is no one absolute, unbendable way to conduct the follow-up process. Because a certain sequence of procedures is logical, however, franchisors tend to observe similar methods of handling prospect inquiries. The following chronology is a standard one.

BASIC STEPS

1. Upon receipt of an inquiry by a prospective franchisee, a master card is typed and the prospect is entered into the file for all future reference.
2. A form letter with individually typed heading is mailed out. Accompanying the letter is a descriptive pamphlet containing a pro-forma and cash investment data plus a qualification form to be completed and returned.
3. When the completed form is received and appears satisfactory, an interview appointment is set up, again by letter. Prospects are expected to pay their own expenses to and from the appointment at the company office.
4. At the initial interview the focus is on assessing the capabilities of the potential franchisee according to subjective criteria. This is not the time to "sell" a franchise but to exchange information. The franchisee should be made aware of the negative aspects of the business as well as the positive ones, along with the nature of franchising costs and other critical information. Allow two hours or more for this interview.

SHOW THE PROSPECT AROUND

If the initial interview seems promising, offer the prospect a tour of home-office facilities and introduce some people. You might suggest visiting an actual operation for answers to on-the-spot questions.

At the end of the meeting ask if the prospect would like further data. If you are satisfied with the interview, provide the prospect with your franchise agreement (two copies), a financial information sheet, and a full application form. Ask the prospect to fill these out at home.

PROCESSING THE PAPERWORK

At this point, prospective franchisees should consult their own attorneys or accountants for legal guidance. If all is in order, the signed agreement will be returned, along with a designated money deposit. A response letter is mailed out when the check is received, indicating that it takes several weeks to approve a full application. During this time a prospect's finances are analyzed.

After the prospect leaves the initial interview, a special form containing relevant information is completed. This is kept in a special file or placed in the franchise agreement jacket with all other completed forms. A useful history is thus established from the very beginning.

# LEAD FOLLOWUP CONTROL
### FRANCHISE SALES DIVISION

| SOURCE CODE |
| REF. 0000 |

PROSPECT'S NAME_____

ADDRESS_____ PHONE_____

CITY_____ ZONE_____ STATE_____

DATE RECEIVED AT HOME OFFICE

SOURCE OF LEAD

| REQUIRED TIMING | PART 1 — FOR USE AT HOME OFFICE | |
| --- | --- | --- |
| Immediate | Logged in Franchise Evaluation Book. Receipt Date Stamped on Inquiry. | |

| | **O.K. FOR FURTHER PROCESSING** | **REJECTED** |
| --- | --- | --- |
| Within 48 Hours | First Response Package Mailed. Date: ☐ New Construction ☐ Existing Motel ☐ First Response Envelope Date: Enclosed. | BY:_____ REASON:_____ _____ |

DISTRIBUTION

| ☐ 1 1st copy of Reply letter, original Inquiry, and original of this form to MASTER FILE in numerical sequence. | ☐ 2 2nd copy of Reply letter, copy of Inquiry, 1st copy of this form to Regional Office at: City_____ Date:_____ | ☐ 3 3rd copy of Reply letter to city-state file. | ☐ 4 4th copy of Reply letter to Alphabetical File. |
| --- | --- | --- | --- |

Rejection Letter Mailed. Date:

This form with copies of Inquiry and Reply to REJECT FILE

## PART 2 — FOR USE AT REGIONAL OFFICE

| Date Received at Regional Office | Name of Salesman | Date Assigned | ☐ Copy of Reply Letter to Alphabetical File |
| --- | --- | --- | --- |

| | **INITIAL PHONE CONTACT** | **PHONE CALL RESULTS** |
| --- | --- | --- |
| Immediate | If Get-Acquainted Form Received | Appointment Made: Date Time |
| 10 Days after Request Date | If Get-Acquainted Form NOT Received | Location |
| | Phone Date / Disposition | Number of People to Attend |
| | _____ _____ | Accommodation Reservations to be made, if necessary, for: —— people |
| | _____ _____ | Disqualified. Reason: |
| | _____ _____ | |
| | | Unable to Reach. Reason: |

## FOLLOWUP ACTION

| Within 24 hrs. of Phone Call resulting in appointment | Confirmation of Appt. Letter Mailed. Date: ☐ Letter #000 if appointment is at Quality Office ☐ Letter #000 if appointment is in Field | CAN'T-REACH-BY-PHONE LETTER MAILED. Date: ☐ Letter #000 if Get-Acquainted Form has been received ☐ Letter #000 if Get-Acquainted Form has NOT been received |
| --- | --- | --- |
| 72 hours prior to appointment | Followup Confirmation Telegram Sent. Date: ☐ #000 if appointment is at QUALITY OFFICE ☐ #000 if appointment is in FIELD | Accommodation Reservation for Prospect made if appointment is to be at Quality Office. — Date Made File returned to Home Office if unable to contact by phone or letter 4 weeks after lead was received — Date Returned |

| **PRESENTATION MADE** Date: | Parties Attending: { _____ |
| --- | --- |

| CLOSING: ☐ Agreement Signed | Check Received $ | ☐ Credit Form Filled Out | ☐ Preliminary Site Inspection Made By: | Date Made |
| --- | --- | --- | --- | --- |

REMARKS:

| If successful sale of Franchise, completed file returned to Home Office, with: ☐ Franchise agreement ☐ Check ☐ Site Report ☐ Credit Form ☐ Map ☐ Corporate Resolutions — Date Mailed: | IF UNSUCCESSFUL, FILE RETURNED TO HOME OFFICE Salesman's Signature: | DATE MAILED: |
| --- | --- | --- |

## PART 3 — FOR USE AT HOME OFFICE

| FINANCIAL REVIEW ☐ Rejected ☐ Accepted | STAFF COMMITTEE ☐ Rejected ☐ Accepted | ☐ 15 Mile Notice | BOARD OF DIRECTORS Date Referred | FEASIBILITY REPORT Date Ordered | AGREEMENT ACCEPTED | NOTICES SENT: Date |
| --- | --- | --- | --- | --- | --- | --- |
| By: | By: | Date Sent | ☐ Conditional Acceptance ☐ Rejected | Source ☐ Satisfactory | Date: By: | ☐ Acceptance ☐ Rejection |
| Date | Date | | Date: | ☐ Unsatisfactory | | ☐ To Licensee ☐ To Salesman |

REMARKS:_____
_____
_____
_____

| **DISPOSITION OF FILE** |
| ☐ To Operations |
| ☐ Other:_____ |
| Date |

**Fig. 9.4** Sample of a lead follow-up control form.

On approval of a franchisee, written notification is made, including a signed copy of the franchise agreement. (If a prospect is not approved, of course, the check is returned with a polite letter of explanation.)

Following approval, a series of letters are sent, outlining various departmental activities on the new franchisee's behalf. If there appears to be some delay in getting a particular franchise underway, some program of activities should be initiated to maintain interest during the wait.

All correspondence with the franchisee is recorded on a special form. All appropriate department heads are notified concerning this new franchisee.

Once the site has been chosen, the new franchisee is asked to approve it and sign a lease or sub-lease, subject to variances. The security deposit is required at this time.

Two months prior to completed construction the franchisee will begin training, and at approximately the same time will be asked to sign an equipment order individually listing all items and their cost. It is the franchisee's responsibility to make the prescribed down payment and pay (or finance) the remaining monies when the equipment is actually installed.

The financing aspects must be completed within two to three weeks; therefore the company must have access to outside finance companies that will handle the financing promptly if the franchisee doesn't have a source. When feasible, the company could consider doing its own financing with a separate leasing or financing subsidiary. This can give the company added profit potential and increased control.

After the home-office training, the franchisee returns to the franchise site to complete the preopening program and hire employees and managers. Supervisors are available to help with this process as well as with such details as equipment installation. On the Saturday or Sunday before opening (traditionally a Monday), the supervisor conducts a training class and then stays all week with the franchisee—training and retraining the new employees. The supervisor makes sure the franchisee knows how to complete and analyze all operational and accounting forms and, before leaving, prepares a supervisor's report.

The supervisor will visit the store at least once more in the first month and once a month thereafter (more frequently if the franchisee has problems). These visits will usually be unannounced. The supervisor's objective is to help the franchisee make money.

The franchisee will submit royalty payments monthly, on a special form. Monthly profit-and-loss statements, yearly audited profit-and-loss statements, and balance sheets are also required. Certain daily operational forms must be filled out and submitted weekly, and other forms are sometimes necessary. An operations analyst will constantly check these forms and reports and notify the franchisees—either directly or through supervisors—of possible areas for improvement. All verbal and written correspondence with the franchisee should be kept in a special franchisee file for reference and documentation. Recordkeeping systems occupy a great deal of space, but they are important to the success of the enterprise.

The relationship with the franchisee continues. It involves numerous special forms for particular circumstances, additional controls and reports, special services offered, and the planned feeding of information and changes to the franchisee. It also includes the correction of emerging problems. Vital to this continuity is the relationship of the supervisor to the home office and to the franchisee. This individual must represent the continuing development of the franchise system and operations and the continuing development and sophistication of the home-office organization. The supervisor must anticipate franchisee unrest and know how to deal with it. The wise franchisor will arrange ample seminars, meetings, and conventions, and will implement advertising programs on such local, regional, and national basis as the market demands.

Faithfully executed these are some of the functions that help ensure a successful franchisee and a healthy franchisor-franchisee relationship.

## SUMMARY OF FRANCHISING PROCEDURES

1. Franchise application and financial application, plus payment of the franchisee fee.
2. Site selection by the franchisor and approval of site signed by the applicant.
3. Lease is signed and lease deposit is paid.
4. Before construction begins, the balance of equipment lease deposit and land lease deposit are required.
5. Evidence of adequate working capital must be presented to the company.
6. Consideration may be given to all rents becoming due at one time in event of forfeiture by franchisee.
7. While unit is under construction, the franchisee is notified to come for training.

## FRANCHISOR SALESPEOPLE

Anyone signing a franchise agreement with a reputable franchisor ultimately will deal with the company home-office specialists. Usually, these individuals include the national director of franchising and the resident counsel.

In some companies, one of these executives has sole responsibility for enfranchising and disenfranchising. When the company is in a rapid expansion phase, however, it is likely to have one or more additional salespeople whose sole responsibility is to sign up new franchisees. Generally, each salesperson will be responsible for a section of the country. They work from leads provided by the home office. The current policy of certain companies is to have the salesperson pursue initial replies to advertisements. Most companies, however, wait for the interested party to request a meeting.

The salesperson is expected to elaborate upon the literature that has previously been sent to the prospective franchisee and is qualified to answer questions or at least obtain the answers. If the prospect wants to inspect a "going" operation, the salesperson can arrange an appointment with a franchisee located nearby.

Like many salespeople, franchise salespeople may tend to oversell through overstating the likely profits or understating the required amount of work.

## THE QUALIFICATION FORM

The qualification form is a useful tool for the franchisor. It can serve a number of purposes, some of which are listed below.

1. *To discourage casual applicants:* Those who are interested mainly in accumulating a lot of literature will not bother to fill out detailed forms.

2. *To screen out unqualified applicants:* Time and money can be saved by eliminating unnecessary interviews and lengthy correspondence with applicants who are obviously not qualified.

3. *As a basis for conducting the interview:* When an applicant looks like a good prospect and an interview is arranged, the qualification form gives the interviewer some concrete points to discuss with the prospect and serves as a basis for further inquiry.

4. *As a source of credit information:* When extension of credit and financing is built into your program, credit information can be gained immediately.

Franchisors often adopt a two-step approach in determining the qualifications of an applicant for their particular business.

1. Submission of a get-acquainted fact sheet similar to the one shown in Fig. 9.5. It requests adequate information to help the franchisor determine basic franchisee feasibility yet refrains from prying.

2. At this stage, the prospective franchisee and franchisor have exchanged preliminary information, met in person, and formed mutual opinions relative to eligibility. It is therefore appropriate to ask for more detailed information, similar to a bank financial statement.

### TITLE

Analysis of some 80 different forms used by leading franchisors show a variety of titles. Among them are the following:

- Confidential Information Form
- Personal History
- Confidential Application
- Franchise Application
- Pre-Interview Form
- Qualification Report
- Confidential Get-Acquainted Application Form
- Credit Application
- Application for Interview Form
- Request for Interview

They are all different ways of describing the same thing. No special title is recommended—it's a matter of the franchisor's personal taste.

### SCOPE OF INFORMATION

The qualification form should seek information about the *applicant* personally. The following information categories are pertinent:

## THIS IS NOT A CONTRACT
## PERSONAL DATA

Date_____

Name_____

| HOME PHONE | |
|---|---|
| area code | number |
| | |

Residence Address_____

City_____State_____Zip_____

Age_____Health_____Physical Impairments_____

Married ☐   Single ☐   Divorce ☐   Widowed ☐   Dependents_____

Names of Fraternal, business, civic organizations to which you belong_____

_____

_____

## BUSINESS DATA

Your present business or corporation_____

Your position_____Telephone_____

Type of business_____

Business Address_____

City_____State_____Zip_____

How long in this business_____Annual Salary_____

Previous Business history_____

_____

_____

_____

_____

Have you ever been bonded?   Yes ☐   No ☐   Amount $_____

## REFERENCES

Business Bank_____

Branch_____Address_____

Savings Bank_____

Branch_____Address_____

Name_____Relationship_____

Address_____

Name_____Relationship_____

Address_____

**Fig. 9.5** A sample get-acquainted sheet.

# CONFIDENTIAL DATA

## FINANCIAL DATA

Your average annual income for the past 5 years? _____ per year.

| YOUR ASSETS (at current market value) | | YOUR LIABILITIES | |
|---|---|---|---|
| Cash on hand | $_____ | Notes payable to banks | $_____ |
| Cash in banks | $_____ | Other notes payable | $_____ |
| Notes receivable | $_____ | Accounts payable | $_____ |
| Loans receivable | $_____ | Loans against Life Insurance | $_____ |
| Life insurance—cash value | $_____ | Real estate mortgages payable | $_____ |
| Securities—listed marketable | $_____ | Taxes payable | $_____ |
| Mortgages owned | $_____ | Interest payable | $_____ |
| Real estate | $_____ | Brokers margin accounts | $_____ |
| Automobiles | $_____ | Other liabilities | $_____ |
| Other assets | $_____ | ............................................. | $_____ |
| ............................................. | $_____ | ............................................. | $_____ |
| ............................................. | $_____ | ............................................. | $_____ |
| TOTAL ASSETS | $_____ | Total Liabilities | $_____ |
| | | NET WORTH | $_____ |

## CONTEMPLATED ENTERPRISE

Do you have a preference as to area or city where you would like to locate your franchise?
Yes ( )    No ( )
List areas in order of preference:

1._____    3._____

2._____    4._____

Investment structure:   Individual ☐    Partnership ☐    Syndicate ☐    Investment Group ☐
Other principals, in addition to yourself:

Name_____ % of interest_____

Address_____ Telephone_____

City_____ State_____ Zip_____

Name_____ % of interest_____

Address_____ Telephone_____

City_____ State_____ Zip_____

(If additional space is needed, use back page and check here ☐ )

NOTE: Completing this form does not obligate you or us in any way. It is intended only to provide information on which to base preliminary discussions. All information will be kept strictly confidential and no verification of statements or references will be made until negotiations are initiated.

## THIS IS NOT A CONTRACT   Signature_____

- Personal history
- Financial status
- Experience
- Activities
- References
- "You and us" (franchisee-franchisor)

However, it's worth noting a couple of variations that may be of interest to some franchisors:

1. Where the franchise is specifically for a husband-wife team, the form was expanded to include detailed information about both individuals.

2. A few forms are called "Application for Option" or "Application for Territory Option." The personal information they request is very brief. A frequent feature of these is a requirement for nominal payment as evidence of good faith. There is, of course, a provision for refund. A more detailed form is filled out later, or the information is obtained during the interview. These forms are useful only to established franchisors who normally get more applicants than they can handle. They are *not* recommended for the new franchisor.

# FRANCHISE PROGRAM ARITHMETIC

# 10

While virtually every aspect of franchise program development and implementation involves some arithmetic nowhere is its use so critical as in the development of the financial roadmaps—the projections, or pro-forma financial statements—that will be used to guide the program through its infancy and growth to its maturity. In addition to their use as predefined financial performance criteria against which actual operating performance may be judged, these statements as a whole represent the franchisor's prior, quantified judgment of the value and viability of the proposed franchise program. Individual sections contain quantified statements concerning total franchisor capital requirements, total franchisee capital requirements, working capital requirements for both parties, and a plethora of additional useful information.

The very minimum financial projections of a prospective franchisor in planning his or her franchise program should consist of the following statements, each of which should be developed for *both* franchisee and franchisor:

- A series of pro-forma statements.
- A series of pro-forma cash flows.
- A source of application of funds statement, or statement of capital requirements.
- A break-even analysis.

In many instances it is found that a series of pro-forma balance sheets are useful and well worth the time and effort expended in their development. In the event that the planned franchise program will include master franchisees or area controllers, projections should be performed for this level of distribution, also.

Whether specific projections relate to franchisor, franchisee, master franchisee, area controller, or any other component of the planned program, they have certain characteristics in common: They consist of two separate and distinct components, and they concern themselves with the prediction and identification of levels of money that will flow through the projected business entity.

The two separate and distinct components of projections are *arithmetic,* or the mathematical manipulation of numbers, and *assumptions,* or the bases of the numbers that are subject to mathematical treatment.

## ARITHMETIC

The arithmetic component is not inherently subject to error. The only error to which it is subject is misuse. The system is governed by a series of rules. If the rules are followed, the conclusions to which use of the system leads will be perfect. The only way that the system can lead to an erroneous conclusion is for its user to say that $1 + 1 = 3$ or make some other rule-defying statement.

## ASSUMPTIVE TECHNIQUE

Assumptions are inherently subject to error, primarily because they often result from inductive—or *a posteriori*—reasoning, rather than deductive—or *a priori*—reasoning. Deductive reasoning flows from the general to the specific and, as with mathematics, adherence to the rules of logic will lead to perfect results.

We may generalize that "the quality of the assumptions utilized in developing projections determines the quality of the projections themselves." The greater the number of observed instances on which an assumption is based, the higher will be the quality of the assumption; the smaller the variation between extremes of observed instances, the higher will be the quality of the assumption; the more precisely defined the nature of the parameter assumed, the higher will be the quality of the assumption; and the higher the quality of the assumptions, the more accurate will be the projections.

Assumptions may be based on any one or a combination of factors. Under any circumstances, however, they must be "credible estimates," and in instances wherein a single assumption may be derived from two or more sources, each derivation should closely resemble the other or others. A prospective franchisor who says, "I have observed that inventory turnover in my pilot operation is six times a year, and will therefore assume that my typical franchisee will experience an inventory turnover six times a year, all other things being equal," is making a credible estimate based on observation and resulting from proper application of the rules of logic to that observation. A prospective franchisor who says, "I have observed that inventory turnover in my pilot operation is six times a year, and will therefore assume that my typical franchisee will experience an inventory turnover *twelve* times a year, all other things being equal," is making an incredible estimate based on wishful thinking and improper application of the rules of logic to that wishful thought. A prospective restaurant franchisor who develops average franchisee sales projections based on average check, number of seats, and turnover data, and then finds that this projection differs drastically from projections based on industry sales-per-seat data for similar operations—and is, in fact, lower or higher than reported extremes—is better advised to reconcile the data than to proceed. Further assumptions cannot be made confidently when two derivations of the same assumption do not resemble each other.

Credible estimates and valid assumptions usually result from experience. This experience may be the prospective franchisor's personal experience, it may be the experience of others, or it may be some combination of first- and second-party experience. A number of outside sources are available for use by a prospective franchisor:

- The research of competitive operations.
- Statistical information compiled by

    Dun and Bradstreet

    National Cash Register Co., Dayton, Ohio

    Trade magazines

    Trade associations

    Department of Commerce

    Small Business Administration

- Information obtained from accountants, consultants, and other professionals who have access to a broad background of both first- and second-party information in specialized fields.

In addition to the common components of arithmetic and assumptions, all projections share a concern with predicting and identifying levels of money, as it will flow through the business entity. In this regard, "money" is categorized according to its source, its use, and the direction of its flow, with pro-forma income statements and pro-forma cash flows assuming positions of primary importance, and pro-forma balance sheets, statements of capital requirements or pro-forma source and application of funds statements, and pro-forma break-even analyses assuming positions of secondary or subsidiary importance.

With respect to the pro-forma income statement, money that results from the sale of goods and/or services by the entity, or from other miscellaneous sources, is categorized as "income."

A franchisor may realize income from any of the following sources:

- Sale of franchises.
- Receipt of royalties or other forms of residual income, or recognition that these *will be* received in the future as a result of current or past events.
- Initial sale of inventory and equipment to franchisees.
- Compensated provision of one-time services, such as site selection or construction supervision, to franchisees.
- Compensated provision of continuing services, such as accounting or auditing, to franchisees.
- Ongoing sale of inventory and/or other items to franchisees.
- Sales or profits realized from operation of pilot unit(s).

All these sources of income will not be available to the typical franchisee, who usually relies on sales to the general public as the sole source of income. In any event, "income" must not be confused with "cash increase." Rather, with some minor exceptions, income is defined as the result of a sale that took place within a specified time period. The outstanding characteristic of income is that it is recorded in the entity's accounting records as a credit to some income account. The offsetting debit is normally to some balance-sheet item, but rather than a debit to cash being required at all times, the offsetting debit or a portion of it may be to accounts receivable, or notes receivable, or cash—or it may be to a liability account, such as a reduction in accounts or notes payable.

Money that is expended or, in most cases, legally committed by the entity as a result of operations, or that represents a theoretical decrease in useful remaining life of an asset, or that represents an expenditure for an item the value of which remains for a number of years, and that flows out of the entity is categorized as "expense." To a franchisor, expenses are commissions paid to franchise salespeople, the cost of materials supplied to franchisees, salaries paid to employees, telephone bills, advertising costs, and so on. If the franchisor's offices are located in a building that is occupied solely by the franchisor and the allowable depreciation schedule applicable to the building is a "twenty-year straight-line" schedule, one-twentieth of the cost of the building is an expense for each of the franchisor's first twenty years of life. If incorporation costs to establish a franchisor corporation are allowed to be "written off" over ten years, then one-tenth of the cost of incorporation is an expense for each of the franchisor's first ten years of life. In the case of the building the expense is called *depreciation*; in the case of incorporation the expense is called *amortization*. In both cases they are expenses, despite the fact that they are either unrelated or only indirectly related to flows of money that have occurred within the time period under consideration.

Expenses may be divided into three distinct categories, and it is often useful to do so in preparing pro-forma income statements:

1. Variable expenses
2. Semivariable or semifixed expenses
3. Fixed expenses

Variable expenses are those that vary proportionally with sales units, sales dollars, or any other measurement of sales. If a franchisor pays a franchise salesman a sales commission of ten percent for each franchise sold, then that ten-percent commission is a variable expense of the franchisor and is stated as being "variable with franchise sales."

Semivariable and semifixed expenses are those franchisor expenses that increase as sales increase. If, for example, a franchisor finds it necessary to increase office space and add salaried personnel when income reaches a specified level, these and associated costs are considered to be semivariable or semifixed expenses and are stated as being "related to gross income."

Fixed expenses are those that do not change in relation to sales and are, as their name implies, fixed in their nature. Depreciation and amortization are examples of this expense category, as is rent paid for existing office space. These expenses are the bills that must be paid each month, regardless of sales.

The same expenses that have been categorized as variable, semivariable and semifixed, and fixed may be regrouped and categorized this way:

1. *Controllable* expenses
2. *Uncontrollable* expenses

Expenses that are subject to management control, such as travel and entertainment expenses, are categorized as controllable expenses. Those that are not subject to management control, such as local taxes and license fees, are categorized as uncontrollable expenses.

The choice of categorization is dictated by the use to which it will be put. The three-category distinction is applicable to the performance of analyses and projections, while the two-category distinction is suitable for judging management performance and performance requirements.

The term "expense" must not be confused with "cash decreases." With some minor exceptions, expense is defined as the result of a purchase of a product or service during the specified time period, and the use of the product or service in the operation of the business. Its outstanding characteristic is that it is recorded in the entity's accounting records as a debit to some expense account. The offsetting credit is normally to some balance sheet item, but rather than a credit to cash being required at all times, the offsetting credit or a portion of it may be to accounts payable, notes payable, or cash; it may even be to an asset account, such as a reduction in accounts or notes receivable.

A pro-forma income statement begins at a specified point in time and ends at a specified point in time, so that its prediction is of the income and expense that will be experienced by the business being projected for a specified time period. To use an analogy, we might say that a pro-forma income statement is like a motion picture, whereas a pro-forma balance sheet is like a photograph. The former depicts the flow of income into a business entity during a given period of time and matches that flow with the flow of expenses out of the business entity during the same period of time. The latter depicts the level of assets that exists with respect to the business entity at a specified instant in time and matches that level with the liabilities of the business entity at the same instant in time. In the case of a pro-forma income statement, the result of subtracting expenses from income is known as the business's *net income* for the time period in question; in the case of the pro-forma balance sheet, the result of subtracting liabilities from assets is known as the business's *net worth* at that instant of time. A pro-forma income statement is prepared for "the first month of operations" or "the fifth year of operations," whereas a pro-forma balance sheet is prepared for "31 December 1981" or "midnight of the last day of the first month following grand opening."

A pro-forma cash flow statement is similar to a pro-forma income statement in that it may be compared with a motion picture rather than a photograph, but its concern is with the flow of cash into a business entity and the comparison of the inward flow to the flow of cash out of a business entity. Whereas the pro-forma income statement predicts flows of income and expense, the pro-forma cash flow predicts cash inflow and cash outflow. It is also similar to a pro-forma income statement in that many (but not all) of the predicted cash inflows result from the business's income, and many (but not all) of the predicted cash outflows result from the business's expense. Even in the event of cash inflows and cash outflows that result directly from income and expense, however, the pro-forma cash flow differs significantly and substantially from the pro-forma income statement. Whereas the pro-forma income statement records a prediction of income as it is experienced (e.g., a $5000 sale made in month one would be recorded as income of $5000 in month one), a pro-forma cash flow records a prediction of the receipt of the cash that results from that sale by the business entity that is the subject of the pro-forma statements. Continuing with the preceding example, it may be that the terms of the $5000 sale in month one were 50 percent down and 25 percent in each of the following two months. In this case the pro-forma income statement would indicate income of $5000 in month one, but the pro-forma cash flow would indicate cash inflows of $2500 in month one, $1250 in month two, and $1250 in month three.

In addition, a pro-forma cash flow records predictions of cash inflows and cash outflows that are unrelated, or only indirectly related, to income and expense. As an example, a prospective franchisor may have made arrangements for a $25,000 line of credit, and may plan to "take down" this line in its entirety in the sixth month of operations. In this example the prospective franchisor's pro-forma cash flow would indicate a cash inflow of $25,000 in month six, but that cash inflow would be unrelated to the projected sales. The outstanding characteristic of the inflow would be that it is represented on the accounting records as a debit to cash, but the offsetting credit would not be to an income account. Rather, it would be to a liability account, such as loan or note payable.

Continuing with the same example, it may be that the prospective franchisor had arranged to repay the $25,000 loan with equal payments to principal of $1000 a month, with interest payable at the rate of 15 percent a year and monthly on the principal balance outstanding. The seventh month of the pro-forma cash flow, then, would indicate a cash outflow resulting from the loan of $1312.50, but only $312.50 of this outflow, or the interest, would be an expense. The remaining $1000 would be reduction in the liability that had been incurred by the franchisor in obtaining the loan. In this case the total credit to cash of $1312.50 would be offset by two debits, the total of which would be $1312.50: a debit to interest expense, an income statement item of $312.50; plus a debit to loan or note payable, balance sheet items, of $1000.

While the time periods for which pro-forma income statements and pro-forma cash flows should be prepared will vary with specific industries and specific operations, it is generally recognized that they should be prepared as a series that spans a total length of time of approximately five years, and that pro-forma cash flows should be prepared so that each increment in the series is of a shorter duration than their related pro-forma income statements. If the time period chosen for the pro-forma income statements is of sufficiently short duration, it is not always necessary to adhere to the latter rule. However, it has been found that pro-forma cash flows performed for durations longer than monthly are seldom as useful as they might be. With respect to both pro-forma income statements and pro-forma cash flows, a general rule is "the shorter the time period chosen, the better the pro-forma."

As an example, say a prospective franchisor has chosen to perform a series of pro-forma income statements and has decided that the business's purposes will be served by a series of five yearly pro-forma income statements. In this case there may be a temptation to perform related cash flows quarterly, resulting in twenty consecutive pro-forma cash flows. However, this analysis rarely serves nearly so well as the development of sixty *monthly* projections.

A prospective restaurant franchisor usually finds that the "natural" accounting period is one week, and is best advised to perform pro-forma income statements on a quarterly basis, and pro-forma cash flows on a weekly basis. Performance of pro-forma income statements on a weekly basis might lead to development of pro-forma cash flows on a daily basis, but it is seldom found that this short a time span is warranted. Rather, in this instance pro-forma cash flows can be developed utilizing the same time period as would be used for the pro-forma income statements in question with little loss of effectiveness or usefulness.

Another effective approach to the question of choosing time periods for projection preparation is to perform them for longer time periods, and then follow with the development of projections for shorter time periods only within the critical phases defined by the longer projections. In fact, the objective and logical nature of this approach recommends it in most instances.

For example, a prospective franchisor might perform a series of five consecutive yearly income statements, and find that the period of greatest negative cumulative net income or lowest positive cumulative net income is reflected in the pro-forma statement for the first year. This individual might then perform a series of quarterly cash flows for the first and second years of operation, and find that the peak cumulative cash outflow occurs in the fifth quarter. At this point, performance of a series of weekly pro-forma cash flows for the fourth, fifth, and sixth quarters (or even for the first through the sixth quarters) is generally observed to fulfill all requirements and yield projected information that differs little in its quality from that obtained from a series of 260 consecutive weekly pro-forma cash flows.

A source-and-application-of-funds statement is a projected analysis of the amount of capital that will be required of a franchisee and a franchisor in order to establish a business, develop it until positive net income and positive cash flow are attained, and maintain adequate working reserves together with a projected analysis of the source or sources from which funds in an amount equal to all requirements are forthcoming. A statement of capital requirements is similar, except that it does not contain an analysis of the source from which funds will be forthcoming. As a general rule, the former is more appropriate to analyzing the franchisor's situation, and the latter more appropriate to analyzing a portion of franchisee prospect qualifications. On the other hand, a prospective franchisee should be most distinctly interested in examining a franchisor's statement of capital requirements, modifying it to suit the particular situation and expanding the modified version to include the sources from which required funds are to be obtained.

Whereas pro-forma income statements and pro-forma cash flows can be compared to motion pictures, a pro-forma source and application of funds is similar to a pro-forma balance sheet in that it can be compared to a photograph. It does not extend, except by implication, over a period of time, but exists at one, discrete point in time. The statement of funds required is not related to time, in other words, so far as the statement per se is concerned. However, the actual provision of the funds stipulated may be related to time as it is defined by the pro-forma cash flow.

In the case of the prospective franchisor who had arranged a $25,000 line of credit for "take down" in its entirety in the sixth month of operation, the source and application of funds would show "take-down of line of credit" or "pre-arranged loan" as a source of funds in the amount of $25,000, with an offsetting application of funds such as "additional working capital." However, the funds in question would not be forthcoming as a practical matter for six months, and the timing of the funds' receipt would have been determined by cash requirements as defined by the prospective franchisor's series of pro-forma cash flows.

A break-even analysis is both static and dynamic; it is explicitly static with respect to time, and only implicitly dynamic with respect to time, but explicitly dynamic with respect to sales volume. It may be presented in one of two forms:

- Arithmetic
- Graphic

It is generally found that presentation in both forms is preferable to concentration on one or the other.

Considering semivariable and semifixed expenses to be mathematically treated as pure variable or pure fixed expenses for the sake of an example, arithmetic analysis of break-even requires that variable expenses be subtracted from sales on a per-unit or per-dollar basis. The result of this per-sales-unit or per-sales-dollar subtraction is "contribution to overhead and profit" on a per-unit or per-sales-dollar basis. If this contribution to overhead and profit figure is divided into fixed overhead, or fixed expense, the result is the "break-even point" of the business, or the amount of business it must do within the time period specified by quantification of overhead in order that it break even, or lose no money and make no money. Sales above those defined levels will provide the business with a net profit, and sales below will provide the business with a net loss.

As an example, the business may be selling items for $100 and exhibit a total variable cost structure of $60, including sales commissions, cost of goods sold, and all other variable cost components. This business may also exhibit a total fixed expense, or total overhead structure, of $1000 a week. In this case the business's contribution to overhead and profit would be $100 − $60 = $40 per unit sold, and its break-even point would be $1000/$40 = 25 units a week. Sale of 26 units a week would yield a net profit before taxes of $40 — sales *above* break-even yield a contribution to profit; sale of 24 units a week would yield a net loss before taxes of $40 — sales *below* break-even yield a contribution to overhead.

Graphic analysis of break-even requires that contribution to overhead and profit be defined as the vertical axis and stated in terms of dollars, and that sales volume be defined as the horizontal axis and stated in terms of sales units or sales dollars. A horizontal line representing total overhead is drawn on the graph, with steps representing semifixed expense level increases. Contribution to overhead and profit is then plotted against sales volume, providing a line with a slope specified by contribution to overhead and profit per sales unit or per sales dollar, and with semivariable expenses altering the slope of the line at specific points. The intersection of the two lines specifies break-even, which will be identical to that obtained by arithmetic means for an identical situation.

The advantage of arithmetic analysis is that it presents information in a form that is easy to comprehend; its disadvantage is that it presents a relatively incomplete picture of the business's dynamics. The advantage of graphic analysis is that it presents a clear picture of the business's dynamics, with the area between the two curves lying below break-even identified as the "loss area" of the business, and the area between the two curves lying above break-even identified as the "profit area" of the business. As a result, the profit or loss of the business at any level of sales can be determined by simply measuring the distance between the two curves.

Break-even analyses, whether they be arithmetic or graphic, may be performed on the basis of cash as well as on the basis of income, and it is often wise to perform this analysis as well—especially in those instances where cash payments to principal may represent a significant portion of the fixed cash outflows of a business. Only the interest portion of these outflows will appear on the pro-forma income statement, whereas total payments to both principal and interest will appear on the pro-forma cash flow.

The pro-forma income statement and the pro-forma cash flow are related mathematically, as is implicit and obvious in the above discussion. The specifics of that relation are stated in the pro-forma balance sheet, and it is for this reason—immediate ability to cross-check the accuracy of mathematical results—that it is often wise to develop a series of pro-forma balance sheets. In addition, of course, the success and proper financial planning of many businesses are highly dependent on the existence of balance sheet ratios that fall within defined, industry-average or ideal ranges, and pro-forma balance sheet ratio analysis has often indicated a requirement for more or less initial capital than might be obvious from the results of projections of income, cash flow, and applications of funds, especially with respect to working capital requirements.

In developing pro-forma statements, a number of basic considerations must be kept clearly in mind. Many of these considerations are specified by the particular industry within which the prospective franchisor is operating and by the specific entity that has been selected as a franchise vehicle. However, two areas are of such critical importance in franchising that they require specific mention, specific and careful consideration, and particular attention:

1. Franchisor personnel requirements and costs directly associated with personnel.
2. Recapture of initial franchisor investment.

With respect to item 1, it must be kept clearly in mind that one of the primary functions of the franchisor is to provide needed service and assistance to franchisees. The proper performance of this function requires that the franchisor be staffed with personnel whose relationships with one another are specified by a comprehensive table of organization, and whose responsibilities are specified by an equally comprehensive set of job descriptions. Further, this table of organization should be dynamic, not static in its nature, so that it is able to expand in a carefully predefined manner as the franchisor's network of franchisees grows and the support and staff requirements grow. All pro-forma analyses must fully reflect this expansion and growth.

In addition, the inclusion of cost items and cash outflow items that reflect salaries alone at the time of indicated requirement is usually unacceptable. Personnel additions often require the expenditure of sums far in excess of simple salaries. Also, new employees must be hired prior to the precise time when they are required, because training or retraining and general acclimation are necessary before personnel can function effectively. This is particularly true with respect to field personnel. It is often found that allowing a poorly or partially trained person to deal directly with franchisees is more deleterious than assigning no personnel to this function. The home-office staff, by means of letter, telephone, and visits, can accomplish more than an untrained field rep.

The addition of a person to a franchisor's staff is virtually never represented by the overhead increase of salary alone. Cost items such as increased payroll taxes and benefits are immediately obvious. Other items are not so obvious: increased secretarial and clerical expenses, increased telephone expenses, increased travel and entertainment expenses, and in some instances increased occupancy expenses are just a few. Increased field personnel expense typically entails other overhead increases resulting from the field personnel's communications with the home office. Increased secretarial and clerical expense usually entails an increased supplies and telephone expense. In fact, it is found that the treatment of personnel additions on the basis of "cost units," consisting of a combination of salary, payroll taxes, benefits, additional staff requirements, and allowances for other employment-associated expenses, is far more realistic than the common "Well, this person can share Lee's secretary" approach. On this basis we find that "salary" often represents only one-half or *less* of the "cost unit."

Now let's consider item 2, recapture of initial franchisor investment. Mathematical treatment of this item is most judicious if total initial franchisor investment is amortized on the pro-forma income statement over a two- to five-year period. This recapture should be totally accomplished on a pro-forma basis within the time period selected. The selection of a total time period for recapture is dependent on a combination of risk and return factors, and its quantification will reflect the franchisor's judgment concerning risk versus return with respect to the investment in developing the franchise program, as well as the specific financial circumstances and economic environment. As a general rule, however—and subject to particular franchisor qualifications—selection of a two-year amortization schedule is found to be appropriate.

**RETURN ON INVESTMENT**

Income, source of income, and division of income are topics of prime importance to any company or individual contemplating a franchise program. The true nature of income, however, can be viewed only in relation to other factors which, taken collectively, may be described as "the factors of production." These factors of production can consist of a wide variety of individual items, among which are the human characteristics of initiative, intelligence, creativity, and labor, and the physical characteristics of plant, machinery, inventory, and materials. Itemization of the factors of production may vary from industry to industry, or from business to business within an industry, but each factor must receive its proper reward if any business is to succeed—and a franchise program can be successful only if it has a successful business at its base.

One of the major differences between an employee and a franchisee is that a franchisee is usually classified as an *"entrepreneur."* The literal definition of this noun, which derives from the French verb *entreprendre* (to undertake), is "one who organizes, manages, and assumes the risks of a business or enterprise." This implies a point of view quite different from that of an employee. An employee's primary interest is in "wages" of one form or another—that is, payment for labor or work done. A franchisee's interest, on the other hand, is in net income, or that money which remains after all rewards and compensations for the physical factors of production pertaining to the franchised business have been made. An employee, in other words (and with some major exceptions), represents *one of the factors of production,* with philosophies and attitudes that may not correspond to those of the employer, whereas a franchisee's business concern is philosophically identical to that of the franchisor. An employee represents an expense to his or her employer, and the employer's natural interest in reducing expense is in direct contrast with the employee's interest in maximizing wages. A franchisee is interested in maximizing net income, and this interest is philosophically identical to that of the franchisor. While an employee must be viewed as an asset to be utilized as efficiently as possible, a franchisee must be viewed as more of a partner, whose primary economic interest is efficient asset utilization.

To date, the most comprehensive measurement of asset utilization efficiency within any business enterprise is "return on investment," or the arithmetic relation of income produced within a given time period to the assets employed in the production of that income. The most common expression of return on investment is in terms of "percent per year," with both income and assets expressed in dollars, and with income stated as a percentage of net assets employed. While a completely accurate statement of return on investment requires that compounding effects be treated arithmetically, employing present-value techniques, or the discounting of future cash flows and their reduction to "present value dollars," a simplified approximation that excludes compounding effects from consideration is commonly used and commonly understood, so that a business that produces $100,000 a year in net earnings and that has a net investment in it of $250,000 is said to exhibit a return on investment of $100,000/$250,000 = 40%.

This return on investment measurement is that which is of primary importance to both franchisor and franchisee in virtually any franchise system. The franchisor's interest is in maximizing the return experienced on his or her investment in the franchise system, and the franchisee's interest is in maximizing the return experienced on his or her investment in the franchised business. In both cases the return experienced is a measurement of the efficiency with which assets are utilized and, consequently, of the reward to which the human factors of production (in this case the franchisor's and the franchisee's efforts) are entitled.

It is useful to predict that a franchisee will earn $100,000 a year, for example, as a result of franchise ownership, but that prediction must be related to a prediction of the total capital investment required before the earnings prediction can be utilized fully, and before it is truly meaningful to either franchisee or franchisor. If required investment is $50,000, the resulting return of 200 percent a year is of extreme interest; if required investment is $10,000,000, the resulting return of 1 percent a year is distinctly unappealing.

Thus we have arithmetic relation of return to investment:

ROI = R/I,

where

ROI = Return on investment,
 R = Return, or net income, and
 I = Investment.

We see that ROI varies in direct proportion to changes in R, and in inverse proportion to changes in I. ROI increases, in other words, either as R increases, or as I decreases. Since the level at which it is predicted will control the investment decision of the potential franchisor in determining whether to develop the program, and of the potential franchisee in determining whether to acquire the franchise, it follows that the goal of each should be maximization of R and minimization of I.

It is found that ROI within specific businesses, whether they are existing or conceptual, must be at or above specified minimum levels for the business to be considered a likely candidate for franchising. While specific levels are often dictated by macro-economic conditions and investment alternative considerations, and may vary from time to time and from industry to industry, it has been found that well-established franchisors in today's economy must predict on sound bases franchisee ROI of 33 percent and upwards to attract franchisees to their systems. The less established the franchise, of course, the greater must be the predicted ROI: payback of one year, or a franchisee ROI of 100 percent, is not unusual.

As we have indicated, ROI can be increased either by increasing net income or by decreasing investment. As the essential consideration of ROI is cash, it follows that introduction of a financing plan for all or a portion of a potential franchisee's cash requirements can affect dramatically the decision to purchase. A hotel franchise, for example, may require a total investment of $10,000,000 and have a cash earnings capacity of $2,000,000 a year. The resulting 20-percent return on investment is probably insufficient to attract investors in today's economy, but introduction of leverage through mortgage financing alters the situation considerably. If the hotel franchise is structured to include 80-percent 20-year financing at 15 percent interest, the franchisee finds that cash requirement is reduced to $2,000,000. Periodic mortgage payments to principal and interest are required, of course, and these payments affect cash return adversely to the extent of approximately $1,000,000 a year. However, ROI will increase from the projected 20 percent to the much more interesting level of 50 percent.

These same ROI considerations are critically relevant not only to prospective franchisors in their determination of whether to develop franchise programs, but also to existing franchisors in determining their systems' modes of operation. A decision to transfer a unit to franchisee ownership from company ownership can be made only after due consideration has been given to the effect that such a transfer will have on the company's return on invested capital. Earlier examples have illustrated alterations in profit levels and cash flow that accrue to both company and franchisee at varying levels of sales when ownership is transferred to the franchisee. While useful, these illustrations are necessarily incomplete because they fail to take into account the investment of the company and of the franchisee, to relate that investment to the cash flows generated, and to express them as return on investment projections.

Those illustrations depict a unit operating at annual sales levels of $250,000, $400,000, and $600,000, with real-estate and equipment depreciation existing at levels of $15,000 and $22,500 a year, respectively. These levels indicate a company investment of approximately $400,000 in the unit, and assumption of this investment allows a return-on-investment analysis to be performed.

In Chapter 1, Fig. 1.1 indicates that annual sales of approximately $335,000 represent a "point of indifference" for the company with respect to whether the unit is company owned or franchisee owned. Figure 10.1 shows this same "point of indifference" and a higher company return on investment at sales in excess of that point under company ownership than under franchisee ownership. Further, however, it indicates an approximate return on investment to the company of only 14 percent at this level with return on investment depressed at increasing sales levels under franchisee as opposed to company ownership, increasing to a level of only 19.5 percent at sales of $600,000.

The company's return on investment will increase, however, as its investment in the operation decreases under franchisee control (see Fig. 10.2),

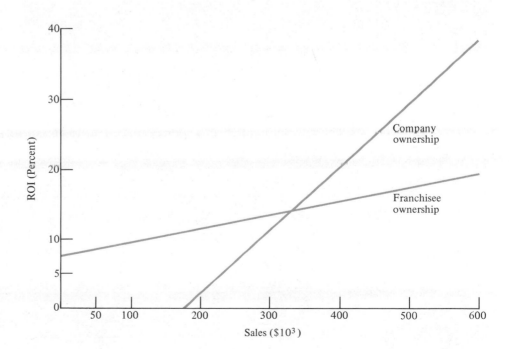

**Fig. 10.1** Return on investment analysis: ROI to company at $400.000 investment. Comparison of company ownership with franchisee ownership.

reaching infinity at an investment of 0. By the same token, the franchisee's return on investment will increase as his or her investment decreases, also reaching infinity at an investment of 0 (see Fig. 10.3). Thus, while it is in the interest of the company to minimize investment and to sell the unit to the franchisee for its investment or more, it is not in the interest of the franchisee to invest in the unit by purchasing it from the company, especially at lower sales volume levels. Resolution of this conflict is usually accomplished by company and franchisee entering into an agreement under the terms of which the franchisee allocates a portion of the unit's profit to the company, "buying out" the company's investment over a period of time. In the example under consideration, this agreement might call for the franchisee to retain all profits to $24,000 a year, but to share profits above that level equally with the company until such time as the company has been paid an amount equal to its investment, or some other prestated amount. Assuming for the sake of illustration that $400,000 has been agreed upon as shown in Fig. 10.4, the company's ROI is indeed maximized. Although the franchisee's ROI is minimized, it is satisfactory because of the nature in which the investment was made. In fact, if the franchisee sustains an annual sales level of $600,000, he or she will be able to "buy out" the company in less than seven years, while experiencing a pre-tax cash income exceeding $80,000 a year for each of the seven years.

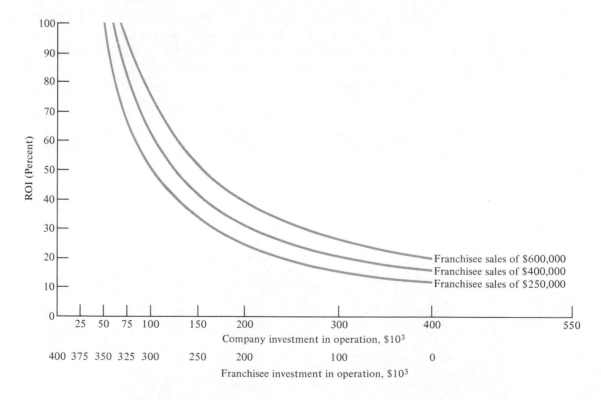

**Fig. 10.2** Return on investment analysis: ROI to franchisee to company at varying investment levels.

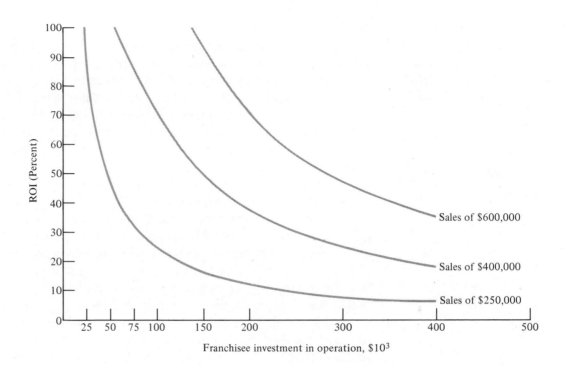

**Fig. 10.3** Return on investment analysis: ROI to franchisee at varying investment levels.

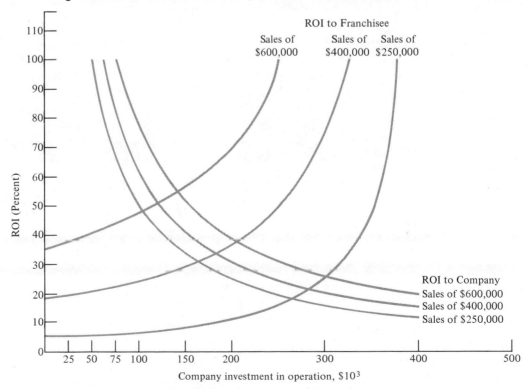

**Fig. 10.4** Return on investment analysis: Comparison of company ROI with franchise ROI at varying investment levels.

## DEVELOPING A FRANCHISOR'S PRO-FORMA INCOME STATEMENT

In planning a franchise program, one of the most critical steps is the development of a pro-forma income statement for the prospective franchisor. This process, while uncomplicated, requires that all aspects of the planned program be considered carefully and that the program's various income and expense categories be appraised realistically. Thus the development of pro-forma income statements serves a dual purpose: (1) The finished product provides guidelines for making present decisions and judging future performance; and (2) the process of evolving the projections forces an analysis of the entire program in all its details as they interrelate with one another.

Typically, organizational efficiency benefits from the improved communications flow that results from the process, and it is not unusual for persons with a somewhat limited view of their functions and of the organization's essential purpose to gain a valuable, overall perspective. Entire conceptual programs have been modified drastically, and in some cases abandoned, as a result of pro-forma analysis; sometimes entirely new and superior programs emerge.

Developing a pro-forma income statement for a franchisor *requires* that a pro-forma income statement for the franchisee be developed as a first step. Major categories of income to the franchisor—the primary one of which is royalty income—represent expense items to the franchisee; and reimbursement to the franchisor for its cost of franchise program development actually represents a capital investment of the franchisee: the payment to the franchisor of a franchise fee.

Following a predefined step-by-step process is an effective method of developing a franchisor pro-forma income statement. The following theoretical example illustrates how a prospective franchisor might proceed:

Let's say the prospective franchisor is a corporation that has developed a successful operating history with one of its assets—a 200-seat restaurant. The corporation's officers and employees as a group are knowledgeable in the restaurant business and in the fields of real-estate investment and construction. Their analysis of market conditions and other factors has convinced them that the success of their restaurant is perfectly duplicable in other markets, and the combination of their experience with the research they have conducted indicates that, on the average, the required physical structure can be built and equipped for an investment of $410,000, as indicated in Fig. 10.5.

They consider their current restaurant to be their pilot unit or prototype, and they have its income statement (see Fig. 10.6) at their disposal. Their analysis of it has convinced them that a properly trained franchisee will be able to duplicate the proven financial performance.

| | |
|---|---:|
| Land | 135.0 |
| Building | 185.0 |
| Lot work | 15.0 |
| Equipment | 75.0 |
| Total | 410.0 |

**Fig. 10.5** Estimated capital requirements for land, building, and equipment ($10³).

|  | $10^3$ |  | % |  |
|---|---|---|---|---|
| Gross sales |  | 500.0 |  | 100.0 |
| Cost of goods sold |  |  |  |  |
|   Food | 219.0 |  | 43.8 |  |
|   Paper | 10.0 | 229.0 | 2.0 | 45.8 |
| Gross profit |  | 271.0 |  | 54.2 |
| Operating expenses |  |  |  |  |
|   Laundry and supplies | 7.0 |  | 1.4 |  |
|   Royalty |  |  |  |  |
|   Breakage | 3.0 |  | 0.6 |  |
|   Rent |  |  |  |  |
|   Property taxes | 3.0 |  | 0.6 |  |
|   Utilities and telephone | 15.0 |  | 3.0 |  |
|   Maintenance and repairs | 4.0 |  | 0.8 |  |
|   Payroll and taxes | 100.0 |  | 20.0 |  |
|   Advertising | 15.0 |  | 3.0 |  |
|   Insurance | 2.0 |  | 0.4 |  |
|   Office expense | 1.0 |  | 0.2 |  |
|   Professional fees | 1.0 |  | 0.2 |  |
|   Interest expense |  |  |  |  |
|   Equipment depreciation | 7.5 |  | 1.5 |  |
|   Real-Estate depreciation | 20.0 |  | 4.0 |  |
|   Miscellaneous | 2.0 | 180.5 | 0.4 | 36.1 |
| Net profit before taxes |  | 90.5 |  | 18.1 |

**Fig. 10.6** Income statement for pilot unit.

Because of their experience with real-estate investment and construction, as well as their desire to minimize required franchisee cash investment, they have established that the corporation will, as normal operating policy, acquire real property, finance the construction of the building, and lease the entire "package" to the franchisee. Their required return for investments of this type is a minimum of 10 percent per year on land and $13\frac{1}{4}$ percent on building, so that each average franchisee will be required to pay a minimum annual rental of $40,000 (see Fig. 10.7). This minimum rental is opposed to eight percent of sales, so that the franchisee will be required to make rental payments of $40,000 per year or eight percent of sales, whichever is greater.

|  | Estimated cost ($10^3$) | Yearly minimum return (%) | Minimum lease requirement |
|---|---|---|---|
| Land | 135.0 | 10.0 | 135.0 |
| Building | 185.0 | $13\frac{1}{4}$ | 245.0 |
| Lot work | 15.0 | $13\frac{1}{4}$ | 2.0 |
| Total | 335.0 |  | 40.0 |

**Fig. 10.7** Determination of minimum requirements.

However, the corporation has determined that it does *not* wish to participate in the financing of the required equipment; the manufacturer will finance $50,000 of its total cost of $75,000 over a five-year period at nine-percent add-on interest.

The corporation is now ready to begin developing its pro-forma income statement for its typical franchisee. As the pilot unit's performance is considered typical of what the average franchisee will experience, it is modified to reflect both the financing of the equipment and the real-estate lease. Real-estate depreciation will not be applicable to a franchisee's operation, as the franchisee will own no real estate; thus that expense item is eliminated and replaced with rent, which will be $40,000 per year at a sales volume of $500,000 per year or less. The additional cost item of $4500 per year, representing interest on funds borrowed from the manufacturer to pay for a portion of the equipment package, is also included. This modified pilot unit income statement is shown in Fig. 10.8.

In addition, and as one of the factors to be considered in determining the royalties payed by the franchisee, the corporation estimates the typical franchisee's annual cash flow before royalty payments as shown in Fig. 10.9.

Considering the income it requires to service franchisees properly and profitably, a first and approximate analysis of the franchisee's return on investment, such competitive factors as royalties charged by other franchisors with similar

| | $10^3$ | | % | |
|---|---|---|---|---|
| Gross sales | | 500.0 | | 100.0 |
| Cost of goods sold | | | | |
|   Food | 219.0 | | 43.8 | |
|   Paper | 10.0 | 229.0 | 2.0 | 45.8 |
| Gross profit | | 271.0 | | 54.2 |
| Operating expenses | | | | |
|   Laundry and supplies | 7.0 | | 1.4 | |
|   Royalty | | | | |
|   Breakage | 3.0 | | 0.6 | |
|   Rent | 40.0 | | 8.0 | |
|   Property taxes | 3.0 | | 0.6 | |
|   Utilities and telephone | 15.0 | | 3.0 | |
|   Maintenance and repairs | 4.0 | | 0.8 | |
|   Payroll and taxes | 100.0 | | 20.0 | |
|   Advertising | 15.0 | | 3.0 | |
|   Insurance | 2.0 | | 0.4 | |
|   Office expense | 1.0 | | 0.2 | |
|   Professional fees | 1.0 | | 0.2 | |
|   Interest expense | 4.5 | | 0.9 | |
|   Equipment depreciation | 7.5 | | 1.5 | |
|   Real estate | | | | |
|   Depreciation | | | | |
|   Miscellaneous | 2.0 | 205.0 | 0.4 | 41.0 |
| Net profit before taxes | | 66.0 | | 13.2 |

**Fig. 10.8** Modified pilot unit income statement.

| | |
|---|---:|
| Net profit before taxes | 66.0 |
| | |
| Plus depreciation | 75.0 |
| Plus interest | 45.0 |
| Less equipment payments | 145.0 |
| | |
| Net cash flow before taxes | 635.0 |

**Fig. 10.9** Estimated franchisee cash flow before royalty ($10³).

programs, plus the maintenance of franchisee profit at acceptable levels, the corporation establishes its royalty at four percent of gross sales, as shown in Fig. 10.10.

| Royalty (%) | Royalty ($10³) | Franchisee net profit before tax ($10³) | Franchisee net cash flow before tax ($10³) |
|:---:|:---:|:---:|:---:|
| 1 | 5.0 | 61.0 | 585.0 |
| 2 | 10.0 | 56.0 | 535.0 |
| 3 | 15.0 | 51.0 | 485.0 |
| 4 | 20.0 | 46.0 | 435.0 |
| 5 | 25.0 | 41.0 | 385.0 |
| 6 | 30.0 | 36.0 | 335.0 |
| 7 | 35.0 | 31.0 | 285.0 |
| 8 | 40.0 | 26.0 | 235.0 |
| 9 | 45.0 | 21.0 | 185.0 |
| 10 | 50.0 | 16.0 | 135.0 |

**Fig. 10.10** Determination of royalty.

Inclusion of that royalty in our Pilot Unit Income Statement (Fig. 10.8) results in the Franchisee Pro-Forma Income Statement shown in Fig. 10.11. Here the franchisee's pro-forma income has been fully developed for the expected average sales level of $500,000. However, using that pro-forma statement combined with its history and experience as bases, the corporation also develops pro-forma income statements for sales levels of $400,000 and $600,000, presented as Figs. 10.12 and 10.13.

Experience with the pilot unit indicates that the franchisee will require approximately $10,000 in inventory and $10,000 in working capital to operate the business. The corporation's officers and employees are quite certain of inventory requirements, but they fully realize that even the most effective grand-opening promotion seldom assures a restaurant of immediate sales at projected levels. Rather, their experience is that sales will be quite high during "grand-opening week," but will taper and then begin to rebuild, eventually reaching projected levels towards the end of the first quarter of operations. Consequently, they prepare a weekly projected operating cash-flow analysis of the franchisee's business for the first quarter of operations to ascertain the franchisee's projected peak cash outflow and determine whether working capital requirements are, in fact, realistically projected at the $10,000 level. This projection is presented in Fig. 10.14, which indicates the realism of projecting a franchisee working capital requirement of $10,000.

| | $10^3$ | | % |
|---|---|---|---|
| Gross sales | | 500.0 | 100.0 |
| Cost of goods sold | | | |
| Food | 219.0 | | 43.8 |
| Paper | 10.0 | 229.0 | 2.0 | 45.8 |
| Gross profit | | 271.0 | 54.2 |
| Operating expenses | | | |
| Laundry and supplies | 7.0 | | 1.4 |
| Royalty | 20.0 | | 4.0 |
| Breakage | 3.0 | | 0.6 |
| Rent | 40.0 | | 8.0 |
| Property taxes | 3.0 | | 0.6 |
| Utilities and telephone | 15.0 | | 3.0 |
| Maintenance and repairs | 4.0 | | 0.8 |
| Payroll and taxes | 100.0 | | 20.0 |
| Advertising | 15.0 | | 3.0 |
| Insurance | 2.0 | | 0.4 |
| Office expense | 1.0 | | 0.2 |
| Professional fees | 1.0 | | 0.2 |
| Interest expense* | 4.5 | | 0.9 |
| Equipment depreciation† | 7.5 | | 1.5 |
| Miscellaneous | 2.0 | 225.0 | 0.4 | 45.0 |
| Net profit before taxes | | 46.0 | 9.2 |

**Fig. 10.11** Franchisee pro-forma income statement at $500,000 gross sales ($10^3$).

\*$50,000 equipment package financed
at 9% add-on interest

†10-year straight-line depreciation

The corporation is now in a position to estimate the total capital required to open and operate an essential duplicate of its pilot unit, as shown in Fig. 10.15. Of equal importance, it is in a position to portion this capital requirement between franchisee and franchisor, as shown in Fig. 10.16, which indicates a franchisor capital contribution to each unit of $335,000 for land and building plus a franchisee capital contribution of $95,000 (of which $50,000 may be credit) for equipment, inventory, and working capital.

However, the corporation will invest $100,000 in the development of its franchise program and the creation of its franchise package, and must recoup this investment by its receipt of franchise fees as opposed to royalties. Further, in recruiting, training, and establishing franchisees it will incur costs that must be reimbursed as well. Considering available data concerning area allotment and franchise sales potential, the officers determine that amortization of the franchise package over the first fifty franchises is reasonable and thus establish the franchise fee at $18,000, as indicated in Fig. 10.17.

Accounting also for the leasehold deposit of $5000 that the corporation will require of franchisees, the corporation is in a position to estimate total franchisee capital requirements as presented in Fig. 10.18. Also at this stage, the corporation is able to review previously estimated performance and relate two data

|  | $10^3$ |  | % |  |
|---|---|---|---|---|
| Gross sales |  | 400.0 |  | 100.0 |
| Cost of goods sold |  |  |  |  |
| Food | 175.2 |  | 43.8 |  |
| Paper | 8.0 | 183.2 | 2.0 | 45.8 |
| Gross profit |  | 216.8 |  | 54.2 |
| Operating expenses |  |  |  |  |
| Laundry and supplies | 6.0 |  | 1.5 |  |
| Royalty | 16.0 |  | 4.0 |  |
| Breakage | 2.4 |  | 0.6 |  |
| Rent | 40.0 |  | 10.0 |  |
| Property taxes | 3.0 |  | 0.8 |  |
| Utilities and telephone | 12.8 |  | 3.2 |  |
| Maintenance and repairs | 3.6 |  | 0.9 |  |
| Payroll and taxes | 84.0 |  | 21.0 |  |
| Advertising | 12.0 |  | 3.0 |  |
| Insurance | 1.6 |  | 0.4 |  |
| Office expense | .8 |  | 0.2 |  |
| Professional fees | 1.0 |  | 0.3 |  |
| Interest expense* | 4.5 |  | 1.1 |  |
| Equipment depreciation† | 7.5 |  | 1.9 |  |
| Miscellaneous | 1.6 | 196.8 | 0.4 | 49.3 |
| Net profit before taxes |  | 20.0 |  | 4.9 |

**Fig. 10.12** Franchisee pro-forma income statement at $400,000 gross sales ($10^3$).

*$50,000 equipment package financed at 9% add-on interest

†10-year straight-line depreciation

to ascertain their acceptablility from the viewpoint of a prospective franchisee. Referring again to Fig. 10.10, we find a pre-tax franchisee positive cash flow of $43,500 per year at a sales volume of $500,000. Operating at projected levels, the franchisee can experience a cash payback of the cash investment in a little over a year and a half—which is acceptable. *If this figure had been unacceptable* (and anything in excess of three years is unacceptable), *the entire program would have to be restructured and rethought.* If the fault were incurable, perhaps the program would be abandoned.

Only now is the corporation ready to begin development of its own pro-forma income statement. As an initial step in this development, its officers and employees must determine the program's income sources. These sources, in the case of the example at hand, may be divided into three general categories: (1) income resulting from the sale of franchises; (2) income resulting from establishing franchisees in operation; and (3) income resulting from franchisee operations. Further, the particular income in question may be received only once, as is the case with franchise fee income, or continually, as is the case with royalty income. The officers of the corporation have arranged for a ten-percent margin payable to the corporation from the equipment manufacturer, and will

|  | $10^3$ |  | % |  |
|---|---|---|---|---|
| Gross sales |  | 600.0 |  | 100.0 |
| Cost of goods sold |  |  |  |  |
| Food | 262.8 |  | 43.8 |  |
| Paper | 12.0 | 274.8 | 2.0 | 45.8 |
| Gross profit |  | 325.2 |  | 54.2 |
| Operating expenses |  |  |  |  |
| Laundry and supplies | 7.8 |  | 1.3 |  |
| Royalty | 24.0 |  | 4.0 |  |
| Breakage | 3.6 |  | 0.6 |  |
| Rent | 48.0 |  | 8.0 |  |
| Property taxes | 3.0 |  | 0.5 |  |
| Utilities and telephone | 16.8 |  | 2.8 |  |
| Maintenance and repairs | 4.2 |  | 0.7 |  |
| Payroll and taxes | 114.0 |  | 19.0 |  |
| Advertising | 18.0 |  | 3.0 |  |
| Insurance | 2.4 |  | 0.4 |  |
| Office expense | 1.2 |  | 0.2 |  |
| Professional fees | 1.2 |  | 0.2 |  |
| Interest expense* | 4.5 |  | 0.8 |  |
| Equipment depreciation† | 7.5 |  | 1.3 |  |
| Miscellaneous | 2.4 | 258.6 | 0.4 | 43.2 |
| Net profit before taxes |  | 66.6 |  | 11.0 |

**Fig. 10.13** Franchisee pro-forma income statement at $600,000 gross sales ($10^3$).

*$50,000 equipment package financed
at 9% add-on interest

†10-year straight-line depreciation

furnish corporate personnel to supervise construction for a fee of 3.75 percent of construction costs. This additional $15,000 income will be experienced for each unit constructed and equipped. It is defined in Fig. 10.19 together with $4000 per year of income that the corporation will experience from each franchisee as a result of furnishing that franchisee with services above and beyond the requirements of royalty receipt justification, plus franchise sales income, real-estate lease income, and royalty income.

Of course the corporation will also experience certain direct costs, and these are defined in Fig. 10.20.

The timing of both income and direct costs is depicted in Fig. 10.21, which is on a per-franchisee per-quarter basis.

The corporation must now estimate the number of franchises that it will sell and the rate at which they will be sold. This estimate on a quarterly basis for four years is presented in Fig. 10.22, where the timing of franchisee establishment is defined as well.

The last step, then, is development of the franchisor pro-forma income statement (see Fig. 10.23), which is presented on a quarterly basis for four years and is, in essence, the composite of all the projections and estimates made previously.

| Week | 1 | 2 | 3 | 4 | 5 | 6 | 7 | 8 | 9 | 10 | 11 | 12 | 13 |
|---|---|---|---|---|---|---|---|---|---|---|---|---|---|
| **Operating cash inflow** | | | | | | | | | | | | | |
| Sales | 10000.0 | 9000.0 | 8000.0 | 7000.0 | 7250.0 | 7500.0 | 7750.0 | 8000.0 | 8250.0 | 8500.0 | 8750.0 | 9000.0 | 9500.0 |
| Total operating inflow | 10000.0 | 9000.0 | 8000.0 | 7000.0 | 7250.0 | 7500.0 | 7750.0 | 8000.0 | 8250.0 | 8500.0 | 8750.0 | 9000.0 | 9500.0 |
| **Cash outflow, cost of goods sold** | | | | | | | | | | | | | |
| Food inventory replacement | | 4380.0 | 3942.0 | 3504.0 | 3066.0 | 3176.0 | 3285.0 | 3395.0 | 3504.0 | 3614.0 | 3723.0 | 3833.0 | 3942.0 |
| Paper inventory replacement | | 200.0 | 180.0 | 160.0 | 140.0 | 145.0 | 150.0 | 155.0 | 160.0 | 165.0 | 170.0 | 175.0 | 180.0 |
| Total COGS outflow | | 4580.0 | 4122.0 | 3664.0 | 3206.0 | 3321.0 | 3435.0 | 3550.0 | 3664.0 | 3779.0 | 3893.0 | 4008.0 | 4122.0 |
| Gross profit inflow | 10000.0 | 4420.0 | 3878.0 | 3336.0 | 4044.0 | 4179.0 | 4315.0 | 4450.0 | 4586.0 | 4721.0 | 4857.0 | 4992.0 | 5378.0 |
| **Operating cash outflow** | | | | | | | | | | | | | |
| Laundry and supplies | | 140.0 | 126.0 | 112.0 | 98.0 | 102.0 | 105.0 | 109.0 | 112.0 | 116.0 | 119.0 | 123.0 | 126.0 |
| Royalty | | 400.0 | 360.0 | 320.0 | 280.0 | 290.0 | 300.0 | 310.0 | 320.0 | 330.0 | 340.0 | 350.0 | 360.0 |
| Replacement of breakage | | 60.0 | 54.0 | 48.0 | 42.0 | 44.0 | 45.0 | 47.0 | 48.0 | 50.0 | 51.0 | 53.0 | 54.0 |
| Rent | 3500.0 | | | | 3300.0 | | | | 3300.0 | | | | 3300.0 |
| Property taxes | 1500.0 | | | | | | | | | | | | |
| Utilities and telephone, deposits | 500.0 | | | | 1000.0 | | | | 250.0 | | | | 1250.0 |
| Maintenance and repairs | 800.0 | 720.0 | 640.0 | 560.0 | 580.0 | 600.0 | 620.0 | 640.0 | 660.0 | 680.0 | 700.0 | 720.0 | 760.0 |
| Payroll and taxes | 2000.0 | 1800.0 | 1600.0 | 1400.0 | 1450.0 | 1500.0 | 1550.0 | 1600.0 | 1650.0 | 1700.0 | 1750.0 | 1800.0 | 1900.0 |
| Advertising, grand opening | 3000.0 | 300.0 | 270.0 | 240.0 | 210.0 | 218.0 | 225.0 | 233.0 | 240.0 | 248.0 | 255.0 | 263.0 | 270.0 |
| Insurance | 500.0 | | | | 100.0 | | | | 100.0 | | | | |
| Office expense | 100.0 | | | | | | | | | | | | |
| Professional fees | 500.0 | | | | | | | | | | | | |
| Equipment payments | 1210.0 | | | | 1210.0 | | | | 1210.0 | | | | 1210.0 |
| Miscellaneous | 40.0 | 36.0 | 32.0 | 28.0 | 29.0 | 30.0 | 31.0 | 32.0 | 33.0 | 34.0 | 35.0 | 36.0 | 38.0 |
| Total operating outflow | 13650.0 | 3456.0 | 3082.0 | 2708.0 | 8299.0 | 2784.0 | 2876.0 | 2971.0 | 7923.0 | 3158.0 | 3250.0 | 3345.0 | 9268.0 |
| Net cash inflow | (3650.0) | 964.0 | 796.0 | 628.0 | (4255.0) | 1395.0 | 1439.0 | 1479.0 | (3337.0) | 1563.0 | 1607.0 | 1647.0 | (3890.0) |
| Cumulative net cash inflow | (3650.0) | (2686.0) | (1890.0) | (1262.0) | (5517.0) | (4122.0) | (2683.0) | (1204.0) | (4541.0) | (2978.0) | (1371.0) | 276.0 | (3614.0) |

Peak cash outflow 5517.0

Plus allowance for minimum cash balances and contingency reserve 4483.0

Working capital requirements 10000.0

**Fig. 10.14** Determination of franchisee working capital requirements.

**Fig. 10.15** Estimated capital requirements for turnkey operation ($10^3$).

| | |
|---|---|
| Land | 135.0 |
| Building | 185.0 |
| Lot work | 15.0 |
| Equipment | 75.0 |
| Initial inventory and supplies | 10.0 |
| Working capital | 10.0 |
| Total capital required | 430.0 |

**Fig. 10.16** Analysis of estimated capital requirements for turnkey operation ($10^3$).

| | Total capital required | Franchisee total | Capital cash | Required credit | Franchisor capital required |
|---|---|---|---|---|---|
| Land | 135.0 | | | | 135.0 |
| Building | 185.0 | | | | 185.0‡ |
| Lot work | 15.0 | | | | 15.0‡ |
| Equipment | 75.0 | 75.0* | 25.0 | 50.0† | |
| Initial inventory and supplies | 10.0 | 10.0 | 10.0 | | |
| Working capital | 10.0 | 10.0 | 10.0 | | |
| Total capital required | 430.0 | 95.0 | 45.0 | 50.0 | 335.0 |

*Depreciable over 10 years, straight-line method.
†Five-year financing at 9% add-on interest.
‡Depreciable over 20 years, straight-line method.

**Fig. 10.17** Estimated franchisor cost of recruiting, training, and establishing a franchisee—development of franchisee fee ($10^3$).

| | |
|---|---|
| Recruitment advertising | 1.0 |
| Franchise sales commission | 3.0 |
| Site selection expense | 3.0 |
| Franchisee schooling and training | 5.0 |
| Legal and administrative costs | 1.0 |
| Amortization of franchise package* | 2.0 |
| Total cost to franchisor | 15.0 |
| Plus contingency reserve | 3.0 |
| Franchisee fee | 18.0 |

*Total cost of franchise package is $100,000, amortized over 50 franchises at $2,000 per franchise.

|  | Total capital required | Cash required | Amount financed | Annual depreciation | Annual interest |
|---|---|---|---|---|---|
| Franchise fee | 18.0 | 18.0 | | | |
| Leasehold security deposit | 5.0 | 5.0 | | | |
| Equipment package | 75.0* | 25.0 | 50.0† | 75.0* | 45.0† |
| Initial inventory | 10.0 | 10.0 | | | |
| Working capital | 10.0 | 10.0 | | | |
| Total capital required | 118.0 | 68.0 | 50.0 | 75.0 | 45.0 |

**Fig. 10.18** Estimated franchisee capital requirements ($10^3$).

*Depreciable over 10 years, straight-line method.
†Five-year financing at 9% add-on interest.

| | Total | Per franchise sold | Per unit constructed | Per functioning franchise | |
|---|---|---|---|---|---|
| | | | | annually | quarterly |
| Resulting from the sale of franchises—franchise sales income | 18.0* | 18.0 | | | |
| Total income, sale of franchises | 18.0 | 18.0 | | | |
| Resulting from franchisee establishment—equipment and construction income | 15.0† | | 15.0 | | |
| Real-estate lease receipts | 40.0‡ | | | 40.0 | 10.0 |
| Total income, establishment | 55.0 | | 15.0 | 40.0 | 10.0 |
| Resulting from franchise operations—royalty income | 20.0§ | | | 20.0 | 5.0 |
| Miscellaneous income | 4.0# | | | 4.0 | 1.0 |
| Total income, operations | 24.0 | | | 24.0 | 6.0 |
| Total income | 97.0 | 18.0 | 15.0 | 64.0 | 16.0 |

**Fig. 10.19** Estimated franchisor income ($10^3$).

*See Fig. 10.16 for details.
†10% markup on equipment, plus construction supervision fee of $3\frac{3}{4}\%$ = (.10) ($75,000−) + (.0375) ($200,000−) = $7,500 + $7,500 = $15,000.
‡10% minimum rental of land cost, plus $13\frac{1}{4}\%$ of construction cost = (.10) ($135,000) + (.1325) ($200,000) = $13,500 + $26,500 = $40,000.
§4% royalty on average franchise sales of $500,000 = (.04) ($500,000) = $20,000.
#Income derived as a result of performing franchisee services for and supplying franchisee needs above and beyond the requirements of royalty receipt justification, estimated at $4000 per franchisee per year.

| | Total | Per franchise sold | Per unit constructed | Per functioning franchisee | |
|---|---|---|---|---|---|
| | | | | annually | quarterly |
| Resulting from the sale of franchises*—recruitment advertising | 1.0 | 1.0 | | | |
| Franchise sales commission | 3.0 | 3.0 | | | |
| Site selection expense | 3.0 | 3.0 | | | |
| Franchisee schooling and training | 5.0 | 5.0 | | | |
| Legal and administrative costs | 1.0 | 1.0 | | | |
| Amortization of franchise package | 2.0 | 2.0 | | | |
| Total franchise sale cost | 15.0 | 15.0 | | | |
| Resulting from franchisee establishment real estate Depreciation | 10.0† | | | 10.0 | 25.0 |
| Total franchisee establishment | 10.0 | | | 10.0 | 25.0 |
| Resulting from franchisee operations‡ | | | | | |
| Total direct cost | 25.0 | 15.0 | | 10.0 | 25.0 |

**Fig. 10.20** Estimated franchisor direct cost ($10$^3$).

*From Fig. 10.16.
†Depreciated on a 20-year, straight-line basis: $200,000 ÷ 20 = $10,000 per year.
‡Totally related to franchisor overhead.

| Quarter | −1 | 0 | +1 | +2 | 3 To +X |
|---|---|---|---|---|---|
| Event | Advertising | Sale of franchise | Construction | Grand opening | Franchisee functioning |
| Franchise sales income | | 18.0 | | | |
| Equipment and construction income | | | | 15.0 | |
| Real-estate lease receipts | | | | | 10.0 |
| Royalty income | | | | | 5.0 |
| Miscellaneous income | | | | | |
| Total income | | 18.0 | | 15.0 | 16.0 |
| Recruitment advertising | 1.0 | | | | |
| Franchise sales commissions | | 3.0 | | | |
| Site selection expense | | 3.0 | | | |
| Franchisee schooling and training | | | 5.0 | | |
| Legal and administrative expense | | 1.0 | | | |
| Real-estate depreciation | | | | | 25.0 |
| Amortization of franchise package | | 2.0 | | | |
| Total direct cost | 1.0 | 9.0 | 5.0 | | 25.0 |
| Gross profit | (1.0) | 9.0 | (5.0) | 15.0 | 135.0 |

**Fig. 10.21** Franchisor income and direct cost timing (per franchisee per quarter, ($10$^3$).

| Year | Quarterly | | Franchises sold | Grand openings | Cumulative grand openings | Functioning franchisees |
|---|---|---|---|---|---|---|
| 1 | 1 | | | | | |
| | 2 | | 3 | | | |
| | 3 | | 6 | | | |
| | 4 | | 9 | 3 | 3 | |
| | | Yearly total | 18 | 3 | 3 | |
| 2 | 1 | | 5 | 6 | 9 | 3 |
| | 2 | | 6 | 9 | 18 | 9 |
| | 3 | | 7 | 5 | 23 | 18 |
| | 4 | | 9 | 6 | 29 | 23 |
| | | Yearly total | 27 | 26 | 29 | 23 |
| 3 | 1 | | 7 | 7 | 36 | 29 |
| | 2 | | 8 | 9 | 45 | 36 |
| | 3 | | 9 | 7 | 52 | 45 |
| | 4 | | 11 | 8 | 60 | 52 |
| | | Yearly total | 35 | 31 | 60 | 52 |
| 4 | 1 | | 7 | 9 | 69 | 60 |
| | 2 | | 8 | 11 | 80 | 69 |
| | 3 | | 9 | 7 | 87 | 80 |
| | 4 | | 11 | 8 | 95 | 87 |
| | | Yearly total | 35 | 35 | 95 | 87 |
| | | Total, four years | 115 | 95 | 95 | 87 |

**Fig. 10.22** Franchise system development derived from estimated franchise sales.

For the sake of conservatism, as well as to allow the corporation latitude in assisting its franchisees during their first quarter of operation, no royalty or real-estate lease income was projected for the quarter in which the franchisee's grand opening took place. In addition, and in order to determine the amount of capital that the corporation must have available for investment in the real-estate portion of the franchisees' operations, those data have been accumulated, as well.

| Year<br>Quarter | 1<br>1 | 2 | 3 |
|---|---|---|---|
| Franchises sold | | 3.0 | 6.0 |
| Cumulative franchises sold | | 3.0 | 9.0 |
| Grand openings | | | |
| Functioning franchisees | | | |
| | | | |
| Capital required for land and building | | | 1005.0 |
| Cumulative capital required for land<br>  and building | | | 1005.0 |
| | | | |
| Franchise sales income | | 54.0 | 108.0 |
| Equipment and construction income | | | |
| Real-estate lease receipts | | | |
| Royalty income | | | |
| Miscellaneous income | | | |
| Total income | | 54.0 | 108.0 |
| | | | |
| Recruitment advertising | 3.0 | 6.0 | 9.0 |
| Franchise sales commissions | | 9.0 | 18.0 |
| Site selection expense | | 9.0 | 18.0 |
| Franchisee schooling and training | | | 15.0 |
| Legal and administrative expense | | 3.0 | 6.0 |
| Real-estate depreciation | | | |
| Amortization of franchise package | | 6.0 | 12.0 |
| Total direct cost | 3.0 | 33.0 | 78.0 |
| | | | |
| Gross profit | (3.0) | 21.0 | 30.0 |
| | | | |
| Salaries | 6.5 | 19.3 | 23.0 |
| Payroll taxes and benefits | 1.0 | 2.9 | 3.5 |
| Rent and office occupancy | 1.5 | 1.5 | 1.5 |
| Telephone | .9 | .9 | 1.0 |
| Travel and entertainment | .5 | .8 | 1.0 |
| Insurance | .2 | .2 | .2 |
| Accounting | 3.0 | 3.0 | 3.0 |
| Management consultant's retainer | 6.0 | 6.0 | 6.0 |
| Office supplies | .6 | .7 | .8 |
| Miscellaneous | 2.5 | 2.5 | 2.5 |
| Total indirect cost | 22.7 | 37.8 | 42.5 |
| | | | |
| Net income before taxes | (25.7) | (16.8) | (12.5) |

**Fig. 10.23** Franchisor pro-forma income statement ($10^3$).

| 4 | Total | 2<br>1 | 2 | 3 | 4 | Total |
|---|---|---|---|---|---|---|
| 9.0 | 18.0 | 5.0 | 6.0 | 7.0 | 9.0 | 27.0 |
| 18.0 | 18.0 | 23.0 | 29.0 | 36.0 | 45.0 | 45.0 |
| 3.0 | 3.0 | 6.0 | 9.0 | 5.0 | 6.0 | 26.0 |
| | | 3.0 | 9.0 | 18.0 | 23.0 | 23.0 |
| 2010.0 | 3015.0 | 3015.0 | 1675.0 | 2010.0 | 2345.0 | 9045.0 |
| 3015.0 | 3015.0 | 6030.0 | 7705.0 | 9715.0 | 12060.0 | 12060.0 |
| 162.0 | 324.0 | 90.0 | 108.0 | 126.0 | 162.0 | 486.0 |
| 45.0 | 45.0 | 90.0 | 135.0 | 75.0 | 90.0 | 390.0 |
| | | 30.0 | 90.0 | 180.0 | 230.0 | 530.0 |
| | | 15.0 | 45.0 | 90.0 | 115.0 | 265.0 |
| | | 3.0 | 9.0 | 18.0 | 23.0 | 53.0 |
| 207.0 | 369.0 | 228.0 | 387.0 | 489.0 | 620.0 | 1724.0 |
| 5.0 | 23.0 | 6.0 | 7.0 | 9.0 | 7.0 | 29.0 |
| 27.0 | 54.0 | 15.0 | 18.0 | 21.0 | 27.0 | 81.0 |
| 27.0 | 54.0 | 15.0 | 18.0 | 21.0 | 27.0 | 81.0 |
| 30.0 | 45.0 | 45.0 | 25.0 | 30.0 | 35.0 | 135.0 |
| 9.0 | 18.0 | 5.0 | 6.0 | 7.0 | 9.0 | 27.0 |
| | | 7.5 | 22.5 | 45.0 | 57.5 | 132.5 |
| 18.0 | 36.0 | 10.0 | 12.0 | 14.0 | 18.0 | 54.0 |
| 116.0 | 230.0 | 103.5 | 108.5 | 147.0 | 180.5 | 539.5 |
| 91.0 | 139.0 | 124.5 | 278.5 | 342.0 | 439.5 | 1184.5 |
| 30.5 | 79.3 | 34.3 | 34.3 | 34.3 | 38.8 | 141.7 |
| 4.6 | 12.0 | 5.1 | 5.1 | 5.1 | 5.8 | 21.1 |
| 1.5 | 6.0 | 2.0 | 2.0 | 2.0 | 2.0 | 8.0 |
| 1.2 | 4.0 | 1.5 | 1.7 | 1.9 | 2.2 | 7.3 |
| 1.3 | 3.6 | 1.5 | 2.0 | 2.1 | 2.3 | 7.9 |
| .2 | .8 | .3 | .3 | .3 | .3 | 1.2 |
| 3.0 | 12.0 | 5.0 | 5.0 | 5.0 | 5.0 | 20.0 |
| 6.0 | 24.0 | 6.0 | 6.0 | 6.0 | 6.0 | 24.0 |
| 1.0 | 3.1 | 1.5 | 1.6 | 1.7 | 1.8 | 6.6 |
| 2.5 | 10.0 | 3.5 | 3.5 | 3.5 | 3.5 | 14.0 |
| 51.8 | 154.8 | 60.7 | 61.5 | 61.9 | 67.7 | 251.8 |
| 39.2 | (15.8) | 63.8 | 217.0 | 280.1 | 371.8 | 932.7 |

| | Year | 3 | | |
| --- | --- | --- | --- | --- |
| | Quarter | 1 | 2 | 3 |
| Franchises sold | | 7.0 | 8.0 | 9.0 |
| Cumulative franchises sold | | 52.0 | 60.0 | 69.0 |
| Grand openings | | 7.0 | 9.0 | 7.0 |
| Functioning franchisees | | 30.0 | 39.0 | 46.0 |
| Capital required for land and building | | 3015.0 | 2345.0 | 2680.0 |
| Cumulative capital required for land and building | | 15075.0 | 17420.0 | 20100.0 |
| Franchise sales income | | 126.0 | 144.0 | 162.0 |
| Equipment and construction income | | 105.0 | 135.0 | 105.0 |
| Real-estate lease receipts | | 300.0 | 390.0 | 460.0 |
| Royalty income | | 150.0 | 195.0 | 230.0 |
| Miscellaneous income | | 30.0 | 39.0 | 46.0 |
| Total income | | 711.0 | 903.0 | 1003.0 |
| Recruitment advertising | | 8.0 | 9.0 | 11.0 |
| Franchise sales commissions | | 21.0 | 24.0 | 27.0 |
| Site selection expense | | 21.0 | 24.0 | 27.0 |
| Franchisee schooling and training | | 45.0 | 35.0 | 40.0 |
| Legal and administrative expense | | 7.0 | 8.0 | 9.0 |
| Real-estate depreciation | | 75.0 | 97.5 | 115.0 |
| Amortization of franchise package | | 10.0 | | |
| Total direct cost | | 187.0 | 197.5 | 229.0 |
| Gross profit | | 524.0 | 705.5 | 774.0 |
| Salaries | | 43.0 | 46.3 | 46.3 |
| Payroll taxes and benefits | | 6.5 | 6.9 | 6.9 |
| Rent and office occupancy | | 3.0 | 3.0 | 3.0 |
| Telephone | | 2.2 | 2.4 | 2.6 |
| Travel and entertainment | | 2.5 | 2.7 | 2.9 |
| Insurance | | .4 | .4 | .4 |
| Accounting | | 6.0 | 6.0 | 6.0 |
| Management consultant's retainer | | 6.0 | 6.0 | 6.0 |
| Office supplies | | 2.2 | 2.4 | 2.6 |
| Miscellaneous | | 4.5 | 4.5 | 5.0 |
| Total indirect cost | | 76.3 | 80.6 | 81.7 |
| Net income before taxes | | 447.7 | 624.9 | 692.3 |

| 4 | Total | 4<br>1 | 2 | 3 | 4 | Total |
|---|---|---|---|---|---|---|
| 11.0 | 35.0 | 7.0 | 8.0 | 9.0 | 11.0 | 35.0 |
| 80.0 | 80.0 | 87.0 | 95.0 | 104.0 | 115.0 | 115.0 |
| 8.0 | 31.0 | 9.0 | 11.0 | 7.0 | 8.0 | 35.0 |
| 54.0 | 54.0 | 63.0 | 74.0 | 81.0 | 90.0 | 90.0 |
| | | | | | | |
| 3015.0 | 11055.0 | 3685.0 | 2345.0 | 2680.0 | 3015.0 | 11725.0 |
| 23115.0 | 23115.0 | 26800.0 | 29145.0 | 31825.0 | 34840.0 | 34840.0 |
| | | | | | | |
| 198.0 | 630.0 | 126.0 | 144.0 | 162.0 | 198.0 | 630.0 |
| 120.0 | 465.0 | 135.0 | 165.0 | 105.0 | 120.0 | 525.0 |
| 540.0 | 1690.0 | 630.0 | 740.0 | 810.0 | 900.0 | 3080.0 |
| 270.0 | 845.0 | 315.0 | 370.0 | 405.0 | 450.0 | 1540.0 |
| 54.0 | 169.0 | 63.0 | 74.0 | 81.0 | 90.0 | 308.0 |
| 1182.0 | 3799.0 | 1269.0 | 1493.0 | 1563.0 | 1758.0 | 6083.0 |
| | | | | | | |
| 7.0 | 35.0 | 8.0 | 9.0 | 11.0 | 7.0 | 35.0 |
| 33.0 | 105.0 | 21.0 | 24.0 | 27.0 | 33.0 | 105.0 |
| 33.0 | 105.0 | 21.0 | 24.0 | 27.0 | 33.0 | 105.0 |
| 45.0 | 165.0 | 55.0 | 35.0 | 40.0 | 45.0 | 175.0 |
| 11.0 | 35.0 | 7.0 | 8.0 | 9.0 | 11.0 | 35.0 |
| 135.0 | 422.5 | 157.5 | 185.0 | 202.5 | 225.0 | 770.0 |
| | 10.0 | | | | | |
| 264.0 | 877.5 | 269.5 | 285.0 | 316.5 | 354.0 | 1225.0 |
| 918.0 | 2921.5 | 999.5 | 1208.0 | 1246.5 | 1404.0 | 4858.0 |
| | | | | | | |
| 47.0 | 182.6 | 48.0 | 49.0 | 50.0 | 51.0 | 198.0 |
| 7.1 | 27.4 | 7.2 | 7.4 | 7.5 | 7.7 | 29.8 |
| 3.0 | 12.0 | 3.5 | 3.5 | 3.5 | 3.5 | 14.0 |
| 2.8 | 10.0 | 3.2 | 3.6 | 3.8 | 4.0 | 14.6 |
| 3.0 | 11.1 | 3.3 | 3.5 | 4.0 | 4.5 | 15.3 |
| .4 | 1.6 | .4 | .4 | .4 | .4 | 1.6 |
| 6.0 | 24.0 | 7.0 | 7.0 | 7.0 | 7.0 | 28.0 |
| 6.0 | 24.0 | 6.0 | 6.0 | 6.0 | 6.0 | 24.0 |
| 3.0 | 10.2 | 3.2 | 3.4 | 3.8 | 4.0 | 14.4 |
| 5.0 | 19.0 | 5.5 | 5.5 | 6.0 | 6.0 | 23.0 |
| 83.3 | 321.9 | 87.3 | 89.3 | 92.0 | 94.1 | 362.7 |
| 834.7 | 2599.6 | 912.2 | 1118.7 | 1154.5 | 1309.9 | 4495.3 |

# ADVERTISING AND PROMOTIONS

The Small Business Administration's Small Marketers' Aid No. 156, entitled "Marketing Checklist for Small Retailers," provides this promotional checklist:

- ☐ Are you familiar with the strengths and weaknesses of various promotional methods?
- ☐ Have you considered how each type might be used for your firm?
- ☐ Do you know which of your items can be successfully advertised?
- ☐ Do you know which can best be sold through personal selling?
- ☐ Do you know which can best be sold by demonstrations?
- ☐ Do you know when it is profitable to use institutional advertising?
- ☐ Do you know when product advertising is better?
- ☐ Do you know which of the media (radio, television, newspapers, yellow pages, handbills) can most effectively reach your target group?
- ☐ Do you know what can and cannot be said in your ads (Truth in Advertising requirements)?
- ☐ Can you make use of direct mail?
- ☐ Is a good mailing list available?
- ☐ Are your promotional efforts fairly regular?
- ☐ Do you concentrate them on certain seasons?
- ☐ Are certain periods of the week better than others?

Today's franchisor recognizes a responsibility for teaching franchisees how to gain profitable marketing coverage of the TOTAL allotted area. During an intensely inflationary period it's almost impossible for a single unit store to succeed if it depends on walk-in traffic alone. Operating expenses are too high, and profit margin is at a preinflationary low.

Passerby traffic can provide only a fragment of the potential market—perhaps five to ten percent. Hence it's important that the franchisee be taught how to achieve coverage of all marketing factors in the community. With

**143**

minimal addition to operating costs, a maximum market coverage of eighty or even ninety percent may be achieved! The store or other unit thus constitutes a "hub" or central headquarters from which all viable marketing tentacles can emanate.

Figure 11.1 is a chart suggesting a number of prospecting sources. The chart in Fig. 11.2 offers some approaches that may prove effective in attracting local attention.

**Fig. 11.1** Prospecting sources for marketing.

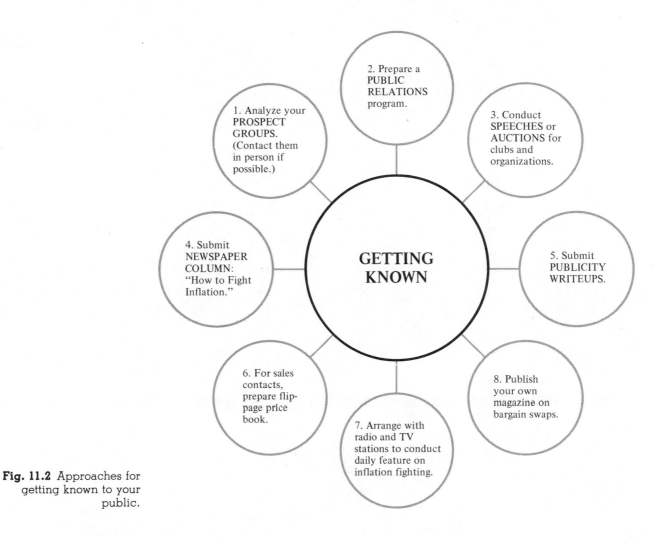

**Fig. 11.2** Approaches for getting known to your public.

# THE GRAND OPENING PROGRAM

# 12

**THE VALUE OF PUBLICITY**   A rookie franchisee will need certain selling tools to alert the local community to a new business in its midst and encourage people to stop by. It is unrealistic to depend solely on the passing traffic for advance publicity. There are certain basic actions that combine to form a pre-opening and grand-opening program. Ideally, a standardized list of suggestions is prepared by the franchisor organization and incorporated into the franchisee operations manual. Some of these suggestions may include the following:

1. Shortly after the contract is signed, a publicity release should be placed in newspapers throughout the franchisee's territory announcing the appointment of Ms./Mr._____ as a franchisee. The franchisor can submit a representative story containing certain pertinent information, and a photo and brief biographical sketch can be added for each individual franchisee.

2. As soon as the store site is leased, signs should be prominently displayed on the franchise structure announcing the impending opening of the business. The copy and designs for the signs should be included in the grand-opening package.

3. About two weeks prior to the opening, or as soon as a firm date is established, signs should be placed in the window fixing the date of the grand opening and advertising door prizes, specials, giveaways, and so on. If any celebrities are to attend the grand opening, their names should be featured.

4. Five days prior to the grand opening, a large ad should appear in all appropriate newspapers. (Be sure to check ahead on the advertising deadline for local weekly papers.) This ad should be at least a quarter-page in size and should feature basic specials. It might also announce drawings for any door prizes that are to be awarded.

5. The day before the grand opening, the premises should be decorated with grand-opening banners and pennants that may be supplied by the fran-

chisor or rented locally by the franchisee. This decorative material should be left up for a full week.

6. Recruits from the local high school could be employed to give out free door-prize tickets in and around the store during the opening week. Some prevailing theme such as old-fashioned apparel, clowns, or animals may be considered.

7. Invite local clubs and organizations to visit the grand opening. Personalized invitations should be sent to the officers of these groups, who often represent "influence leaders" in a community. And don't forget the elected town or city officials.

8. Handbills announcing the grand opening can be placed under windshield wipers of autos parked in commercial and industrial lots.

9. The itinerant clown often yields fine results. A clown moves around town, performing antics and handing out announcements about family specials offered during the grand-opening event.

10. "Teasers"—a series of attention-getting small-space ads—can be placed in local newspapers to arouse interest in the impending opening.

11. Place a "Treasure Chest" in the store. Give a key with each purchase. Lucky keys that open the chest win prizes. This entire set-up, including 1000 keys, can be purchased for about $60.

12. A "preview party" can be especially effective in small towns. The press and important local luminaries are invited for an opening-day preview party with free refreshments provided.

13. Radio spot announcements are quite inexpensive in smaller communities and should be considered particularly during the grand opening.

14. A roving vehicle (perhaps an antique auto) with eye-catching decorations and signs announcing the opening can travel around town. The driver may distribute introductory get-acquainted coupons offering some free enticement. Parked in front of the premises, the vehicle doubles as a stationary billboard.

## A TIMETABLE FOR OPENING PROCEDURES

The multiple responsibilities faced in opening a new restaurant—obtaining all necessary equipment, furnishings, supplies, and stock, plus training all levels of personnel and handling many other details—demand a great deal of time and energy. It is therefore important that a well-developed timetable be followed carefully in order not to miss any important steps in effecting a smooth and timely opening. It is vital that everything be accomplished sequentially to allow full operating efficiency from the very start.

For a detailed step-by-step example of activities leading to a well-planned grand opening, let's examine the timetable necessary for a new franchised unit of a restaurant. Figure 12.1 graphically illustrates the process.

CHECKLISTS   At certain points on the timetable there appear boxes labeled "Checklist A," "Checklist B," and so on. These checklists contain not only the main items on the visual chart, but also a number of specific details that are no less crucial to the process. It is important to review them carefully.

CHECKLIST A
THINGS TO BE DONE THREE TO FOUR MONTHS BEFORE GRAND OPENING:

☐ Approval of construction plans by various municipal departments.
☐ Construction begins.
☐ Two weeks' franchisee training at home office.
☐ Fixtures and equipment ordered by home office.
☐ Contact post office for exact mailing address.
☐ Obtain advisory services.
☐ Preliminary arrangements for essential services and utilities.
☐ Register name.
☐ Establish bank account.
☐ Apply for necessary licenses.
☐ Construction progress inspection.

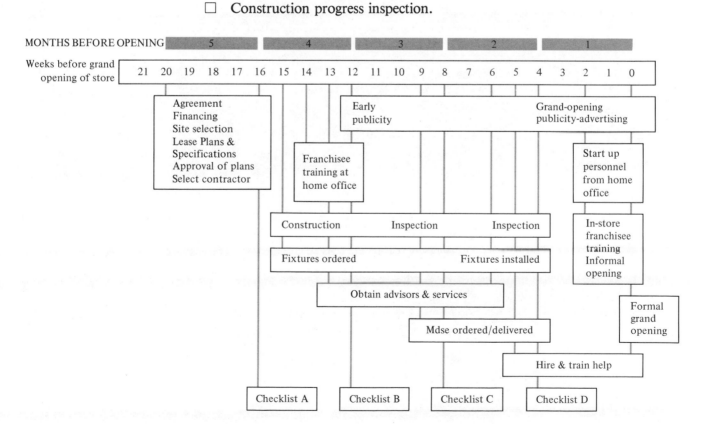

**Fig. 12.1** Timetable for preopening of a new franchise.

☐ Select insurance program.

☐ Arrange for security service.

## CHECKLIST B
## THINGS TO BE DONE TWO TO THREE MONTHS BEFORE GRAND OPENING:

☐ Construction continues.

☐ Release early publicity announcing franchisee appointment and construction of store.

☐ Put "Coming Soon" sign in window.

☐ Fixtures start arriving.

☐ Check on services and utilities.

☐ Inventory is ordered by home office. List furnished by you.

☐ Obtain legally required inspections (municipal).

☐ Check floor-covering installation date with contractor to be ready for installation of equipment.

☐ Obtain IRS forms and schedules and withholding permits.

☐ Obtain employment wage and hour regulation sheets, and Workman's Compensation notices for posting.

☐ Join selected local organizations, including Chamber of Commerce and Better Business Bureau.

## CHECKLIST C
## THINGS TO BE DONE ONE TO TWO MONTHS BEFORE GRAND OPENING:

☐ Inventory starts arriving.

☐ Check incoming merchandise against shipping lists.

☐ Notify home office and supplier of shortages and damage by registered mail.

☐ Begin to stock shelves in accordance with layout and plans given to you by home office.

☐ Check on sales tax permits.

☐ Arrange balance of services such as laundry, trash disposal, and window cleaning.

☐ Frame and display permits and licenses.

☐ Start to hire, bond, and train appropriate personnel.

☐ Establish list of sources of emergency repair for such essentials as plumbing and air conditioning.

CHECKLIST D
THINGS TO BE DONE DURING THE THIRTY-DAY PERIOD BEFORE
GRAND OPENING:

- [ ] Home office training director or field supervisor arrives to give start-up assistance, remains through your grand opening.
- [ ] Two weeks in-store franchisee training.
- [ ] Informal opening (unadvertised). Start ten-day dry run before grand opening.
- [ ] Put "NOW OPEN" sign in window.
- [ ] Continue employee training as needed.
- [ ] Check on housekeeping; have windows washed.
- [ ] Study your grand opening program.
- [ ] Put grand opening program into effect.
- [ ] Formal grand-opening ceremonies.

# FRANCHISEE TRAINING

# 13

**THE IMPORTANCE OF FRANCHISEE SELF-CONFIDENCE**

The training of new franchisees is a complex and multifacted challenge. Of course the franchisor must educate the franchisee thoroughly in the diverse areas of inventory control, advertising and promotion, bookkeeping, and all other aspects of management that operating a franchise will involve. But this alone is not enough. Of equal importance is the franchisor's success in instilling a sense of confidence, self-respect, and worth of purpose in the franchise. As a result of training, the franchisee should feel that operating the franchised business is an opportunity to become a successful and astute businessperson, rendering a needed service to the community and deriving from the business a personal profit as well as providing jobs and opportunities for others.

**THE TRAINING MANAGER**

These attitudes so vital to the success of a franchisee cannot be "taught" in the usual sense. Rather, they must be *infused* throughout the training period. Thus it is imperative that the selection of a training manager be undertaken with great care. The effective training manager inspires confidence, respect, and a feeling of rapport; the franchisee must feel that this individual is worthy of emulation. In addition to this ability, the training manager should possess expertise in all practical aspects of the operation. These include personnel management, community relations, public relations, bookkeeping, housekeeping, inventory control, and customer service.

**DEVELOPING A TRAINING PROGRAM**

A satisfactory training program should be based on the hypothesis that the franchisee has little or no business background. A part of the training period must be devoted to such basic business-management principles as the profit motive and cost control. Franchisees must recognize that profit consists of those monies that remain in their business after ALL expenses are paid and that their own labor must be compensated by the business. A salary based on market conditions should be established and considered as an expense of the business; only by this method can the true profit of the business be measured.

**153**

In all subjects of instruction, the training manager must teach in terms of elementary basics. "Trade lingo" and the use of esoteric management and accounting terminology should be avoided. Classes must be timed so that they are short enough to maintain peak attention, yet long enough to allow complete absorption of the material covered in each session. It is wise to set aside a segment of each session for questions and answers so that the trainees can clarify any uncertainties about the material and the instructor can evaluate how much learning is taking place.

## HOME-OFFICE TRAINING

Since it is in the best interests of both parties to activate the franchised business as an income-producing entity as quickly as possible, total time devoted to training at a location removed from the franchisee's premises should be as brief as thorough training will permit. Home-office training periods vary widely from industry to industry and program to program. Effective training programs may range from five days to two weeks. Normally, time is divided between "hands-off" (classroom) instruction and "hands-on" (learn-by-doing) training. A five-day program might, for example, consist of three days of classroom study and two days of actual working experience in the franchisor's pilot unit or prototype.

From the viewpoint of educational psychology as well as franchisor economics, it is best that home-office training be conducted with *groups* of franchisees. Three is generally considered the minimum number to comprise such a group. Economic franchisor advantages evolve from the lower training cost per franchisee when instructing groups rather than individuals; franchisees benefit psychologically from the interplay of ideas and the group vitality engendered by working with a number of peers.

## IN-STORE TRAINING

Following home-office training, the franchisee and staff typically receive additional in-store training prior to (and sometimes during) the grand opening. This focuses primarily on practical application of the knowledge and skills acquired by the franchisee through home-office training. The franchisor's field representative or trainer remains on the scene to assist the franchisee throughout this critical time.

## A SAMPLE TRAINING CURRICULUM

The following training curriculum has been used successfully by a restaurant franchisor. It can be adapted, however, to suit nearly any type of operation.

- *Introduction*

  Basic business facts.

  Basic facts about the restaurant business in general.

  Facts about your franchisor.

  Franchisor personnel and whom to contact.

  Communicating with the home office.

  Licenses, permits, and other legal requirements.

- *Marketing*

  Getting established—preopening procedures.

  Getting established—opening and postopening procedures, including the grand opening.

  Merchandising, advertising, and sales promotion.

  Customer relations.

- *Production*

  Ordering equipment.

  Supervising construction.

  Ordering procedure—from the home office.

  Ordering procedure—from local suppliers.

  Food-storage methods.

  Inventory control.

  Kitchen operation.

  Sanitary control.

  Food-preparation methods.

  Portion control.

  Mixing the beverage formulae.

  Serving.

- *Finance*

  How to read and analyze your balance sheet: assets, liabilities, contingent liabilities, net worth, balance-sheet ratios.

  How to prepare and analyze your profit-and-loss statement: income, costs—direct and indirect, profitability, operating ratios, break-even point.

  Record keeping—the system and how to use it.

  Bookkeeping procedures.

  Functions and use of the cash register.

  Cash-register tapes—how to read them.

  How to set up your cash register in the morning.

  How to close out your cash register in the evening.

  Sales checks.

  Cash disbursements.

  Register control—cash versus sales checks.

  Petty cash.

  Petty-cash vouchers—two ways to use them.

  Bank-deposit slips.

  Night deposits.

Workmen's compensation.

Social security.

City, state, federal, and withholding taxes.

Insurance—why and how much.

Your lease—what it means and how to live with it.

- *Personnel*

Personnel job specifications.

Personnel recruitment.

Personnel selection.

Personnel training.

Personnel management.

Motivating your employees.

Labor laws and practices.

Professional and personal services requirements.

# FUNCTION OF THE OPERATIONS MANUAL

In an earlier chapter we emphasized the importance of preparing and maintaining a comprehensive operations manual for franchisee use. As a training tool, this operations manual should feature detailed coverage of all necessary areas and thus should be designed for use as a text during the home-office training period. Further, it should continue to serve as a permanent ready reference, providing the necessary guidelines for the proper operation of the established franchised unit. It should cover the administrative as well as the merchandising methods that set the standard for the franchise program.

Because the operations manual will be used as an ongoing reference, its logical format is that of a loose-leaf volume, allowing additions and deletions to be made as necessary. In this way the franchise "bible" can be updated as necessary, keeping pace with any changes in merchandising and promotion.

The manual should detail all procedures and other substantive material. It should describe the complete personnel-management program from specific job qualifications and responsibilities to the technique for hiring employees. The manual should contain the specifics on all subjects covered in training and provide promotional material for the franchisee's local use.

**SUGGESTED OUTLINE FOR STORE OPERATIONS MANUAL**

- Section A—*Introduction*

  Foreword.

  Company history.

  The people behind the operation.

  Company's obligation to franchisee.

  Franchisee's obligation to company.

- Section B—*Preopening procedures*

  Timetable, from agreement to grand opening.

  Receiving fixtures and inventory.

Obtaining advisory services.

Obtaining insurance program.

Obtaining licenses and permits.

Obtaining utilities and other services.

Trade publications and recommended reference books.

Checklists of actions to take: 3 to 4 months before opening, 2 to 3 months before opening, 1 to 2 months before opening, within 30 days before opening.

- Section C—*Store policies*

Image.

Quality standards of products.

Price policy.

Brand policy.

Service and courtesy.

Delivery to customers.

Customer credit.

Check cashing.

Complaints and refunds.

Guarantees.

Maintenance.

Relationship with community.

Store hours.

Employee discounts.

- Section D—*Store routine and housekeeping*

General housekeeping.

Basic duties of personnel: store manager, clerks, etc.

Daily store-opening procedure—checklists.

Daily store-closing procedure—checklists.

Checking out register and daily report.

Maintenance of store and equipment.

Self-inspection.

- Section E—*Sales routine*

Order-taking procedure (writing up order).

Operating cash register.

Making change.

Sales taxes.

Charge-account procedure (if applicable).

Mail-order procedure (if applicable).

Exchanges, adjustments, and refunds procedures.

Bags and packages.

Supply requisition.

- Section F—*Supplies and inventory*

Initial orders, showing supply source and quantity (by category and item).

Purchase-order forms—how to use them.

Checking in shipments.

Payment.

Pricing procedures.

Taking inventory—procedure and forms.

Inventory-control and order-planning guide; form showing minimum quantities (item by item), how much to build to when minimum is reached, etc.

Preventing losses (through poor records, pilferage, shoplifting).

- Section G—*Administration*

Personnel: job chart, hiring—qualifications and interviewing, application form; checking references, hours, shifts, timekeeping, vacations, sick pay, time off, employee discounts, payroll taxes; laws concerning employees, rules of conduct for employees, training.

Field supervisor's inspection.

Communications and reports (forms to use): between stores and home office, between stores and warehouse, periodical reports to home office.

Record keeping and accounting.

- Section H—*Sales promotion*

Grand-opening promotion plans (with timetable).

General promotion: newspaper, radio, direct mail.

Seasonal events—major holidays, etc.

Display.

**SPECIFIC DETAILS ARE NECESSARY**

Every franchise program is unique. Many products and services are similar, of course, and well-developed programs will have a number of common features. But the finesse points—those areas to which a particular franchisor devotes an extra measure of concern—may contribute significantly toward establishing a competitive edge.

By supplying the franchisee with comprehensive details, especially in the form of visual aids such as charts and illustrations for quick reference, a franchisor better ensures that established standards will be followed. Figure 14.1, for example, defines the specified cleaning and maintenance schedule for a hot-dog and fruit-juice franchise unit. It would be difficult to overlook any details that are spelled out this clearly.

| | |
|---|---|
| **Items to be done daily** | Clean grill. |
| | Clean orange-juice squeezer. |
| | Clean counter above and below. |
| | Clean coffee urn. |
| | Clean mustard and other containers. |
| | |
| | Empty all trash. |
| | Wipe inside, front, and back of coolers. |
| | Clean refrigerator inside and out. |
| | Clean signs. |
| | Mop floors. |
| | Wipe surface in front of counter and around coolers. |
| | General outside cleaning. |
| | Spray for roaches if necessary. |
| | |
| **Items to be done weekly** | Wash all windows inside and out. |
| | Scrape gum from floor and under counter. |
| | Clean all ornaments. |
| | Wash outside thoroughly. |
| | Check outside sign. |
| | Check all light bulbs. |
| | Clean spouts of coolers. |
| | Clean coffee urns with cleanser. |
| | Check trash cans for cleanliness. |
| | |
| **Items to be done monthly** | Clean exhaust-fan filter. |
| | Clean grease from exhaust. |
| | Wash interior walls. |
| | Check gas jets—if flame is not high or if it's the wrong color, call gas company or grill maintenance. |
| | Wipe dust from cooler motors. |
| | Exterminator service (oftener if necessary). |
| | |
| **Items to be done every six months** | Oil cooler motors. |
| | Take oranges down from the ceiling and clean them. |
| | Check and touch up signs if needed. |
| | Vacuum grass on walls. |
| | Professionally clean and wax floor. |
| | |
| **Items to be done yearly** | Redecorate as necessary. |
| | Maintain signs. |
| | Replace ornaments as needed. |
| | Spray-paint the grass on walls. |

**Fig. 14.1** Housekeeping and maintenance frequency chart for a hot-dog and fruit-juice franchise unit.

Figures 14.2 through 14.10 illustrate how one restaurant franchisor set the standards for each item on the menu. The size of both the budget and the chain itself will have much bearing on the lengths to which such illustrations go. Nationwide franchise manuals may feature color photographs with expensive transparent overlays. However, there is no reason why a low-budget operation cannot use its creative ingenuity to provide a manual just as specific and just as easy to use, regardless of its inability to afford the "slick" presentation.

# WAFFLES

| ITEM | CODE | DESCRIPTION |
|------|------|-------------|
| PLAIN WAFFLE | | Prepare according to package recipe. Mix with water, beat to smooth texture. |
| | | Waffle irons must be hot; they should remain on all day. |
| | | With pastry brush, spread grid w/Kay–Gold, bottom & top. |
| | | Pour 1 ladle batter on iron, close, set timer for 3 minutes. |
| | | Shake handle of iron, remove waffle w/fork or spatula. |
| | | Lay on plate, butter well, serve. Serve syrup with order. |
| FANCY WAFFLE (STRAWBERRY, for example.) | | Prepare waffle same as plain. Place large scoop strawberry ice cream in center. Place large ladle frozen-fresh strawberries and juice around waffle and on top of ice cream. Place whipped-cream rosettes around waffle and on top of ice cream. Top ice cream with strawberry. |
| OTHER FANCY WAFFLES | | Follow same procedure, substituting rasberry, blueberry, banana, pineapple, etc. |

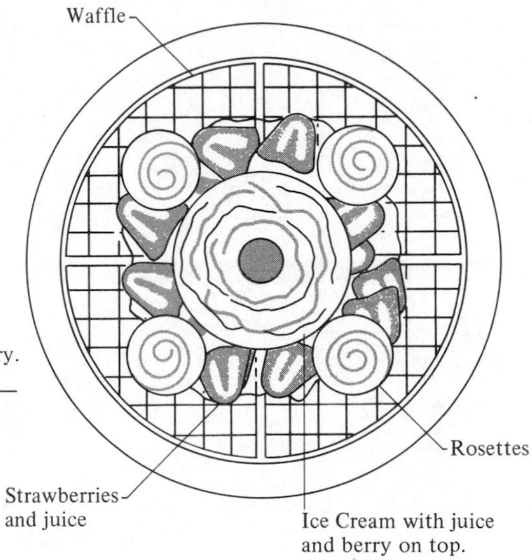

Waffle — Rosettes — Strawberries and juice — Ice Cream with juice and berry on top.

**Figure 14.2**

# FRIED-EGG PLATES

| ITEM | CODE | DESCRIPTION |
|---|---|---|
| FRIED EGGS (served with toast) | | Start with clean grill — wipe with old apron grill cloth. Have grill nice and warm, but <u>not hot</u>. Time your toast order to coincide with finished eggs depending upon style (sunny—side, turned over, etc.). Place generous pat butter (teaspoonful) on grill, spread and melt. Crack eggs, place on buttered grill.  Serve as illustrated. |
| FRIED EGGS WITH BACON | | Same, except  add 3 slices crisp bacon |
| FRIED EGGS WITH HAM | | Same, except add 2 or 3 good slices ham, heated and turned over. |
| FRIED EGGS WITH SAUSAGE | | Same, except add 3 well-fried sausages. |

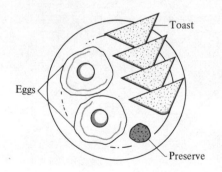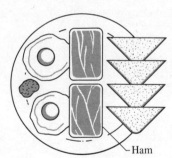

**Figure 14.3**

# SALAD COMBINATIONS

| ITEM | CODE | DESCRIPTION |
|------|------|-------------|
| # 1<br>TUNA FISH SALAD<br>COMBINATION | | Bed of lettuce on ½ plate.<br><br>3-oz. tuna salad centered on lettuce.<br><br>Sliced tomato slices around mound of tuna.<br><br>Sliced egg around mound of tuna.<br><br>Add one tablespoon each of potato salad and cole slaw; lemon wedge with frilled toothpick; potato chips; pickle.<br><br>Serve as illustrated. |
| #2<br>SARDINE SALAD<br>COMBINATION | | Same as # 1,<br>except use whole can sardines instead of tuna. |
| # 4<br>EGG SALAD<br>COMBINATION | | Same as # 1,<br>except use mound of egg salad instead of tuna. |
| # 6<br>HAM SALAD<br>COMBINATION | | Same as # 1,<br>except use ham salad instead of tuna. |

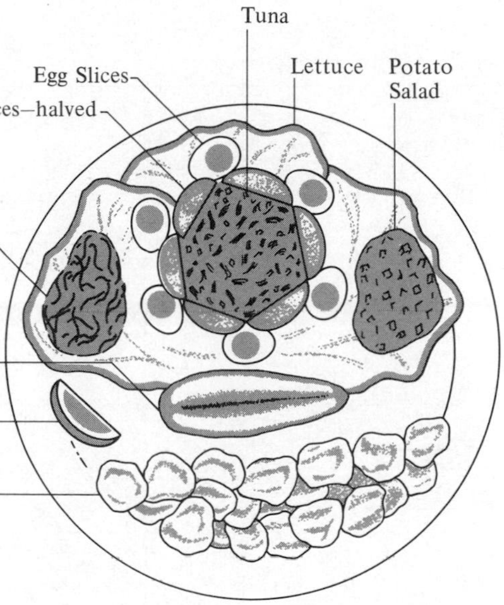

**Figure 14.4**

# SALAD COMBINATIONS

| ITEM | CODE | DESCRIPTION | |
|---|---|---|---|
| # 3<br>HAM & CHEESE SALAD<br>COMBINATION | | Use 2 slices ham cut into halves and 2 slices American cheese, cut into half angles. | |
| # 5<br>SALAMI SALAD<br>COMBINATION | | Same as # 3 , except use 4 slices salami. | |
| # 8<br>SANDWICH<br>STEAKS SALAD<br>COMBINATION | | Charbroil 2 sandwich steaks rare, medium or well.<br><br>Toast bread of customer's choice and place buttered halves on plate.<br><br>Arrange lettuce on side of plate, with 3 nice slices of tomato and sliced pickle.<br><br>Place steaks on top of toast.<br><br>Place large pat of butter atop steaks.  Serve. | |

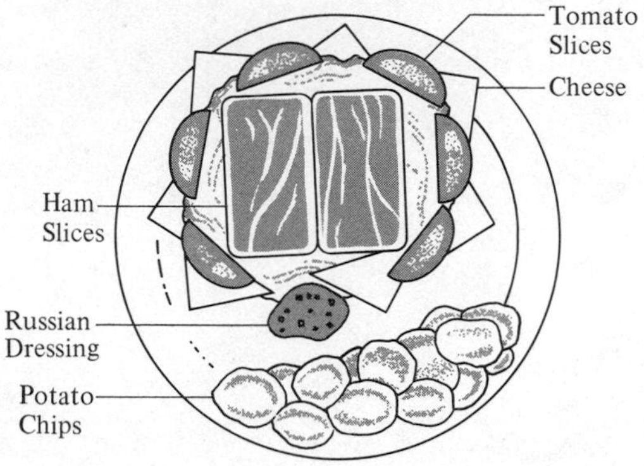

**Figure 14.5**

# SALAD COMBINATIONS

| ITEM | CODE | DESCRIPTION |
|------|------|-------------|
| # 7<br>TWO HAMBURGERS<br>COMBINATION PLATE | | Prepare same as H–2<br><br>Use top and bottom half of roll.<br><br>Serve open-faced with chips & pickle. |

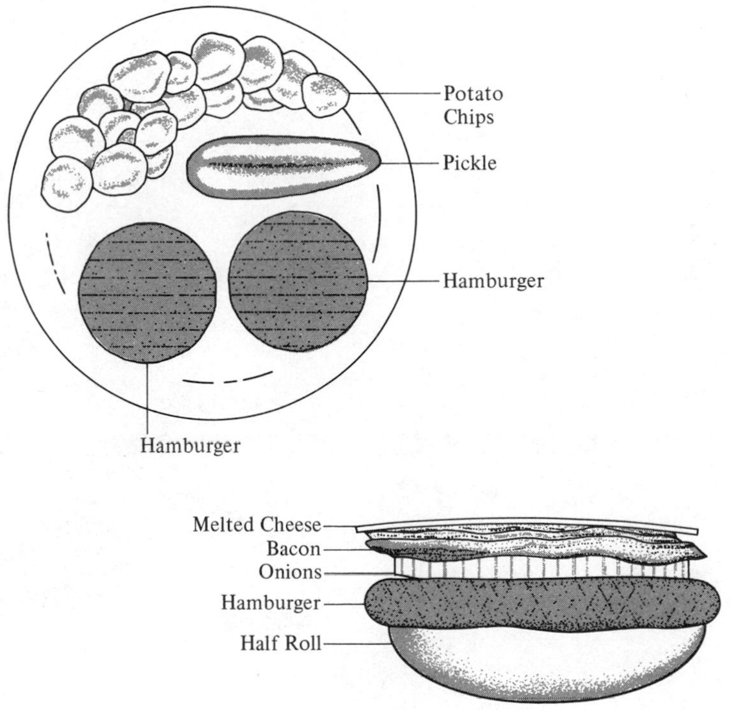

Potato Chips

Pickle

Hamburger

Hamburger

Melted Cheese
Bacon
Onions
Hamburger
Half Roll

**Figure 14.6**

# SALAD COMBINATIONS

| ITEM | CODE | DESCRIPTION |
|---|---|---|
| #10 OPEN HOT CLAM-ROLL SALAD COMBINATION | | Portion order clams, fry golden brown.<br><br>Toast hot-dog bun; butter.<br><br>Place clams on roll, with generous portion of butter.<br><br>On side of plate: Lettuce with 3 tomato slices; 1 tablespoon each of coleslaw, potato salad, and tartar sauce: add potato chips and lemon wedge with frilled toothpick.<br><br>Serve as illustrated. |

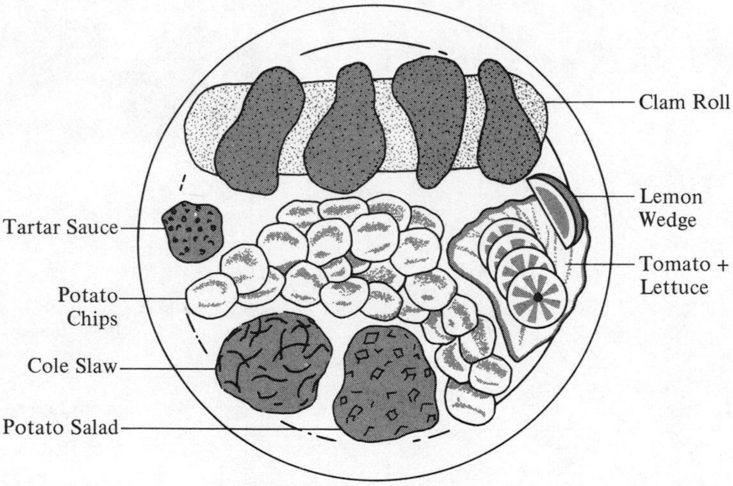

Clam Roll

Lemon Wedge

Tomato + Lettuce

Tartar Sauce

Potato Chips

Cole Slaw

Potato Salad

**Figure 14.7**

# SALAD PLATES (BOWL)

| ITEM | CODE | DESCRIPTION |
|---|---|---|
| SALAD BOWL | | Use salad bowl. <br><br> Chop ¼ head lettuce into large pieces. <br><br> Add half a tomato, sliced. <br><br> Top with teaspoon pepper greens, teaspoon chopped celery, 6 to 8 croutons.  Choice of dressing. <br><br> (Large salad:  Use larger bowl & 1½ times ingredients.) |
| STUFFED-TOMATO SALAD <br><br> (Using prepared salads of customer's choice) | | Place bed of lettuce on half of plate. <br><br> Remove stem core from a good–sized tomato.  Slice whole tomato 3 slices across about ¾ way down.  Place on lettuce bed. <br><br> Stuff tomato with 3 to 4 oz. prepared salad choice. <br><br> Slice hard-boiled egg around tomato. <br><br> Add one tablespoon each of coleslaw and potato salad. <br><br> Add pickle slice & potato chips. <br><br> (If fish salad such as tuna or crab, add lemon wedge with frilled tooth–pick on top of salad) |

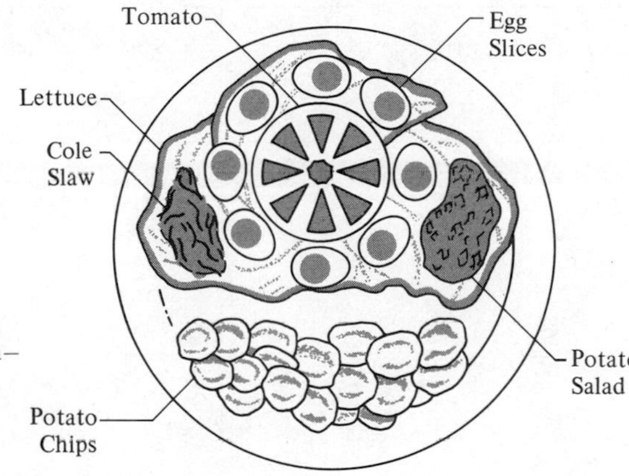

**Figure 14.8**

# HOT DOGS

| ITEM | CODE | DESCRIPTION |
|------|------|-------------|
| PLAIN HOT DOG | | Toast bun on top of grill or broiler.<br><br>Cook hot dog on grill, rolling often so as to brown well without burning.<br><br>Remove roll from grill.<br><br>Place hot dog on roll.<br><br>Arrange on plate as shown.<br>Serve quickly to retain warmth.<br><br>Place relish, ketchup, and mustard on table. 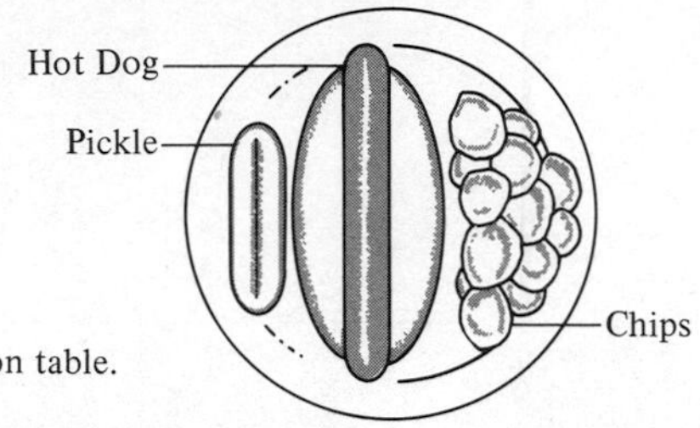 |
| HOT DOG & BACON | | Same procedure, but add a crisp slice of bacon. |
| HOT DOG & CHEESE | | Same procedure, but place 1½ slices cheese over hot dog in roll.<br><br>Place under grill until melted. Serve quickly. |
| HOT DOG & SAUERKRAUT | | Same procedure, but serve with large forkful of hot sauerkraut. |

**Figure 14.9**

# SANDWICHES

Bread is always the customer's choice!

| ITEM | CODE | DESCRIPTIONS |
|---|---|---|
| CREAM CHEESE & JELLY ON DATE NUT BREAD | | 3 slices date nut bread , cut in half.<br><br>Spread cream cheese on all open sides.<br><br>Add grape jam over cream cheese.<br><br>Close, slice on angle.<br>Stand sections on edge, arranged on plate like spokes of a wheel (see illustration). 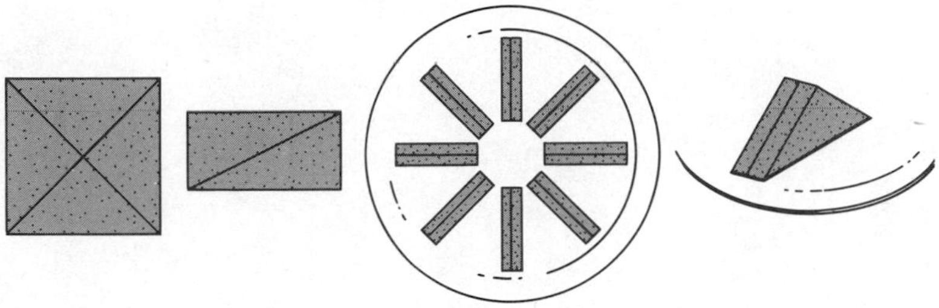 |
| BACON & EGG<br><br>HAM & EGG<br><br>SAUSAGE & EGG | | On toast unless otherwise specified.<br><br>Fry egg in butter; add<br>3 slices crisp bacon or 2 good slices warm ham<br>or 3 well-fried breakfast sausages. |

**Figure 14.10**

# PROVIDING SUPPORTIVE BACKUP TO FRANCHISEES

# 15

A new type of relationship exists between today's successful franchisor and franchisee.

No longer do we find these two entities functioning in a vertical structure wherein the autocratic franchisor resides at the top of a hierarchy. Today's franchisor does not oversee and discipline its franchisees as a grim parent might monitor the behavior of children.

Rather, the relationship has become *horizontal*. A sense of equality must prevail between franchisor and franchisee, because they are mutually interdependent. The franchise concept cannot succeed if either of its factions fails.

In view of the interlocking nature of this relationship, the backup support provided by the franchisor has become increasingly important. Effective support not only helps the franchisee to succeed, but also helps the franchisor to justify the receipt of royalties. The need for pragmatic, ongoing supportive measures sensitive to both business and personal needs of the franchisee can best be understoood by examining the new realities of today's franchisor–franchisee relationship.

**TWELVE "REALITIES" OF TODAY'S FRANCHISOR– FRANCHISEE RELATIONSHIP**

One prominent franchisor has identified and characterized the twelve realities of a contemporary franchisor–franchisee relationship as follows:

1. Be professional.
2. Negotiate equally.
3. Institute self-improvement programs.
4. Provide a marketing umbrella.
5. Maintain high franchisor status.
6. Establish constant communication flow.
7. Plan for growth potential.
8. Plan for diversification.

9. Suggest immediate tax benefits.
10. Help franchisee see "money now."
11. Provide strong leadership.
12. Help franchisee become a community VIP.

1. **Be professional.** Franchisees have rising demands similar to emerging nations. They demand professionalism. They expect the franchisor to bring quality marketing strategies into the management of the business. They will not settle for incompetence and mediocrity.

2. **Negotiate equally.** The franchisor–franchisee relationship should be one in which the parties deal with one another much as labor and management negotiate over a bargaining table. Try to sell the merits of the proposition rather than dictating them. Take your franchisees into your confidence, and be sincere.

3. **Institute self-improvement programs.** Franchisees seek self-improvement programs for improving their management capacities and their profits. They also seek help in personal financial budgeting. A correspondence course and post-graduate courses in these areas can prove extremely worthwhile.

4. **Provide a marketing umbrella.** Franchisees seek competent and effective advertising coverage on a national and regional basis. They need the type of coverage that they could not afford on their own.

5. **Maintain high franchisor status.** The franchisee expects the franchisor to maintain a reputation on the highest level. Any reduction in franchisor status reflects on the franchisee and can affect his or her substantial investment.

6. **Establish constant communication flow.** Franchisees want to participate in future plans. They've developed an expertise that seeks to be tapped. They want to be consulted, and they want their advice to be considered in planning the company's future. Communication must be a two-way street.

7. **Plan for growth potential.** Franchisees like their company to expand. They resent a business that is on a treadmill. Hence, innovativeness is required.

8. **Plan for diversification.** Franchisees seek diversification for add-on profits and earnings and to ensure that the business is constantly upgraded to meet current needs. This is particularly pertinent in view of today's escalating overhead costs. McDonald's, for example, introduced its breakfast, constituting an add-on business for essentially the same overhead, and new structural formats conforming to community needs. Ben Franklin converted from small five-and-dime variety stores to sophisticated shopping-center stores with potential sales volumes three to four times greater than before.

9. **Suggest immediate tax benefits.** Franchisees often want to be relieved from some of the tax constraints that go with ordinary income. Franchisors

usually have the experience and information to advise franchisees on the subjects of capital gains and tax shelters.

10. **Help franchisee see "money now."** Some franchisees want money now from the business they built. They also seek monies beyond the ordinary income of salaries and dividends; they want the opportunity for capital gain. There should be a phased-in plan to help attain this goal to the best interests of both parties.

11. **Provide strong leadership.** Franchisees seek diversification, for add-on profits and add-on earnings, and to ensure that the business is constantly upgraded. This is particularly pertinent in view of today's escalating overhead costs. The cases of McDonald's and the Ben Franklin stores, mentioned in item 8, are just two of the many examples where strong leadership has given these franchisees what they want.

12. **Help franchisee becomes a community VIP.** Franchisees want to be assisted in becoming local VIPs. Help them become "joiners"; prepare special speeches they can deliver to local groups, a newspaper column containing the franchisee's picture, etc., to help enhance local status and reputation.

## MANAGEMENT DIRECTION

Franchisee support is an ongoing process that begins with initial training and continues through subsequent training and field assistance. Its quality, thoroughness, and practicality gauge its effectiveness, and at its core must be a comprehensive, in-depth operations manual that discusses every aspect of the franchised business in a sequential, understandable, and readily usable manner.

One of the most critical ingredients of effective training is *management direction*. Figure 15.1 is a summary of franchisee complaints as compiled by the Federal Trade Commission. It clearly identifies "management services" as the single area in which most franchisee complaints are received.

Chief among the problems faced by today's small-business owners—a category into which the majority of franchisees fall—is the profit squeeze im-

| Misrepresentation | Number | Percent of total items classified |
|---|---|---|
| Management services | 69 | 16.9 |
| Earnings claims | 51 | 12.5 |
| Refundable fees | 42 | 10.3 |
| Site not located | 33 | 8.1 |
| Training provided | 31 | 7.6 |
| Terms of contract | 24 | 5.9 |
| Advertising assistance | 10 | 2.5 |
| Investment required | 7 | 1.7 |
| Poor design of franchise unit | 5 | 1.2 |
| Site located by franchisee not accepted | 4 | 1.0 |
| Amount of work or hours required | 3 | 0.7 |
| Others | 55 | 13.4 |
| Total items classified as misrepresentation | 334 | 81.8 |

**Fig. 15.1** Franchisee complaints of management direction.

posed by a cost escalation often not matched by proportional sales increases. In view of the franchisor's implicit emphasis on generating greater and greater sales volumes, one of the more important franchisor functions is providing franchisees with effective advertising and sales-promotion packages. It is important that these supports be pretested and of proven effectiveness. They should offer a set of marketing tentacles that extend throughout the franchisee's entire community, grasping every marketing opportunity therein. No longer is it possible for the franchisee to sit passively in the store awaiting the arrival of customers. The operating overhead of business is too great to permit this luxury. Rather, the store or office should be a central headquarters, generating sales efforts that impact the entire locality.

In this chapter, we will discuss franchisee motivators and cite some examples of successful motivational aids. We will explore supervision as a form of support, district and regional seminars, and the possibilities afforded by offering "a piece of the corporate rock" to the franchisee. Quality control will be explained, and a comprehensive insurance plan will be described. Emphasis is given to the importance of providing the franchisee with a workable record-keeping system.

At the end of the chapter, you'll have a chance to examine the package offered by General Business Services, Inc., a comprehensive example of far-sightedness in supportive backup.

## PRINCIPAL FRANCHISEE MOTIVATORS

The motivating forces behind all franchisees can be divided into three principal categories: *profit, growth potential,* and *recognition.* The franchisor who maintains a balanced backup program that responds equally to these three motivators has developed an excellent formula for success.

### PROFIT

The profit motive is, of course, the strongest force in business. All business is based on a desire for profit. As long as your franchisees can make money with you, they will continue to exhibit self-motivation and put forth effort.

### GROWTH

Everyone has a craving to build and to grow—a desire to forge steadily ahead. This is what causes people to leave one job for another; very likely it is why many leave high-salaried jobs to become franchisees. It is most essential, therefore, that the franchisor provide the products, the services, and the facilities that carry inherent, built-in facilitators for growth.

### RECOGNITION

Like growth, recognition is something everyone craves. Deeply rooted in every human being is a desire for acceptance and recognition—a desire to be wanted and needed. If this longing isn't fulfilled, the gulf that separates the franchisee from the home office widens often exaggerating actual geographical distances. This gulf must be bridged by recognition through praise, instruction, encouragement, and ongoing communication.

SOME
SUCCESSFUL
MOTIVATIONAL
AIDS

There are nearly as many types of effective response to these needs as there are successful franchisors. The important thing is to determine which combination of them will work best for you. We're including ten suggestions that have a proven record of effectiveness, and hope you'll add a few of your own.

1. *Company A* distributes a house organ to franchisees. It contains newsy and inspirational material and is an effective forum for franchisee news and views.

2. *Company B* distributes recorded cassettes to their franchisees, conveying instructive and inspirational messages to help spur them on in their sales.

3. *Company C* conducts contests for their franchisees (based on fulfillment of designated objectives). The winners and their families receive expense-paid resort vacations.

4. *Company D* arranges for conference telephone hookups on a regional basis, bringing franchisees in touch with their office and one another through "seminars" via the phone.

5. *Company E* sends a home-office representative into the territory of each franchisee approximately once every three months to extend assistance and help solve recurring problems.

6. *Company F* provides life and medical insurance benefits to franchisees as a means of enhancing their sense of security.

7. *Company G* provides regular bonuses to franchisees, based on sales escalations.

8. *Company H* conducts nationwide publicity programs that increase franchisee self-esteem and status as well as attract leads for further sales.

9. *Company I* conducts semi-annual franchisee get-togethers featuring interesting speakers, good food, and music. These give the franchisees a sense of "belonging" to a large business family and provide them an opportunity to exchange ideas.

10. *Company J* offers a three-phase, built-in expansion program: Phase one, starting six months after a franchise has been assumed, shows how the franchisee is now prepared to expand through the hiring of one employee, tending to increase business approximately 25 percent. Phase two, six months thereafter, instructs the franchisee in another phase of expansion, tending to further increase sales and profits. Phase three, six months thereafter, helps to achieve further expansion factors.

SUPERVISION AS
A FORM OF
SUPPORT

Constructive supervision will not be regarded by the franchisee as harassment. In fact, it is one of the elements that makes franchise ownership more attractive than an independent business venture. Properly conducted, it represents the franchisor's single most important method of supportive backup.

The basic requisite of supervision is *communication*. The better the home office communicates with the franchisee, the more effective will be the supervision.

Communication can be established through the following media:

- Mail contacts.
- Phone contacts.
- Home-office personnel visits.
- Franchisees helping one another.
- Group get-togethers.

SUPERVISION VIA
MAIL CONTACTS

The franchisor must recognize that if a franchisee is in the territory and deprived of correspondence with the company, diminished morale will impede sales efficiency. It's extremely important that a regular system of letters and other material be established. Such mail contacts may include the following:

1. **House organs,** running from four to eight pages ($8\frac{1}{2} \times 11$) and containing news and views of the company and other franchisees. Franchisee accomplishments and personal news plus new sales and administrative ideas can be featured.

2. **Flash bulletins,** generally one-sheet mimeographed messages, can convey special instructive or inspirational messages of current value to the franchisee.

3. **Letters** sent regularly from the home office of the franchisee. For maximum effectiveness these letters should emanate from a number of sources—e.g., President, Sales Manager, Franchisee Coordinator, etc. These letters should be written in a chatty, personalized vein, giving franchisees the feeling that they are of utmost importance to the company and that their progress is noticed constantly.

4. **Self-check activity forms,** provided by many franchise organizations so that franchisees can report weekly contacts and results (e.g., sales, call-backs, turn-downs, etc.). A copy is returned to the sales manager each week. This gives the home office a perspective on the franchisee's area activities—exposing possible weaknesses. At the end of each month the sales manager prepares an "Activities Profile" on the franchisee, highlighting individual weaknesses and strengths. It sets forth specific constructive recommendations for improving the picture and congratulates the franchisee whenever excellence is shown.

SUPERVISION VIA
PHONE CONTACTS

The telephone constitutes a powerful force for inspiring, motivating, instructing, and guiding franchisees—keeping them contented and in proper perspective. Properly used, it more than "pays its way" in achieving increased franchisee results. Telephone contacts can be classified as follows:

1. **Phone contacts set up by letter.** Many franchisors have found it effective to arrange person-to-person chats with each franchisee at least once a month. This helps to build a valuable rapport with the franchisee and does much to expose and solve franchisee problems and gripes. A letter is written to the franchisee advising the date and time of a planned phone call. This approach has two benefits: First, it spurs the franchisee to greater effort and

accomplishments in anticipation of this call, so that maximum results can be reported. Second, it provides a sense of pleasant anticipation (something favorable that is going to occur several days hence), giving the phone call utmost morale value.

2. **Spontaneous phone calls** (unscheduled by previous letter). Phone calls of this nature—especially when they emanate from an unexpected source such as a company executive—greatly boost franchisee morale and increase their pride in "belonging" to the organization. Contacts of this type can be friendly chat-type calls, or they may refer to current business events of interest to the franchisee.

3. **Conference phone calls** have proved highly effective. Franchisors set up conference phone calls including from five to twenty franchisees in a given region. A letter will alert the franchisees regarding the date and time. Such phone calls are often used to inform franchisees of some new, important development. One objective for which conference calls have proved useful is to announce a franchisee contest, a new product, service, or means of enhancing their sales and income. Telephone company rates for such conference calls are moderate and the results are well worth this comparatively small expense.

SUPERVISION VIA HOME-OFFICE PERSONNEL VISITS

Physical followup and backup from home office is instrumental in promoting maximum franchisee accomplishment. This is a "must" to supplement the mail and phone contacts. Such contact should be made on a regular, systematic, prescheduled basis.

At different intervals, visits should be made by either or all of the following members of the franchisor organization: Sales Manager, President, Vice-President, Franchisee Coordinator, Franchisee Service Supervisor. The effect of such visits should be:

1. **Trouble-shooting** to ascertain and solve problems that have impeded franchisee programs or caused recurring objections and complaints from customers.

2. **Sales backup** to help franchisee overcome sales difficulties due to inadequacies in approach, presentation, close meeting objections, etc.

3. **Service backup** to help franchisee solve existing service problems or to help land a current big job through assistance in installation and estimating problems.

SUPERVISION VIA FRANCHISEES HELPING ONE ANOTHER

A number of organizations have found it highly effective to enlist the assistance of strong franchisees to help support weaker ones. Some franchisees tend to resist advice and assistance from the home office, interpreting it as "theoretical" or prejudiced toward home-office objectives rather than in the best interests of the franchisees themselves. Hence there is value in assigning a successful franchisee to help a less successful one. Such an individual often respects and trusts the fellow franchisee's recommendations since they have similar objectives and common goals. There is truth to the old adage, "You can't argue with success." If the assisting franchisee is successful, there will be a tendency to follow the advice and emulate the actions in an attempt to improve his or her own operation.

Franchisor organizations accomplish such franchisee-help programs through the following means:

1. Setting up a "Big-Brother" status among franchisees.
2. Arranging for franchisees in contiguous territories to help one another.
3. Setting up franchise "clinics" supervised by the regional franchisee.
4. Home-office territorial supervisors.

### BIG-BROTHER STATUS

Under this plan, key franchises in each area are selected on a basis of their experience and proven accomplishments among a given number of franchisees (usually four to seven). As Big Brother, this franchisee is available to advise member franchisees and help solve recurring problems. Thus a localized tightly knit nucleus is established for continuing franchisee guidance. The home office should provide an instruction program for these Big Brothers. A reward plan should also be implemented so that participants can benefit from the increased results they achieve among their member franchisees.

### ADJOINING TERRITORIES

Franchisees are encouraged they can "talk out" their problems with other franchisees in adjoining areas. This gives them a sense of belonging to a large family and helps their attitude and pride toward their work. Many of the franchisor organizations set up the mechanics for adjoining territorial franchisees to get together. They should feel free to contact one another whenever the need arises. One franchisor in the closed-circuit television field established such a "working together" arrangement between franchisees, enlisting the technical expertise of one who was weak in sales and the sales ability of another, who was weak in technical skills. Their mutual assistance overcame weaknesses and increased strengths.

### REGIONAL CLINICS

This highly effective plan is used by many organizations. At regular intervals (usually monthly or bimonthly), franchisees in adjoining territories meet together in a central location for a regional clinic. The meetings are presided over by the most successful franchisee in that area (for example, the Big-Brother type previously described) or by a representative of the home office (usually the Sales Manager). Such clinics provide a forum for an interchange of common business problems and methods of solving them.

### HOME-OFFICE SUPERVISORS

These "roving ambassadors" of the franchisor organization assist franchisees in problem solving and encourage them in all constructive endeavors. Their functions include (a) examining books and activity records to ascertain "what is wrong" and what improvement is best indicated; (b) counseling the franchisee in sales or service problems; (c) creating an improved "bridge" between the franchisee and the home office; (d) helping the franchisee improve customer relations.

A SUMMARY OF
SUPPORTIVE
SUPERVISION

Continuing guidance is an important part of franchisee support. A successful franchisor will supervise constantly and creatively. The franchise organization that experiences failure in its programming is generally one that has lacked "hold" over its franchisees, resulting in a number of detached, separated, semihostile units rather than satisfied, interfunctioning, cohesive members of a large, closely knit family.

Proper supervision of franchisees achieves the following:

1. Builds morale.
2. Decentralizes home-office functions.
3. Enables regional control and followup.
4. Achieves constant channels for "communication" between the franchisor organization and the franchisee.
5. Assures maximum morale on the part of the franchisee; nips discontent in the bud and subdues hostility before it has a chance to blossom.
6. Acts to place franchisees in a winning momentum during the first six months of their franchise operation—normally the critical period when franchisees can fail irretrievably if they are not properly and closely supported.

DISTRICT AND
REGIONAL
SEMINARS

A large part of the ongoing franchisee training is accomplished by the franchisor's field representatives, but many franchisors have found it extremely effective to develop supplementary programs of advanced franchisee education and continual training. A multitude of individual techniques can be utilized to accomplish this: refresher and graduate courses at the home office, continual revision and updating of the operations manual, and use of house-organ magazines or newsletters.

Among the most effective of these techniques, however, is the *district and regional seminar*—or clinic—approach. Long-range franchise plans should provide them. These clinics afford an unexcelled opportunity for discussion of common problems and methods of operation between franchisor and franchisee. They provide the franchisor with an exceptional forum from which sales-promotion programs, advertising campaigns, and other franchisor-generated, system-improvement plans can be presented.

Clinics not only establish or embellish franchisee-franchisor rapport, but also provide franchisees the chance to meet with and learn from one another. Many unique, valuable, tested methods of operation have been brought to the fore at seminars, and the opportunity for franchisees to "talk shop" with fellow operators usually proves worthwhile for all concerned.

Seminars and clinics must be properly planned and controlled; then their motivational value and their practical function as an information-exchange medium proves them to be among the most productive efforts of many franchise programs.

**A "PIECE OF THE ROCK" FOR THE FRANCHISEE**

A variety of methods can be devised for allowing franchisees to share in corporate success, but it should be understood at the outset that the assumption of franchisor success automatically subsumes that the individual franchisees, each of whom is a part of the franchise network, already have "a piece of the rock." Their membership in the system yields them benefits of increased sales volume, operational efficiency, cost effectiveness, and increased profitability—all of which they would be unable to share if they conducted independent businesses. To this extent—and it is a very real and very large extent—the officers, employees, and other assets of the franchisor organization exist to serve them and assist them, and from this relationship they derive not only "a piece of the rock," but a very large and important piece, at that.

Perhaps, then, it would be better to restate the objective. Rather than considering how to allow franchisees to share in corporate success, perhaps we should consider how to allow franchisees to obtain a *greater* share of corporate success. In fact, if for any reason this restatement cannot be made, there exists a major flaw in the franchise program, the franchise system, or the administration of the franchisor company. Such a situation requires a diagnosis, prognosis, and cure before consideration is given to anything else.

Assuming, however, that a franchisor has rephrased the purpose with full understanding of the implications of that rephrasing, there are two essential, recommended means by which a franchisee can share a franchisor's success: (1) the receipt of cash or credits, and (2) the receipt of common stock in the franchisor company. Both methods require the disclosure of information to the franchisee, the extent of which is determined by the particular approach adopted; both methods exhibit varying tax consequences.

By disclosure, we mean the requirement for disclosure to the franchisee, or perhaps to the public, of operating and financial details concerning the franchisor company. Given the question of tax corporate and capital structures of the franchisor, it is wise to obtain competent legal and tax counsel before adopting any plan.

The franchisor may establish a cash fund based on its profitability. A percentage of net profits can be predetermined and preset by the franchisor, thus establishing a cash fund for distribution to the franchisee. This fund would, of course, be separate and distinct from any fund established to award sales-incentive or performance-incentive prizes to the franchisee group, and the fund could be distributed annually, semiannually, or even quarterly to the franchisees in the form of cash. The division of the total fund among the individual franchisees would be determined by the application of percentages to it. The percentages, in their turn, would be previously determined by franchisor management based on the criteria which it considers to be most important to the success of the franchise system as a whole. As an example, fifty percent of the fund might be reserved for distribution based on total sales, with each franchisee receiving that percentage of that portion of the fund so reserved represented by his or her percentage of the total sales of all franchisees to the public for the period of time questioned. Another fifty percent of the fund might be reserved for distribution based on growth, with each franchisee receiving that percentage of the total percentage growth of all franchisees.

It is not necessary, on the other hand, that this cash fund be distributed to the franchisees in cash. Rather, it might better serve the franchisor's purposes (and be more advantageous from the viewpoint of taxation) to distribute the fund in the form of deposits to Individual Retirement Accounts established by the franchisor for the benefit of individual franchisees with a reputable financial institution, such as a commercial bank, savings bank, etc.

A common-stock distribution to the franchisees is far more complex, but equally feasible. The franchisor must first determine what portion of the equity of the franchisor company is to be distributed, and must then accept the fact that the operation time of this "sharing-the-equity" plan will be limited—if not from a practical viewpoint, then at least from a theoretical viewpoint. If, for example, the franchisor has determined to give the franchisees as a total group ten percent of the franchisor company, then the plan must necessarily stop when a total of ten percent of the stock of the company has been distributed. Under this plan, it is probably best to recapitalize the franchisor company with classes of common stock, rather than the more usual one class. The additional class of stock, call it "A" common, would represent ten percent of the franchisor company's equity, but would consist of a larger number of authorized shares. These shares, which would differ markedly from "B" shares in voting rights and dividends priority, would then form a fund analogous to the cash fund discussed previously. Management could determine, as an example, that share distribution would take place over a period of ten years. Thus ten percent of the shares in the fund would be distributed in each of the ten years of the program's life, each distribution to be based on percentages determined essentially the same as those which would apply for a cash distribution or deposit distribution.

At the end of the ten-year period, the franchisor may revert to a cash- or credit-distribution plan, or establish an additional stock fund representing additional equity points to be granted to the franchisees.

The stock-distribution plan is also workable with respect to the receipt of franchise fees, and any of these approaches may be combined.

## QUALITY CONTROL AS A SUPPORTIVE MEASURE

Properly administrated quality-control procedures provide a form of benevolent "policing" that achieves constructive, positive results by assuring uniform quality throughout a franchise chain. By setting and maintaining high standards, a franchisor does its franchisees a service. They actually appreciate this parental concern and authoritativeness. If quality control is explained clearly and enforced strictly, it gives franchisees the secure knowledge that their reputation will not be harmed by a sloppy performance elsewhere within the franchise chain.

Because quality control is so vital in achieving a consistently favorable image that invites return patronage and encourages word-of-mouth advertising, many operations are adopting innovative quality-control measures. One of the leaders in this field is Sky Chefs, a subsidiary of American Airlines. Sky Chefs is among the largest food purveyors in the United States, serving in-flight meals for some thirty airlines and providing a food service for thousands of travelers daily in its many airport restaurants.

A 25-point quality-control standards program has been devised under the direction of Sky Chefs' President, J. J. O'Neill. The program requires observations in the following areas of performance:

1. Catering Kitchen management shall conduct observations in Airline Catering categories and Public Facilities management shall conduct observations in Public Facility categories.

2. Observations must be made on a random basis at various times of the day so that all shifts are included.

3. Reporting must be accurate and accomplished on a systematic basis as set forth in the instructions.

4. Corrective action must be taken immediately on those areas found to be below standard.

5. Management on all levels must become totally involved with the program and view it as constructive and positive.

Mr. O'Neill comments:

It is not the purpose of our quality-control program to "police" unit management. It is rather an Awareness Program. As these standards are checked off and graded daily by the management, there is a growing awareness of the problem areas and corrective measures required—e.g., untidy waitress uniforms, an unclean spatula, and so on. Our main-office evaluator appears at each unit, at unscheduled intervals, to recheck the "grades."

Mr. O'Neill states that this program serves the dual purpose of instilling both quality control and enhanced morale among personnel, achieving a sense of team effort. Figures 15.2 through 15.4 show some of the forms that Sky Chef uses to ensure proper quality control.

Thus quality control, for restaurants and purveyors alike, is one of the most important factors in projecting a caring, quality management and operation. If you project an attractive appearance, an appealing decor, considerate and helpful personnel, an interesting product or service, and a quality operation, you have a good opportunity for gaining a large and loyal clientele.

## PLANNING YOUR INSURANCE PROGRAM

The term "insurance" has a greatly expanded significance in the franchise field. There are generally three broad categories of insurance pertinent to franchisees and franchisors. They include:

- Business insurance—Protective of the franchisee's business assets.
- Personal insurance—Protective of the franchisee's personal and family security.
- Consumer insurance—This type of insurance provides needed credibility to protect the franchisee's customers, in effect it warrants that the product and

service are reliable as represented, and offers indemnification against faulty or unsatisfactory work.

More and more franchisors recognize the benefits of providing *all* the aforesaid insurance protections in behalf of their franchisees. They deem it a big program "plus." They recognize that the more secure and relaxed the franchisee—and the franchisee's customers—the more mutually profitable, harmonious and enduring will be the franchisor–franchisee relationship.

In many instances a "blanket" type insurance policy is obtainable by franchisors and available to franchisees—both current and future—on an

## Cafeteria—Observation Record

SKY CHEFS

Unit —————————————

Month of ———————————

|  |  |  |  |  |  |  |  |  |  |  |  | DINNER |  |  |  |
|---|---|---|---|---|---|---|---|---|---|---|---|---|---|---|---|
|  | 1 | 2 | 3 | 4 | 5 | 6 | 7 | 8 | 9 | 10 | 11 | 12 | 13 | 14 | 15 |
| DATE/OBSERVER |  |  |  |  |  |  |  |  |  |  |  |  |  |  |  |
| a Attendant Personality |  |  |  |  |  |  |  |  |  |  |  |  |  |  |  |
| b Personal Appearance |  |  |  |  |  |  |  |  |  |  |  |  |  |  |  |
| c Additional Sales Attempted |  |  |  |  |  |  |  |  |  |  |  |  |  |  |  |
| d Appearance of Food And Steamtable |  |  |  |  |  |  |  |  |  |  |  |  |  |  |  |
| e Clean Tables And Filled And Clean Condiments |  |  |  |  |  |  |  |  |  |  |  |  |  |  |  |
| f Menu Board |  |  |  |  |  |  |  |  |  |  |  |  |  |  |  |
| g Cash Handling |  |  |  |  |  |  |  |  |  |  |  |  |  |  |  |
| h Tableware Available And Clean |  |  |  |  |  |  |  |  |  |  |  |  |  |  |  |
| i General Neatness And Cleanliness |  |  |  |  |  |  |  |  |  |  |  |  |  |  |  |
| Name or initials of Individual Observed |  |  |  |  |  |  |  |  |  |  |  |  |  |  |  |
| Record Entire Observation as Std. (√) or Below Std. (X) |  |  |  |  |  |  |  |  |  |  |  |  |  |  |  |

Comments:

No. Observations Standard A ☐

Total No. Observations B ☐

% Monthly Performance C ☐
A ÷ B = C

Record C on Line B-7 of Form QSS

**Fig. 15.2** Form used by Sky Chef to ensure quality control.

optional basis. In effect this policy provides all-inclusive "umbrella" protection to individual franchisees at a lower rate than if the same policy was issued individually on a one-to-one basis.

FRANCHISEE
PERSONAL
INSURANCE

*Franchisee personal insurance* is exemplified in many types of policies. Generally, they provide:

Group major medical.

Group hospital–cash supplemental.

## Food Handling Procedures/Conformance To Specifications

SKY CHEFS

| OBSERVATION NO. | 1 | 2 | 3 | 4 | 5 | 6 | 7 | 8 | 9 | 10 | 11 | 12 | 13 | 14 | 15 | 16 | 17 | 18 | 19 | 20 | 21 | 22 | 23 | 24 | 25 | 26 | 27 | 28 | 29 | 30 |
|---|---|---|---|---|---|---|---|---|---|---|---|---|---|---|---|---|---|---|---|---|---|---|---|---|---|---|---|---|---|---|
| 1. Receiving Procedures Followed | | | | | | | | | | | | | | | | | | | | | | | | | | | | | | |
| 2. Recipes & Specifications Followed | | | | | | | | | | | | | | | | | | | | | | | | | | | | | | |
| 3. Food Handling Procedures Followed | | | | | | | | | | | | | | | | | | | | | | | | | | | | | | |
| 4. Cooking Equipment Functioning | | | | | | | | | | | | | | | | | | | | | | | | | | | | | | |
| 5. Useable Food Not Discarded | | | | | | | | | | | | | | | | | | | | | | | | | | | | | | |
| 6. Over Portioning Controlled | | | | | | | | | | | | | | | | | | | | | | | | | | | | | | |
| 7. Over Production Minimized | | | | | | | | | | | | | | | | | | | | | | | | | | | | | | |
| 8. Proper Cleaning Habits Followed | | | | | | | | | | | | | | | | | | | | | | | | | | | | | | |
| 9. Meals Prepared with Care | | | | | | | | | | | | | | | | | | | | | | | | | | | | | | |
| 10. Security & Control Adequate | | | | | | | | | | | | | | | | | | | | | | | | | | | | | | |
| OBSERVTION STANDARD (√) OR BELOW STANDARD (X) | | | | | | | | | | | | | | | | | | | | | | | | | | | | | | |
| OBSERVERS INITIALS | | | | | | | | | | | | | | | | | | | | | | | | | | | | | | |

Indicate Observation as Standard (√) or Below Standard (X) in the appropriate columns.

No. Obervations Standard   A ☐

Total Observations   B ☐

% Monthly Performance   C ☐
A ÷ B = C

Record this figure on line A-14 Form QSS

**Fig. 15.3** Form used by Sky Chef to ensure quality control.

Group long-term disability insurance plan.

Life insurance plans: whole life, individual/group term life, decreasing term, family life plan, other.

**FRANCHISE BUSINESS INSURANCE**

Franchisee business insurance includes:

1. **Fire insurance:** Have your property properly appraised so that it is insured for its full value. Be sure that you reexamine your fire insurance periodically, to make sure it covers new, current value. Add to the coverage as

---

## AFEH Uniform Appearance Performance

SKY CHEFS

Unit ————————
Month of ————————

| | | 1 | 2 | 3 | 4 | 5 | 6 | 7 | 8 | 9 | 10 | 11 | 12 | 13 | 14 | 15 | 16 | 17 | 18 | 19 | 20 | 21 | 22 | 23 | 24 | 25 | 26 | 27 | 28 | 29 | 30 |
|---|---|---|---|---|---|---|---|---|---|---|---|---|---|---|---|---|---|---|---|---|---|---|---|---|---|---|---|---|---|---|---|
| DATE/OBSERVER | | | | | | | | | | | | | | | | | | | | | | | | | | | | | | | | |
| Shirt: Sky Chefs Specs | A | | | | | | | | | | | | | | | | | | | | | | | | | | | | | | |
| Pants: Sky Chefs Specs | B | | | | | | | | | | | | | | | | | | | | | | | | | | | | | | |
| Bump Cap: Specs With Logo Affixed | C | | | | | | | | | | | | | | | | | | | | | | | | | | | | | | |
| Security Badge Visible | D | | | | | | | | | | | | | | | | | | | | | | | | | | | | | | |
| Torn or Dirty Clothes Worn | E | | | | | | | | | | | | | | | | | | | | | | | | | | | | | | |
| Haircut, Sideburns or Mustache per Local Management | F | | | | | | | | | | | | | | | | | | | | | | | | | | | | | | |
| Initials of Driver/Helper | G | | | | | | | | | | | | | | | | | | | | | | | | | | | | | | |
| Record Entire Obs. as Std. (√) or Below Std. (X) | | | | | | | | | | | | | | | | | | | | | | | | | | | | | | | |

OBS. NO. ACTION TAKEN & DATE OF REVIEW

No. Observations Standard  A☐

Total No. Observations  B☐

% Monthly Performance  C☐
A ÷ B = C

Record on Line A-8 of Form QSS

**Fig. 15.4** Form used by Sky Chef to ensure quality control.

needed. Determine to what extent, if any, a landlord's insurance covers you; then obtain added insurance in the amount you wish.

2. **Inventory insurance:** It is advisable that your inventory insurance should be slightly higher than your normal inventory. To protect your periodical inventory fluctuations, arrange to obtain periodical extended coverage from your insurance broker. Keep an accurate account of inventory so that exact replacement value is known at all times.

3. **Burglary insurance:** To give yourself maximum coverage, bear in mind that this insurance includes protection against loss resulting from the following crimes:

    a) *Burglary*, which requires forcible entry—for example, if your safe is broken open or a person breaks into your place of business after it is closed, carrying off merchandise or office equipment.

    b) *Robbery*, the taking of property by violence of the threat of violence.

    c) *Theft and larceny*, stealing property while it is unprotected—for example, if a person finds the door of your business establishment open and steals your property. If you rent a store, the Storekeeper's Burglary and Robbery Policy may answer your need. If you operate an office, you may want an Office Burglary and Robbery Policy.

4. **Workmen's compensation:** Generally, an employer is required by state law to carry this insurance. It protects employees against loss resulting from job-connected accidents and certain types of occupational illness. Premium rates are influenced by the percentage of weekly pay allowed as a benefit. Amounts paid for medical treatment also affect its cost. The only way to reduce this insurance expense is to reduce accidents.

5. **Accident and health insurance:** This type of insurance helps to reimburse an employee for expenses resulting from an off-the-job injury or a major illness and for loss of income if the individual is unable to work. A sound health and insurance plan will serve as an inducement to prospective employees, help reduce employee turnover, and promote better morale and loyalty to the company (thus increasing productivity).

6. **Use and occupancy insurance:** Should your business be interrupted or suspended due to serious damage, this insurance will provide you with the profits you would expect to receive if there were no interruption. A total stoppage of business is not mandatory in order to receive benefits. You can collect on partial shrinkage of business profits resulting from damage by fire, machinery breakdown, vandalism by striking employees, explosions, broken water pipes, and a variety of other misfortunes.

7. **General liability insurance:** This type of insurance is usually comprised of two parts: *bodily injury*, which covers claims for the accidental injury or death of persons other than employees, and *property damage*, which covers accidental injury to property that is not being used by the insured or in his

care. Within the scope of this insurance, the following are most important:

a) *Basic coverage*, insuring liability for accidents occurring on the business premises or arising out of the use of the premises for business purposes. This is ordinarily obtainable through the Owners', Landlords', and Tenants' Liability Policy. The premium is normally figured on the number of square feet in the area to be insured; in some cases there is an additional charge for frontage.

b) *Products liability*, which insures against accidents or mishaps arising from the use of your products or services. Some examples are accidents from defective electrical apparatus, poisoning from food or dyes in textiles, plus a variety of miscellaneous hazards.

8. **Automobile insurance:** There are two principal forms of automobile insurance: *liability* and *physical damage*. Liability insurance protects the car owner or operator against damage suits arising from automobile accidents. Physical-damage insurance reimburses the owner for loss of or damage to his or her own car. The three types of physical-damage insurance are fire, theft, and collision.

9. **Contractual liability:** This type of insurance covers liability imposed by law for negligence. Most popular is the Comprehensive General Liability Policy, which provides automatic coverage for many unanticipated hazards that may develop after you have purchased your policy.

10. **Business life insurance:** This is necessary protection for a business, or the family of a business owner. Without it, financial loss can result from the death of someone associated with the business. With it, you maintain business continuity and your *full value in business* for your family. There are several areas of business-life coverage:

a) Key-personnel protection, which reimburses for loss upon the death of a key employee.

b) *Partnership* insurance, which retires a partner's interest at death.

c) *Corporation* insurance, which retires a shareholder's interest at death.

d) *Proprietorship* insurance, which provides for maintenance of business upon the death of a sole proprietor.

e) Insurance to aid a firm's credit status—covers owner or key personnel during the period of a loan or the duration of a mortgage.

f) Where the estate of a business owner consists almost entirely of his or her interest in a business, insurance is payable to the family in the event of the owner's death, providing them with cash and aid in liquidation of interest in the business.

11. **Fidelity insurance:** This protects against losses of property and money because of fraud or dishonesty by one or more employees. Your best coverage could be a "blanket bond" that covers losses resulting from the dishonest act of *any* employee, regardless of name or position.

INSURANCE CHECKLIST

Here is a helpful insurance checklist for use in reviewing with your agent or broker. All the phases of protection may not be required in your business, but it's helpful to be fully acquainted with all insurance protection offered.

- *Buildings*
  - ☐ Fire
  - ☐ Improvements and betterments
  - ☐ Extended coverage
  - ☐ Vandalism and malicious mischief
  - ☐ Earthquakes and floods
  - ☐ Sprinkler leakage and water damage
  - ☐ Glass
  - ☐ Business interruption (contingent B.I. agreed amount)
  - ☐ Extra expense
  - ☐ Rent and leasehold
  - ☐ Replacement cost
  - ☐ Debris removal
  - ☐ Demolition

- *Business*
  - ☐ Key-personnel life
  - ☐ Business continuation
  - ☐ Life: proprietorship, partnership, closed corporation

- *Employees* (Protection of human life values)
  - ☐ Group life
  - ☐ Salary savings
  - ☐ Pension plan, company O.A.S.I.
  - ☐ Group disability
  - ☐ Medical payment
  - ☐ Workmen's compensation
  - ☐ Nonoccupational disability
  - ☐ Unemployment compensation

- *Liability against wrongful actions*
  - ☐ Owners, landlords, and tenants
  - ☐ Manufacturers
  - ☐ Contractual
  - ☐ Contingent
  - ☐ Elevator
  - ☐ Comprehensive, general

- *Equipment*
  - ☐ Boiler and machinery
  - ☐ Auto physical damage
  - ☐ Aircraft damage
  - ☐ Marine hull
  - ☐ Auto liability
  - ☐ Nonownership
  - ☐ Neon sign
  - ☐ Use and occupancy

- *Merchandise*
  - ☐ Inland marine
  - ☐ Transportation, parcel post
  - ☐ Sales samples
  - ☐ Exhibition floater
  - ☐ Robbery and safe burglary
  - ☐ Installment sales floater
  - ☐ Ocean marine cargo
  - ☐ Burglary, robbery, and theft
  - ☐ Open-stock burglary
  - ☐ Money and securities, 3-D broad form

- *Protection against human failure*
  - ☐ Honesty, ability, and financial strength
  - ☐ Supply bond
  - ☐ Contract bond
  - ☐ License and permit bond
  - ☐ Schedule position bond
  - ☐ Blanket position bond
  - ☐ Primary commercial blanket bond
  - ☐ Depositors forgery bond

**CONSUMER INSURANCE**

Franchisors in increasing numbers recognize the importance of also providing insurance to protect franchisees' *customers*. This type of insurance assures the customer of the credibility of representations made and work done by the franchised dealer. This insurance has particular application to service-type businesses that are usually characterized by inconsistency of price and work quality: for example, automotive services, building modernization, etc.

Many insurance companies now provide policies that undertake to indemnify customers against dissatisfaction and faulty work. Some insurance companies go beyond this in cooperating with franchisors. They will provide frameable certificates for display by individual franchisees in their offices, stating that the insurance was extended because of the "documented quality" of services performed by the particular franchisor and franchisee.

The dealers of a number of franchisors contribute to a "reimbursement fund" constituting a financial reserve to compensate customers for having unsatisfactory work properly redone; this guarantee is honored by any dealer in any locality who receives compensation from the reserve fund.

This consumer insurance program helps to build consumer confidence and patronage flow. It also impresses franchisees with the initiative taken by the company to upgrade their business and community status.

Consumer insurance has particular applicability to automobile repairs and related services because of the basic "mystique" in the field surrounding workmanship, price, etc. It helps to establish dealer credibility in a field where heretofore dealer credibility was sadly impugned. It also helps to assure increased consistency of work quality.

## THE FRANCHISOR "BILL OF RIGHTS"

At the outset of this chapter, we commented that today's franchisor recognizes the need for a new cohesive relationship with franchisees. Franchisors and their franchisees no longer have a vertical relationship with the franchisor looming overhead and the franchisee cowering underneath. They now have a more horizontal relationship with equal franchisor–franchisee status.

Several leading franchisors have taken the initiative to promulgate and present the equivalent to a Bill of Rights to their franchisees that lists and describes program benefits and supportive functions planned in their behalf by the franchisor. Because the franchisor has voluntarily prepared these "rights," it helps to clear the air, achieve a meeting of minds between the franchisor and franchisee, and avert misunderstandings and resentments.

One leading franchisor, General Business Services, Inc. of Rockville, Maryland, takes pride in the quality and continuity of its franchisee supportive services as exemplified by their document, which follows.

**memo from the president**

This Corporate Philosophy is a public pronouncement of the views and attitudes that govern GBS in the conduct of its affairs. Serving as a guideline in the decision making process at all levels, it represents a promise to the thousands of lives touched by General Business Services, Inc. Our intent to be a worthwhile corporate citizen is no less than our desire to be the best managed firm in America. We will strive to accomplish both.

## its mission

To provide owners of small businesses a selection of business services which will help them operate in an orderly, efficient and profitable manner.

## its goals

A. Conduct corporate activities to fulfill the approved mission while achieving a steady growth rate in volume and profits.

B. Offer all services at a fair price and of best quality.

C. Seek and select the best qualified candidates available for granting franchises to market services offered.

D. Conduct corporate affairs in a manner to achieve distinction in the business community for advanced business concepts, management leadership and progressive operating techniques which result in improved business services to clients.

# its conduct

In all phases of operation — accept moral responsibility, preserve integrity, and recognize legitimate interests of all parties in meeting obligations to clients, franchisees, staff members, affiliates, governmental agencies, stockholders and the business community.

# its responsibilities

### A. TO CLIENTS -

Continue developing and offering business services through qualified franchisees with integrity and sincere interest in their clients' welfare.

### B. TO FRANCHISEES -

Provide training for franchisees to enable them with proper self-motivation and effort to develop a profitable and satisfying business using the programs and services offered.

Establish policies, practices and managerial leadership to effect a steady corporate growth and development that will ensure continuing opportunities for the individual franchisee and his employees, if any.

Maintain and encourage a free and timely two-way flow of communications of corporate information with approved plans and programs in matters affecting the well being, success, harmony and working relationship of all.

Foster the development of a "partner relationship" with franchisees so that both parties better understand their proper obligations, recognizing that loyalty, conscientious effort, improved productivity and greater efficiency are common responsibilities of all members in the organization.

Promote the corporate trade name and trademark so that all franchisees will benefit by conducting their operations in accordance with the prescribed operating standards.

For the protection of their equity and future business, development and potential, develop and prescribe control operational standards to be maintained by all franchisees.

Encourage the development and improved application of each franchisee's professional skills so they are better equipped to succeed in accomplishing their individual goals while contributing to the corporate goals.

### C. TO STAFF MEMBERS -

Establish policies, practices, and managerial leadership to effect a steady corporate growth and development that will insure continuing opportunities for the individual.

Respect, protect and support the continuing advancement of the human dignity of the individual and his rightful freedoms including maintenance of equal employment and advancement opportunity for all.

Establish competitive compensation rates (including fringe benefits) consistent with prevailing community rates and the performance of each individual.

Provide educational and training opportunity to encourage continuing professional development and cultural advancement of each individual.

Maintain promotional opportunities from within the organization which reward the best qualified individual on the bases of performance, merit and contribution to corporate goals.

Provide efficient, safe and pleasant working conditions with the best facilities and equipment to accomplish assigned tasks.

Maintain and encourage a free and timely two-way flow of communications of corporate information, approved plans and programs; and of matters affecting the well being, success, harmony and working relationships of all.

Inform and encourage staff members by indoctrination, training, supervision and counseling so that each understands his obligation, including loyalty, and to make suggestions for greater efficiency and profitability of the entire organization.

### D. TO SUPPLIERS AND AFFILIATED COMPANIES -

Adopt policies and practices which permit the greatest possible contribution by all such firms, recognizing they possess specialized knowledge and resources needed by our organization.

Buy without prejudice while seeking the maximum value for each dollar spent.

Be honest in all transactions, avoiding favors, entertainment or gratuities that would compromise the independence of any action.

### E. TO THE GOVERNMENT -

Act as a good corporate citizen respecting and supporting the laws and enforcement bodies, and accepting responsibility for tax obligations in support of our free enterprise system.

Encourage all to take an active interest and participate in the affairs of government as responsible citizens.

### F. TO STOCKHOLDERS -

Operate and manage corporate affairs to achieve the maximum yield on the stockholders' investments to encourage purchase and retention of shares. Priority will be given to reinvesting profits whenever such action will strengthen the financial condition and will give impetus to meeting corporate goals.

### G. TO THE COMMUNITY -

Strive to be a responsible corporate citizen and neighbor maintaining an active interest and participation in the community. Demonstrate integrity toward all neighbors including businesses having relevancy to GBS, as well as competitive organizations.

**GENERAL BUSINESS SERVICES, INC.**
51 Monroe Street
Rockville, Md. 20850
Telephone (301) 424-1040

### Continuing Support Services to Franchisees

#### a. Materials and Supplies

All materials and supplies needed either by the franchisee or his clients are provided and the Systems Development Committee improvements are ongoing. Over 300 items available to franchisees are listed in the Operations Manual.

#### b. Operations Manual

All volumes of the confidential GBS Operations Manual are provided each Field Director. The know-how of many experts and years of experience by franchisees provide proven programs and techniques. Changes to the volumes of the Operations Manuals are made as needed, and it is the responsibility of the Field Director to study and incorporate the new material promptly. The manuals are held in the custody of the Field Director but remain the property of GBS, Inc. and MUST be returned upon request.

#### c. Tax Research Department

The Tax Advisory Service is a no-charge unique program to assist Field Directors and their registered GBS clients with income tax problems on a year-round basis. Also available from the Research Department is the Tax Research Service for Attorneys.

#### d. Return Preparation Service

This service, backed by the GBS Guarantee of Accuracy, relieves the franchisee of becoming a tax expert and preparing client income tax returns.

#### e. Tax Bulletin Service

Each registered GBS client receives monthly the Washington Alert. Each Field Director receives three copies, enclosed with a GBS News each month. The Alert offers tax-saving ideas and business management information specifically for small business owners.

#### f. Training

The monthly meetings of the region, the Expanded Regional Meetings, and the two tax seminars each year provide ongoing training that contribute to the franchisee's professional development.

#### g. Lending Library

Franchisees can check out books, tapes, and other material to aid their professional development.

#### h. Promotional Efforts

Promotional efforts on a continuing basis enhance the GBS image and are designed to help franchisees obtain clients and be quickly identified with the GBS trademark in local communities.

#### i. Computer Services

Computerized Bookkeeping Service is a time-saving, efficient, and accurate recordkeeping method for more complex clients. The accounts receivable program known as Generalbill helps clients collect from customers.

#### j. Franchise Sales Service

A list of areas for sale is regularly sent to Regional Directors to help franchisees who wish to sell their franchise.

### k. Monthly Billing Service

Franchisees may have clients billed monthly by the National Office and thereby avoid becoming a collection agent.

### l. Field Services

Technical guidance on handling particular clients and transactions is available. In addition, professional staff members are available on a special assignment (per diem) basis to help franchisees in personal visits with clients.

### m. Personal Insurance Programs

Six insurance coverages, including Professional Liability, are available on a group basis.

### n. Regional Directors

In addition to training and counseling, Regional Directors coordinate many promotional and other activities within a region to benefit the group. The Regional Director also handles liaison with state and local governments to learn about new rules and regulations; this saves the individual franchisee time and effort.

### o. National Account Program

Contacts with national organizations help franchisees to both sell and service more clients.

### p. Governmental Affairs

The increasing number of state and federal laws and regulations involving tax preparers, franchisees, etc., are monitored to protect franchisees.

### q. Approved Vendor Sources

Suppliers who will provide quality products or services to franchisees at substantial savings are selected and listed in the Operations Manual.

### r. Research and Development

The National Office coordinates the research and development of new products and services. Individual franchisees, through Pilot Programs, also test new products and services. This allows a franchisee to quickly learn if a new product or service has already been investigated.

### s. Financial Assistance

To help solve a cash flow problem, franchisees may take advantage of the Service Contract replacement plan under the Monthly Billing Service. Collection of notes from the sale of franchise rights can be processed through the National Office. Use of credit cards is also available. Loans through the Small Business Administration or banks are more easily obtained when a GBS franchise is involved as opposed to an individual on his own.

### t. Other Support

Four Divisional Vice Presidents work closely with Regional Directors to help franchisees increase client registrations and improve their operations. The President's Advisory Council provides important input to the Management Committee of GBS. One of the most important benefits of being a GBS franchisee is the informal support and help from neighboring franchisees, both on a continuing basis and particularly in time of crisis.

# PREPARING THE BREAK-EVEN CHART

# 16

What IS the break-even point? How do you calculate it? The break-even point is the position in your business operation at which you neither make nor lose money. It means that you have covered your expenses and that additional sales beyond this point will represent profit.

**HOW TO DETERMINE THE BREAK-EVEN POINT OF YOUR BUSINESS**

Let's say you own a small operation and are doing an average business of $10,000 a month, or $120,000 in annual sales.

To find YOUR break-even point, take the following steps:

1. Decide what your FIXED EXPENSES are. By fixed expenses we refer to rent, insurance, various operating taxes you pay, utilities, depreciation—items that remain constant and do not change with the amount of business you do. Let's say that your fixed expenses amount to $4000 a month, or $48,000 a year. Write these figures down.

2. Next, write down your MAXIMUM SALES VOLUME for the year. (100 percent of potential sales volume). This would be $10,000 × 12 months, or $120,000 a year.

3. Next, figure your VARIABLE EXPENSES (expenses that ordinarily increase as your sales increase). These include outside labor, operating supplies, gross wages, repairs and maintenance, advertising, car and delivery, bad debts, administrative and legal expenses, and some miscellaneous expenses. Let's assume that your variable expenses amount to $3000 a month, or $36,000 a year ($3000 × 12 months).

Equipped with your annual fixed and variable cost figures, you are now ready to construct your visual break-even chart (see Fig. 16.1). You don't need sophisticated chart paper; just draw an oblong box, with 12 vertical divisions and 10 horizontal divisions. Make the horizontal divisions about twice as wide as the height of the vertical divisions.

**197**

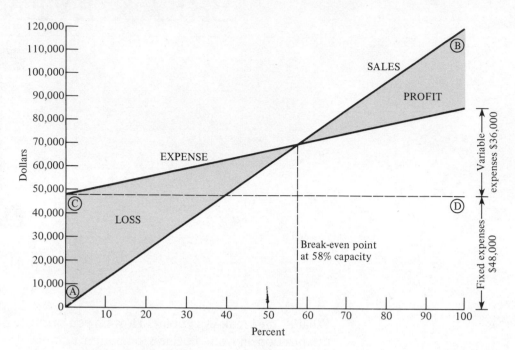

**Fig. 16.1** A visual break-even chart.

The vertical divisions on the left-hand side of the chart represent $10,000 increments of annual sales. The bottom line is zero sales, the next division is $10,000 sales, next is $20,000, and so on, to the top line, which is labeled $120,000—the figure you have calculated as your total annual sales capacity.

The bottom horizontal line of the chart represents increments of percent of sales capacity. Since it is 10 increments wide, each line represents 10 percent of sales. Thus the beginning of the first increment is labeled zero; the first line to the right is 10 percent, the second is 20 percent, and so on to the tenth or last line on the right, which is labeled 100 percent and which represents 100-percent annual sales capacity.

4. Next comes the most important line—*the sales line*. It starts from the point of zero sales and the point of zero percent of capacity and extends in a straight line to the point of $120,000 full capacity on the right-hand side of the chart. It is the line extending from point A to point B in Fig. 16.1.

5. Next, we consider the problem which exists at zero sales and zero percent of capacity. Because we are at this zero point on the chart does not mean that there are zero expenses at zero sales. There are important expenses at this point. These are the *fixed expenses*, the expenses that do not vary with sales. These are costs which must be paid whether or not you do one cent of sales. Rent is one good example of a fixed expense.

In the example it has been calculated that fixed expenses come to $48,000 annually ($4000 a month × 12 months). Now plot $48,000 on the left-hand vertical axis of the chart. That means the point should be placed four lines up plus $\frac{8}{10}$ of the next space. This point equals $48,000 on the chart. This means that *at zero sales* you have $48,000 of fixed expenses.

6. Now think a bit further. If you have $48,000 of fixed expenses at zero sales, these costs are not going to disappear when you operate at 100-percent capacity. They will still be there, so move to the right-hand axis of the chart, at the 100-percent line, and mark off $48,000 on the vertical axis line. For convenience in later calculation, you can draw a line across the chart, connecting the two points on the left-hand axis and the right-hand axis. This will be a level line shown as C–D in Fig. 16.1.

7. Next, we must consider the *variable expense* items. These are the expenses that vary directly with sales volume, the expenses that will have to be paid as you do more business. In the present example they have been calculated as $36,000 at 100-percent capacity ($3000 a month $\times$ 12 months). These costs are entered only on the right-hand vertical axis because at 100-percent capacity they amount to $36,000 and at zero percent of capacity they amount to zero.

    Remember, at 100-percent capacity you have two types of expenses—fixed and variable—while at zero percent of capacity you have only your fixed expenses. So on the right-hand vertical "capacity" axis, the variable expenses must be *superimposed* upon the fixed expenses. In constructing the expense line, the $36,000 of variable expenses must start at the point of $48,000 charted for fixed expenses.

8. From the point of $48,000 on the right-hand vertical axis, count three spaces plus $\frac{6}{10}$ of the next space up, and place your point. Do not make the mistake of counting upward from the bottom line. You count upward $3 \frac{6}{10}$ spaces *above the fixed expense point* (or point D in Fig. 16.1).

9. Now take your straight-edge and line up the fixed-expense point on the left-hand vertical axis and connect a line from there to the $36,000 point on the right-hand vertical "capacity" axis.

10. Now you can read the chart! Where this expense line intersects the sales line you find your BREAK-EVEN POINT. You can draw a vertical line from this point downward; where it intersects the bottom percentage line, it indicates the percentage point at which your business is operating on a break-even basis. The break-even point is the percent of capacity where you are neither making a profit nor losing money. At any percentage point of capacity lower than the break-even point, the distance between the sales line and the expense line will indicate the amount of money the business is losing. The same applies at any point to the right of the break-even point. Here the distance between the expense line and the sales line will indicate the amount of profit the business is making at the particular percent of capacity operations.

The same chart can be constructed monthly and can help if the full-year capacity sales projection requires revision. These break-even charts are a critical tool in controlling expenses. The extent of their usefulness depends upon the accuracy of sales and expense projections. Therefore an accurate record-keeping system is necessary.

# LEGAL CONSIDERATIONS

**LEGAL REQUIREMENTS**

The information provided in this section is intended to constitute general guidelines of possible legal and regulatory constraints or "red flags" to be observed in entering this field. They make no claim to being complete, or current, or legally valid. As previously commented, it is vital to obtain the advice of legal counsel to help conform to current regulations.

The business format of franchising embraces a complex range of nomenclature. Basic to this marketing system are the trademarks and the trade secret, from which flow licensing agreements, franchise offerings, fees and royalties, quality standards, prices and designated suppliers of goods and services to franchisees, tie-in and advertising arrangements, exclusive territories, dual distribution marketing techniques, conditions for termination and renewal, transferability and other practices. All of these are susceptible to regulation by governmental bodies.

Beginning with the initial franchise offering, there are regulations, at both Federal and state levels, requiring the franchisor to disclose to the prospective franchisee complete and accurate information about the franchisor and the franchise agreement. Of significance, in this respect, was the promulgation in late 1979 of the Federal Trade Commission's Trade Regulation Rule on disclosure requirements and prohibitions concerning franchising.

Figure 17.1 is a list noting which states have initially adopted franchise disclosure laws and whether or not preregistration is required.

The following is an explanation of the Federal Disclosure Regulations as provided by the Federal Trade Commission, Washington, D.C.

**TERRITORIAL RESTRICTIONS, COMPETITION, AND THE FTC**

The allocation by franchisors of exclusive territories for franchisees, a marketing practice referred to as a "vertical" or nonprice restriction, is an important element of the franchise system.

Since a franchisor's ability lawfully to direct the growth of his network of distribution is basic to his success, most franchisors have developed some method of controlling the selection of franchisee locations. This practice is often

| | Registration | General | Petroleum | Other |
|---|---|---|---|---|
| Alabama | | | x | |
| Alaska | | | x | |
| Arizona | | | | |
| Arkansas | | | | |
| California | x | | | |
| Colorado | | | | |
| Connecticut | | | | |
| Delaware | | | | |
| Florida | | x | | |
| Georgia | | | | |
| Hawaii | | x | | |
| Idaho | | | | |
| Illinois | x | | | |
| Indiana | x | | | |
| Iowa | | | | |
| Kansas | | | | |
| Kentucky | | | | |
| Louisiana | | | | |
| Maine | | | | |
| Maryland | x | | | |
| Massachusetts | | | | |
| Michigan | x | | | |
| Minnesota | x | | | |
| Mississippi | | x | | |
| Missouri | | | | |
| Montana | | | | |
| Nebraska | | | | |
| Nevada | | | | |
| New Hampshire | | | x | x |
| New Jersey | | | | |
| New Mexico | | | | |
| New York | | | x | |
| North Carolina | | | | x |
| North Dakota | x | | | |
| Ohio | | | | |
| Oklahoma | | x | | |
| Oregon | x | | | |
| Pennsylvania | | | | |
| Rhode Island | x | | | |
| South Carolina | | | | |
| South Dakota | x | | | |
| Tennessee | | | x | |
| Texas | | | | |
| Utah | | | | |
| Vermont | | | x | |
| Virginia | x | | | |
| Washington | x | | | |
| West Virginia | | | x | |
| Wisconsin | x | | | |
| Wyoming | | | | |
| Puerto Rico | | | | |

**Fig. 17.1** States having franchise laws concerning disclosure.

referred to as "selective distribution," "location clause," "spacing of dealers," or "elbow room policy." Franchisors usually ascribe two purposes to such arrangement: (1) to limit and protect the franchisee's area of operation and (2) to assure that the franchisee will maintain the quality of the franchisor's product or service and the goodwill associated with his name or trademark.

For years the legality and economic justification of this practice have been debated in the Congress, in the courts, and in the Federal Trade Commission. Until recently the Justice Department and the Federal Trade Commission held in common the view that franchises which limit the dealer to sales within a fixed area are unlawful restraints in and of themselves without regard to economic justification, and therefore are in violation of the Sherman Act. Territorial restrictions are now permissible under a recent Supreme Court decision (*Continental T.V., Inc.* v. *GTE Sylvania, Inc.*), unless they fall under the "rule of reason" test. The legality of territorial restrictions hinges on a number of factors, including pricing practices and customer restraints in designated territories.

In the 1967 *Schwinn Bicycle* case, the U.S. Supreme Court held vertical restraints on distributor's territories (those imposed by the franchisor) to be *per se* violations of antitrust law because (a) the manufacturer attempted to restrict franchised retailers' reselling Schwinn bicycles to other non-franchised retailers, a technique known as "customer restriction," and (b) the manufacturer, by supplying bicycles to the distributors, had yielded to them, "title, dominion and risk" over those bicycles.

*Per se* violation, mentioned above, means that mere existence of the territorial arrangement, irrespective of any economic justification, is grounds for a finding that it violates the antitrust laws. The alternative to the *per se* rule is the "rule of reason" approach. This requires a balancing of all relevant factors to determine if the arrangement is an unreasonable restraint of trade.

In the 1977 *GTE Sylvania* case, the U.S. Supreme Court overruled the *per se* rule of the Schwinn decision with respect to exclusive territorial restrictions. Sylvania's franchise relationship in the sale of television sets was understood as applying only to such locations as were mutually agreeable. Sylvania did not, however, inhibit the freedom of an authorized Sylvania dealer operating from a franchised location to sell to anyone, wherever situated. The franchise agreement restricted dealer location alone. In deciding that Sylvania's conduct did not meet the test of *per se* illegality, the Court noted that the market impact of vertical restrictions is complex because of their potential for a simultaneous reduction of intrabrand competition and stimulation of interbrand competition.

### Franchise Rule Summary*

The Franchise Rule, which is formally titled "Disclosure Requirements and Prohibitions Concerning Franchising and Business Opportunity Ventures" [16 C.F.R. § 436], has been promulgated in response to widespread evidence of deceptive and unfair practices in connection with the sale of the types of businesses covered by the Rule. These practices often are able to exist because prospective franchisees lack a ready means of obtaining essential and reliable information about the business in which they are asked to invest their money and, frequently, their labor. This lack of information reduces the ability of prospective franchisees either to make an informed investment decision or otherwise verify the representations of the business' salespersons.

The Rule attempts to deal with these problems by requiring franchisors and franchise brokers to furnish prospective franchisees with information about the franchisor, the franchise business, and the terms of the franchise agreement. Franchisors and franchise brokers must furnish additional information if they have made any claim about actual or potential earnings, either to the prospective franchisee or in the media. All disclosures must be made (i) before any sale is consummated and (ii) by means of disclosure documents whose form and content are set forth in the Rule.

The Rule requires disclosure of material facts. It does not regulate the substantive terms of the franchisor-franchisee relationship. It does not require registration of the offering or the filing of any documents with the Federal Trade Commission in connection with the sale of franchises.

The effective date of the Rule is July 21, 1979.

### A. Businesses Covered by the Rule [§ 436.2(a)]

Either of two types of continuing commercial relationships are defined as a "franchise" and covered by the Rule.

The first type involves three characteristics:

1. The franchisee sells goods or services which meet the franchisor's quality standards (in cases where the franchisee operates under the franchisor's trademark, service mark, trade name, advertising or other commercial symbol designating the franchisor "mark") or which are identified by the franchisor's mark;

2. The franchisor exercises significant control over, or gives the franchisee significant assistance in, the franchisee's method of operation; and

3. The franchisee is required to make a payment of $500 or more to the franchisor or a person affiliated with the franchisor within six months after the business opens.

The second type also involves three characteristics:

1. The franchisee sells goods or services which are supplied by the franchisor or a person affiliated with the franchisor;

2. The franchisor secures accounts for the franchisee, or secures locations or sites for vending machines or rack displays, or provides the services of a person able to do either; and

3. The franchisee is required to make a payment of $500 or more to the franchisor or a person affiliated with the franchisor within six months after the business opens.

Relationships covered by the Rule include those which are within the definition of "franchise" and those which are represented as being within the definition when the relationship is entered into, regardless of whether, in fact, they are within the definition.

The Rule exempts:

1. Fractional franchises;

2. Leased department arrangements; and

3. Purely verbal agreements.

The Rule excludes:

1. Relationships between employer/employees, and among general business partners;

2. Membership in retailer-owned cooperatives;

3. Certification and testing services; and

4. Single trademark licenses.

### B. The Disclosure Document [§ 436.1(a)]

All franchisors must furnish the document described in this section. The disclosure document requires information on the following 20 subjects:

1. Identifying information about the franchisor;

2. Business experience of the franchisor's directors and key executives;

3. The franchisor's business experience;

4. Litigation history of the franchisor and its directors and key executives;

5. Bankruptcy history of the franchisor and its directors and key executives;

6. Description of the franchise;

7. Money required to be paid by the franchisee to obtain or commence the franchise operation;

8. Continuing expenses to the franchisee in operating the franchise business that are payable in whole or in part to the franchisor;

9. A list of persons who are either the franchisor or any of its affiliates, with whom the franchisee is required or advised to do business;

10. Realty, personalty, services, and other items which the franchisee is required to purchase, lease, or rent, and a list of any persons with whom such transactions must be made;

11. Description of consideration paid (such as royalties and commissions) by third parties to the franchisor or any of its affiliates as a result of a franchisee's purchase from such third parties;

12. Description of any franchisor assistance in financing the purchase of a franchise;

13. Restrictions placed on a franchisee's conduct of its business;

14. Required personal participation by the franchisee;

15. Termination, cancellation, and renewal of the franchise;

16. Statistical information about the number of franchises and their rate of terminations;

17. Franchisor's right to select or approve a site for franchise;

18. Training programs for the franchisee;

19. Celebrity involvement with the franchise; and

20. Financial information about the franchisor.

The disclosures must be made in a single document, with a cover sheet setting forth the name of the franchisor, the date of issuance of the document, and a statement—whose text is set forth in the Rule—advising the prospective franchisee of the contents and purpose of the document. The document may not include information other than that required by the Rule or by State law not preempted by the Rule. However, the franchisor may furnish other information to the prospective franchisee which is not inconsistent with the material set forth in the disclosure document.

The disclosure document must be given to a prospective franchisee at the earlier of either:

1. The prospective franchisee's first personal meeting with franchisor; or

2. Ten days prior to the execution of a contract or payment of consideration relating to the franchise relationship.

At that time, the franchisor or franchise broker must give the prospective franchisee copies of the franchisor's standard franchise agreement.

The information in the disclosure document must be current as of the completion of the franchisor's most recent fiscal year. In addition, a revision of the document must be prepared quarterly whenever there has been a material change relating to the franchise business of the franchisor.

*C. Earnings Claims* [§ 436.1(b)–(e)]

The Rule prohibits earnings representations about the actual or potential sales, income, or profits of existing or prospective franchisees unless three prerequisites are met:

1. There is a reasonable basis for the representation;

2. The representation has been prepared in accordance with generally accepted accounting principles;

3. The franchisor has evidence to substantiate every representation and such evidence is available to the prospective franchisee or to the Federal Trade Commission upon reasonable demand.

Whenever the franchisor or franchise broker makes a representation about earnings, either in the media or directly to a prospective franchisee, an earnings disclosure document must be furnished to every prospective franchisee. This document must include:

1. A statement describing the material bases and assumptions for each earnings representation made, including the number and percentage of outlets achieving the same results as those claimed,

2. Cautionary language—whose text is set forth in the Rule—concerning the projectibility of the representation to the prospective franchisee's future experience,

3. A notice that evidence to substantiate the representation is available for inspection upon reasonable demand, and

4. A cover page setting forth the name of the franchisor, the date of the document, and a statement—the text of which is set forth in the Rule—advising the prospective franchisee of the importance of the document.

Any earnings representation, other than one used in advertising, must be relevant to the geographic market in which the prospective franchisee's franchise will be located. The earnings disclosure document may not contain any information other than that required by the Rule or by State law not preempted by the Rule, and must be given to every prospective franchisee to whom the representation has been made at least ten days before the execution of a contract or the payment of any consideration relating to the franchise, or at the first personal meeting following the making of the representation, whichever occurs first.

### D. Acts or Practices Which Violate the Rule

It is an unfair or deceptive act or practice within the meaning of § 5 of the Federal Trade Commission Act for any franchisor or franchise broker:

1. To fail to furnish prospective franchisees, within time frames established by the Rule, with a disclosure document containing information on the 20 different subjects relating to the franchisor, the franchise business, and the terms of the franchise agreement [§ 436.1(a)];

2. To make any representations about the actual or potential sales, income, or profits of existing or prospective franchises except in the manner set forth in the Rule [§ 436.1(b)–(e)];

3. To make any claim or representation (such as in advertising or oral statements by salespersons) which is inconsistent with the information required to be disclosed by the Rule [§ 436.1(f)];

4. To fail to furnish prospective franchisees, within the time frames established by the Rule, with copies of the franchisor's standard forms of franchise agreements and copies of the final agreements to be signed by the parties [§ 436.1(g)]; and

5. To fail to return to prospective franchisees any funds or deposits (such as down-payments) identified as refundable in the disclosure document [§ 436.1(h)].

Violators are subject to civil penalty actions brought by the Commission of up to $10,000 per violation.

The Commission believes that the courts should and will hold that any person injured by a violation of the Rule has a private right of action against the violator under the Federal Trade Commission Act, as amended, and the Rule. The existence of such a right is necessary to protect the members of the class for whose benefit the statute was enacted and the Rule is being promulgated, is consistent with the legislative intent of the Congress in enacting the Federal Trade Commission Act, as amended, and is necessary to the enforcement scheme established by the Congress in that Act and to the Commission's own enforcement efforts.

### E. State Franchise Laws

The Commission's goals are to create a minimum Federal standard of disclosure applicable to all franchisor offerings, and to permit States to provide additional protection as they see fit. Thus, while the Federal Trade Commission Trade Regulation Rules have the force and effect of Federal law and, like other Federal substantive regulations, preempt State and local laws to the extent that these laws conflict, the Commission has determined that the Rule will not preempt State or local laws and regulations which either are consistent with the Rule or, even if inconsistent, which would provide protection to prospective franchisees equal to or greater than that imposed by the Rule.

Examples of State laws or regulations which would not be preempted by the Rule include State provisions requiring the registration of franchisors and franchise salesmen, State requirements for escrow or bonding arrangements, and State required disclosure obligations exceeding the disclosure obligations set forth in the Rule. Moreover, the Rule does not affect State laws or regulations which substantively regulate the franchisor/franchisee relationship, such as termination practices, contract provisions, and financing arrangements.

### F. The Uniform Franchise Offering Circular

The Uniform Franchise Offering Circular ("UFOC") now is accepted in satisfaction of the disclosure requirements in 14 States which have franchise registration and disclosure laws. The UFOC format is not identical to the disclosure format prescribed in the Rule. For example, there are minor differences in language on similar disclosure requirements; there are subjects about which the UFOC requires more disclosure than the Rule, and subjects where the Rule requires more disclosure than the UFOC. Even though the two documents are not identical in language, they are quite similar; in any event, both documents are designed to achieve the same result regardless of any minor variations in the means used to attain that result. Accordingly, the Commission will permit franchisors to use the UFOC format in lieu of the disclosure document provided by the Rule. This alternative use is limited to the UFOC version adopted by the Midwest Securities Commissioners Association, Inc., on September 2, 1975, plus any modifications thereof which do not diminish the protection accorded to the prospective franchisee which may be made by a State in which such registration has been made effective.

Certain provisions of the Rule will still control even if the UFOC format is used in lieu of the Rule's disclosure document, such as:

1. The persons required to make disclosure;
2. Transactions requiring disclosure;
3. The timing of the disclosure; and
4. The types of documents to be given to prospective franchisees.

The Commission's decision to permit use of a State disclosure document in lieu of its own document does not constitute Commission deferral to State law enforcement. The Commission is expressly providing for concurrent jurisdiction between the Commission and the States in appropriate instances. The Commission's action does not and is not intended to deprive the Commission of its responsibility to determine whether particular franchisors have complied with the Rule.

### G. Commission Assistance

The Commission has prepared proposed interpretative guidelines to the Rule in an effort to assist franchisors and franchise brokers in complying with the Rule....

*Source:* Federal Trade Commission, Washington, D.C. 20580.

The Commission will furnish a formal advisory opinion about the relationship of the Rule to specific fact situations in accordance with its Procedures and Rule of Practice.

The Commission's franchise staff will furnish informal staff opinions, in appropriate circumstances, upon written request.

In general, the rule covers three types of relationships:

- "Package" or "business format" franchises
- "Product" franchises
- "Business opportunity ventures"

## "PACKAGE" OR "BUSINESS FORMAT" FRANCHISES

This type of franchise is described in three elements:

1. The franchisee sells goods or services that meet the franchisor's quality standards, and does business under the franchisor's trademark.
2. The franchisor has a significant degree of control over the franchisee's method of operation, or gives the franchisee significant assistance in his or her method of operation.
3. To obtain the franchise, the franchisee is required to pay the franchisor or an affiliated person.

## "PRODUCT" FRANCHISES

Three elements define this type of franchise:

1. The franchisee sells goods or services identified by the franchisor's trademark.
2. The franchisor has a significant degree of control over the franchisee's method of operation, or gives the franchisee significant assistance in his or her method of operation.
3. To obtain the franchise, the franchisee is required to pay the franchisor or an affiliated person.

## "BUSINESS OPPORTUNITY VENTURES":

Relationships of this type have three elements:

1. The franchisee sells goods or services supplied by the franchisor, or by suppliers required by the franchisor, or by suppliers who are affiliated with the franchisor.
2. The franchisor secures retail outlets or accounts for the goods, or secures locations for vending devices or racks, or provides the services of a person to do either.
3. To obtain the franchise, the franchisee is required to pay the franchisor or an affiliated person.

The obligation to comply with the rule is imposed on both "franchisors" *and* "franchise brokers." Compliance by one does not relieve the other of obligation. A "franchisor" is any individual, group, association, partnership, corporation, or other business entity who participates in *all* of the elements set out in the definition of a franchise. A "franchise broker" is one of the aforementioned, other than a franchisor, who sells, offers for sale, or arranges for the sale of a franchise. This definition does not include a franchisee who sells his own franchise, but would apply to a franchisee who grants subfranchises.

**FRANCHISE TERMINATION ISSUES**

In the 95th Congress, the House Subcommittee on Consumer Protection and Finance of the Interstate and Foreign Commerce Committee considered legislative proposals to protect all franchisees against arbitrary and unfair termination. However, because of a lack of agreement over scope of coverage, definitions and standards contained in the bills, particularly the Mikva bill (H.R. 5016), action on the legislation came to a standstill and the bills died.

Specifically, concern centered on this bill's definition of "good cause" for termination, which some Subcommittee members believed would create problems and encourage litigation. It was also noted that the conditions such as "continued" failure to comply with "reasonable and essential" requirements could place franchisors in situations where they would not know whether they have a legal right to terminate or refuse renewal.

One Subcommittee member raised questions about the ability to apply such law to franchises in existence at the time a bill became law. Such an application, he thought, may be unconstitutional. To avoid such a problem it was suggested that franchisors and franchisees be granted a period of time after the bill becomes law within which to modify or terminate their agreements and thus avert the constitutional issue of retroactive application. But, it was pointed out, such an approach could produce unintended, adverse effects—wholesale terminations—which would be directly contrary to the basic purpose of the legislation.

There was, however, recognition within the Subcommittee of differences between business format franchises, which encompass the entire business operation of a franchisee, and product distributorship franchises which may account for a small fraction of a franchisee's business. The bill's definition of "franchise" apparently had not taken such differences into account.

Following the failure to enact franchise termination legislation, the chairman of the Subcommittee declared that such legislation would be a high priority item for the Subcommittee in the 96th Congress.

In the meantime, however, some states have their own laws concerning franchise termination. Figure 17.2 gives some information about those states.

**SAMPLE CONTRACTS**

On the following pages you will find three examples of agreements that have been used by Edu-Center, Inc., Ben Franklin, and General Business Services, respectively. We wish to stress that no claim is made as to current legal validity. They are reproduced here merely to indicate various contractual formats and to give you some idea of what elements are involved.

In the preparation of your own agreements and contracts it is imperative that you engage professional counsel.

| | General | Vehicle | Petroleum | Other |
|---|---|---|---|---|
| Alabama | | | | |
| Alaska | | | x | |
| Arizona | | x | x | x |
| Arkansas | x | x | x | |
| California | | x | x | |
| Colorado | | x | | |
| Connecticut | x | | x | |
| Delaware | x | | x | |
| Florida | | x | | |
| Georgia | | x | x | |
| Hawaii | x | x | x | |
| Idaho | | x | | x |
| Illinois | | | | |
| Indiana | x | | | x |
| Iowa | | x | x | |
| Kansas | | | | |
| Kentucky | | x | | |
| Louisiana | | x | | |
| Maine | | x | x | |
| Maryland | | | x | x |
| Massachusetts | | x | x | |
| Michigan | x | x | | |
| Minnesota | x | x | | x |
| Mississippi | x | x | | x |
| Missouri | x | | | x |
| Montana | | x | | |
| Nebraska | x | x | | |
| Nevada | | x | x | x |
| New Hampshire | | x | | |
| New Jersey | x | | | |
| New Mexico | | x | | x |
| New York | | x | x | x |
| North Carolina | | x | | x |
| North Dakota | | x | | |
| Ohio | | | | x |
| Oklahoma | | x | | |
| Oregon | | | | |
| Pennsylvania | | x | x | |
| Rhode Island | | x | x | |
| South Carolina | | x | | x |
| South Dakota | | x | | x |
| Tennessee | | x | x | x |
| Texas | | x | | |
| Utah | | | | |
| Vermont | | x | | x |
| Virginia | x | x | x | x |
| Washington | x | x | | x |
| West Virginia | | x | | x |
| Wisconsin | x | x | | |
| Wyoming | | | | |
| **Figure 17.2** Puerto Rico | x | | | |

# FRANCHISE AGREEMENT
# EDU-CENTER, INC.

THIS AGREEMENT, MADE IN THE City of ............................................... ,

State of ........................, by and between EDU-CENTER, INC., with principal offices located at 250 West 57th Street, New York, N. Y., hereinafter referred to

as the "COMPANY", and ...........................................................................................

......................................................................................................................................

residing at ...........................................................................................................
hereinafter referred to as the "FRANCHISEE".

WHEREAS the COMPANY has obtained from Sight & Sound Education Limited of England the exclusive right and license to promote and develop the use of the Parkes System for touch typing instruction within the United States and Puerto Rico, and

WHEREAS the COMPANY has obtained from Sight & Sound Education Limited of England the exclusive right and license to use and lease instruction machines and apparatus connected therewith, in connection with the system of touch typing referred to above, and

WHEREAS the COMPANY owns and has the exclusive right and power to use the name EDU-CENTER and EDU-CENTERS, and

WHEREAS the COMPANY is desirous of establishing a nationwide group of franchised EDU-CENTERS, utilizing said system and equipment, and

WHEREAS the FRANCHISEE is desirous of establishing a typing center, using the name, system and methods referred to above and to enjoy the commercial benefits related thereto,

NOW, THEREFORE, in consideration of the sum of One Dollar ($1.00) and other good and valuable consideration, and the covenants and conditions herein contained, it is agreed as follows:

1. A. The COMPANY hereby grants to the FRANCHISEE the exclusive right and license to establish and operate an EDU-CENTER to be located within the County of ............................., City of ..........................................., State of ............................. While this agreement is in force, no other such right and license will be granted to any other franchisee within the territory as shown in Schedule A hereto; provided that it is specifically agreed that the COMPANY will have the right to lease Sight & Sound equipment and systems of instruction to commercial, industrial and governmental organizations, and public, private and parochial schools, colleges and universities located within the FRANCHISEE's territory for the exclusive use by these organizations, schools, colleges and universities for the training of their own employees or full time students.
B. The COMPANY will not lease Sight & Sound equipment and systems of instruction to any school or college specializing in typing or secretarial training, which is located in the territory as shown in Schedule A hereto.

2. The COMPANY grants to the FRANCHISEE the following unassignable rights and privileges:
   A. Use of the name EDU-CENTER and the EDU-CENTER trademark, logo, signs, etc. in order that the FRANCHISEE may conduct his business under the name of "EDU-CENTER". This privilege is contingent upon compliance with the terms of this Agreement and is limited to the term of this Agreement. However, use of name EDU-CENTER is not exclusive — FRANCHISEE agrees to cooperate and supply any and all consents and agreements necessary for additional franchisees, who may be assigned to operate under the name of EDU-CENTER in the FRANCHISEE's state of incorporation, outside the territory assigned to the FRANCHISEE. While FRANCHISEE shall have the free use of the trademark during the term of this Agreement, it is specifically understood and agreed that FRANCHISEE shall not have the right or privilege of adopting or using EDU-CENTER as part of a corporate name.
   B. To use the COMPANY plan, methods, systems, and sales tools in the conduct of its business.
   C. To lease from the COMPANY all Sight & Sound equipment pertinent to the operation of an EDU-CENTER, as listed in Schedule B, hereto and under the conditions enumerated in Par. 5 and Schedule C hereto.

3. The COMPANY shall further provide to the FRANCHISEE:
   A. An initial supply of the following materials:
   - 1000 booklets for Trainee recruitment
   - 3 Presentation Books for industrial organization contacts
   - 500 "Invitation" letters to mail to corporation executives
   - 500 letters to mail to private schools
   - Newspaper ad mats for trainee recruitment
   - Radio Scripts and tapes for trainee recruitment
   - Grand Opening Program
   - Publicity kit to help obtain local publicity
   - Promotion kit
   - 2000 direct mailers for trainee recruitment
   - 1000 letterheads
   - 1000 envelopes
   - 500 business cards
   - One Comprehensive Operations Manual
   - 5 personnel-use Manuals
   - 1000 Trainee Registration forms
   - One Record Keeping System
   - One month's average supply of control and administrative forms
   - All Trainee leads obtained by Home Office originating in the FRANCHISEE's territory.
   B. The following services:
   - Design plan for layout of Center including recommendations for furniture and equipment.
   - Assistance in selection of Center and in lease negotiation.
   - Approximately one week training for the FRANCHISEE or his representative in the Home Office.
   - Assistance of a Field Executive who will help FRANCHISEE establish operations.
   - Hotel accommodations while in New York attending training.
   - Supply periodic bulletins, reports, memos, etc. covering trends in developments of all phases of the business, as published by EDU-CENTER.
   - Provide periodic visits to the FRANCHISEE's location by an executive of the COMPANY and consultation, advice and information concerning the growth and operation of the FRANCHISEE's business.
   - Organize and sponsor, when deemed feasible by the COMPANY, regional and national meetings of the FRANCHISEES for the dissemination and exchange of ideas, experiences, techniques and developments.

4. In consideration of all the foregoing rights and privileges granted hereunder, the material to be furnished hereunder and the undertakings to which the COMPANY has committed itself hereunder, the FRANCHISEE shall make payments to the COMPANY as follows:
   A. A fee of $9,500 to be paid as follows:
   1. Initial payment of $6,000, receipt of which is hereby acknowledged.
   2. Payment of $3,500 one week prior to attendance at training center.

5. The FRANCHISEE agrees that he will lease from the Company the equipment referred to in Paragraph 2C and listed in Schedule B hereto at an annual rental of $4,900, payable as follows:
   A. First $4,900 payment to be due one week prior to attendance at Training Center.
   B. Second payment to be due at the commencement of the twelve month period beginning one year from the date of shipment of the equipment leased hereunder;
   C. Each subsequent payment to become due at the commencement of each successive twelve month period thereafter, during the term of the lease.

6. The term for the leasing of the equipment listed in Schedule B hereto shall coincide with the term of this franchise agreement, and shall be renewed automatically with the renewal of this Franchise Agreement as specified in Paragraph 15 hereof. The leasing of said equipment to be subject to such other conditions as set forth in Schedule C.

7. The FRANCHISEE hereby agrees:
   A. That he will obtain, with COMPANY's assistance and advice, suitable space for the Center of type and size specified by the COMPANY within 60 days of the effective date of this agreement. That he will furnish said space at his own cost and expense in accordance with specifications laid down by the COMPANY, and mutually agreed upon.
   B. That he will use his best efforts to promote the sale of EDU-CENTER typing courses and that he will not offer any other competitive courses, and not be concerned in any way with any competing business or any business which in the opinion of COMPANY would conflict with its interest hereunder.
   C. That he will confine his business activities to the territory described in Schedule A hereto.
   D. That he will maintain the COMPANY's suggested schedule of tuition prices unless local factors make changes advisable in which case written COMPANY approval must be obtained.
   E. That he will operate his business in every respect in accordance with the procedures set forth in the Operating Manual furnished to the FRANCHISEE, including reasonable changes and modifications that might be made from time to time; and that said Operating Manual plus reasonable revisions becomes part of this agreement.

F. That upon commencement of his business activities he will recruit and train with COMPANY guidance a qualified staff in accordance with procedures specified in the Operating Manual.

G. That his books and records will be kept accurately and currently. Quarterly profit and loss statements on report forms provided by the COMPANY shall be forwarded to the COMPANY within thirty days after the expiration of each respective quarterly period. A balance sheet and Profit and Loss statement shall be furnished to the COMPANY as of the end of each fiscal year, no later than 30 days from the end of each such fiscal year.

H. That the FRANCHISEE will not at any time divulge any secrets, information, experience or details of EDU-CENTER, its machines or business methods, to any company, firm or person, in any way whatsoever, and that he will not make or cause to be made any copy or reproduction of any machines or methods of the Center or film, tape, record, print, photograph, or broadcast any material, sound signal or method incorporated in or produced by the machines, and it is hereby expressly agreed that the undertakings of this Paragraph 7H shall remain in force, notwithstanding the termination, for any cause, of this agreement.

I. That the FRANCHISEE will require employees, at time of hiring, to sign a form containing substantially the same agreement as expressed in Paragraph 7H above.

J. That the FRANCHISEE or his employees, salesmen, agents, or representatives will not conduct themselves in any manner that would be detrimental to, or reflect adversely upon, the reputation of the COMPANY.

K. That the FRANCHISEE or his representative will attend the Home Office Training Center for a period of approximately one week.

L. That he will achieve the following minimum standard of gross receipts from tuition:
   1. First twelve (12) month period – $52,500.
   2. Each twelve (12) month period thereafter – $70,000.

M. Visits of EDU-CENTER executives, requested by FRANCHISEE, shall be at FRANCHISEE's expense.

8. In addition to the sums to be paid pursuant to the provisions of Paragraph 4 hereof, the FRANCHISEE shall pay to the COMPANY, simultaneously with the submission of each monthly report form, a royalty based on gross receipts. Such royalty shall be 6% of the gross tuition receipts with a minimum annual royalty of $4200; provided that the FRANCHISEE shall have a three month grace period commencing on the date of shipment of the equipment leased hereunder, so that the minimum royalty for the first year shall be $3150. Such payments and reports are to be made within ten days from the end of each month.

9. It is agreed that the FRANCHISEE will advertise regularly in the territory described in Schedule A hereto, in such media as will most effectively publicize his services. The COMPANY has the right to require the FRANCHISEE to expend for advertising the amount of $1,000 a month or 15% of gross receipts, whichever is greater. The advertisements used will be only those supplied by or approved by the COMPANY; the tear sheets and copies of all paid invoices for advertising will be submitted to the EDU-CENTER Home Office immediately after the last day of each month.

10. It is agreed that the COMPANY will establish a fund to provide national and/or regional advertising and promotion for the benefit of the franchisees. This fund will be administered by the COMPANY as it deems best. The COMPANY will use its best efforts to keep the FRANCHISEE informed as to media schedules and expenditures for such advertising and/or publicity. Money not expended will remain in the fund for future allocation in fulfillment of the purpose of this fund. The FRANCHISEE will pay into this fund 3% of his gross tuition receipts. Payments will be made monthly with the submission of the monthly report form. This payment will not be required during the first 3 months of the FRANCHISEE's operation.

11. It is agreed that all advertising material, promotional material, signs, forms and all other documents furnished to the FRANCHISEE by the COMPANY shall not be used for any purpose other than to promote the services of EDU-CENTER nor shall they be copied without prior written permission of the COMPANY.

12. It is agreed that authorized COMPANY personnel shall be permitted to enter upon the premises of the FRANCHISEE during regular business hours for the purpose of examining the premises, conferring with the FRANCHISEE and his employees, inspecting and checking furniture, fixtures, equipment, operating methods and books and records.

13. The COMPANY and the FRANCHISEE are each independent contractors and the FRANCHISEE shall not be the agent for the COMPANY in any manner or capacity whatsoever, nor shall either be responsible for the debts, bills or liabilities incurred by the other. No partnership, joint venture or relationship of principal and agent is intended. The COMPANY's and the FRANCHISEE's interest in each other shall be limited to the purpose set forth herein.

14. The FRANCHISEE shall indemnify and save the COMPANY harmless from or against all or any loss and/or damages, claims, demands, costs and expenses in connection with the operation of this agreement, and the equipment leased hereunder, or following therefrom.

15. The FRANCHISEE shall obtain and maintain in full force and effect during the term of this agreement, an insurance policy protecting the COMPANY and the FRANCHISEE against all loss, liability or expense whatsoever for personal injury, death, property or equipment damage or otherwise arising or occurring in connection with FRANCHISEE's business or the occupancy of its premises. The COMPANY shall be an additional named insured in such policy. The following limits shall be observed: Workmen's compensation as required by statute; fire insurance for 80% of value per Schedule C; general liability, $200,000 each person and $500,000 each accident. The FRANCHISEE may, at his option obtain any other insurance as he deems necessary or advisable. Within ten days from the opening of the FRANCHISEE's place of business, certificates of insurance will be furnished to the COMPANY. The insurance shall not be terminable without at least ten days' prior notice to the COMPANY.

16. The FRANCHISEE acknowledges that the word "EDU-CENTER" is a valid trade name and service mark owned by the COMPANY and the FRANCHISEE hereby expressly acknowledges the validity of any and all patents and trade marks relating to the machine and related apparatus, and that the COMPANY has granted the use thereof to the FRANCHISEE. The FRANCHISEE will use this name only in the manner and to the extent specifically permitted by this Agreement.

17. This agreement, and the appointment of the FRANCHISEE hereunder, shall be for an initial term of five (5) years commencing upon the delivery of the first machine and thereafter this agreement may be extended automatically for successive one (1) year terms upon payment of $1.00 renewal fee for the grant of such extension, provided that the covenants and undertakings assumed by the FRANCHISEE in this agreement are truly and faithfully performed.

18. Failure to meet the yearly quota shall give the COMPANY at its option, on 30 days' written notice by registered mail addressed to FRANCHISEE at his place of business, the right to terminate this agreement.

19. If the FRANCHISEE fails to abide by any terms of this agreement or if bankruptcy or insolvency proceedings are commenced by or against the FRANCHISEE or if the FRANCHISEE makes assignment for benefit of creditors, the COMPANY, at its option, shall have the right to cancel this agreement by giving ten (10) days' written notice by registered mail addressed to FRANCHISEE at his place of business as set forth on this agreement. Failure to exercise this option shall not constitute a waiver of the right upon a recurring breach nor shall the cancellation of this agreement for cause constitute a waiver of the right to pursue such other remedies as the COMPANY may have.

20. Upon termination of this agreement, FRANCHISEE agrees as follows:

A. FRANCHISEE shall surrender all rights and privileges granted under this agreement and shall cease the use of the trademark and name EDU-CENTER in any and all connections.

B. FRANCHISEE shall return, without delay, all material described as property of the COMPANY.

C. The COMPANY shall have the option to repurchase from the FRANCHISEE any or all material, equipment and furnishings in the possession of the FRANCHISEE, which was purchased from or through the COMPANY at prices paid by the FRANCHISEE less twenty-five percent.

D. The COMPANY shall have the option to sublease the premises described herein and all rights and priviledges contained in the original lease, set forth on Schedule D attached hereto, shall be transferred to the COMPANY upon exercise of this right. Said original lease shall contain the landlord's express permission for the COMPANY to sublease the aforesaid premises.

E. The COMPANY shall have the option to retain all rights to the telephone number assigned to the FRANCHISEE, and to such advertising privileges as are concurrent therewith.

21. This agreement shall be binding upon the respective heirs, assigns, personal representatives and successors of the parties, but no sale, assignment or other transfer of the rights granted hereunder may be made without the prior written consent of the COMPANY.

22. This agreement is divisible, and if any provision herein is held to be violative of the law or unenforceable for any reason such illegality or unenforceability shall affect the portion in conflict only, and the remaining portions of this agreement shall remain in effect.

23. Any controversy or claim arising out of or relating to this agreement, or the breach thereof, shall be settled by arbitration in New York, New York in accordance with the rules then prevailing of the American Arbitration Association and the laws of the State of New York, and judgment upon the award rendered by the arbitrator may be entered in any court having jurisdiction thereof.

24. This agreement is subject to the approval and confirmation of the COMPANY at its home office and shall not become binding unless and until it is officially countersigned.

25. This instrument contains all of the agreements, representations, and conditions by or between the parties hereto. Neither party shall be liable for any representations made unless set forth herein and all modifications and amendments hereto must be in writing.

IN WITNESS WHEREOF, the parties have signed this Agreement effective the ...................................................

day of .........................................., 19

Witness: ................................................................. FRANCHISEE ........................................................

Witness: ................................................................. FRANCHISEE'S ADDRESS ....................................

...............................................................................................

APPROVED: EDU-CENTER, INC.

By ..............................................................................

Title .................................... Date ...................................

## SCHEDULE A

TERRITORY referred to in Paragraph 1, as described below and/or outlined in attached map, which becomes part of this Agreement.

## SCHEDULE B

LEASED EQUIPMENT as referred to in Paragraph 2-C and 5.

### ROOM A EQUIPMENT

  1 Electronic Console
  1 Electronic Panel
  1 Reserve Electronic Unit for Console
  1 Cable (to link Console to Panel)
  1 Exercise Board
  6 Tapes (Lessons 1 to 6)
  6 Reserve Tapes (Lessons 1 to 6)
  1 Take-up Spool
  1 Reserve Take-up Spool
25 Yards Twinflex Wire (to link Console with alarm
     bell outside Room A — each tape has built-in-signal
     at end of tape)

### ROOM B EQUIPMENT

  1 Console consisting of 4 Transmission Decks
  1 Reserve Transmission Deck for Console
  1 Main Cable (linking Console to 6 other cables)
  6 Other Cables, each one having 6 Selector Units
36 Head Sets
36 Reserve Head Sets
150 Ear Pips
  6 Twin Track Tapes for different speeds
  6 Reserve Twin Track Tapes for different speeds
  5 Take-up Spools
  1 Reserve Take-up Spool
260 Exercise Sheets
260 Reserve Exercise Sheets

### SPARE PARTS

| | |
|---|---|
| 12 Transistors | 12 Fuses (mixed) |
| 8 Diodes (Silicon Rectifiers) | 6 Lamp Holders |
| 6 Electrolitic Capacitors | 3 Indicator Bulbs |
| 2 Tape Replay Heads | 3 Volume Control |
| 2 Tape Deck Drive Belts | 12 Main Plug & Sockets |
| 2 Operating Arm Coil Springs | 12 Jack Sockets |
| 2 Relays | 2 Control Switches |
| 3 Space Bar Bulbs | |
|    (special bulbs) | |

# FRANCHISE AGREEMENT

# EDU-CENTER, INC.

## SCHEDULE C

**CONDITIONS OF LEASING EQUIPMENT** referred to in Paragraph 5, as agreed upon between the COMPANY and FRANCHISEE.

The component parts of the machine and related equipment and apparatus, as listed in Schedule B, are hereinafter collectively referred to as the "machine" or "the machine".

1. The machine shall remain the property of the COMPANY or its lessor and the value of the machine is stipulated and agreed to as $14,700.

2. The COMPANY shall not be liable for any consequential loss arising from breakdown of the machine or from any delay in carrying out repairs.

3. The FRANCHISEE shall not remove (or cause to be removed) the machine from the installation address without authorization of the COMPANY.

4. In the event of termination of the FRANCHISE agreement the FRANCHISEE shall return the machine in working order and good condition to the COMPANY at such location specified by the COMPANY, at his own cost and expense.

5. Installation of the machine will be at the expense of the COMPANY, in accordance with procedures laid down in the operations manual. Local sources at the FRANCHISEE'S location, authorized in advance by the COMPANY, may be utilized for simple maintenance and repair, as specified by the operations manual. Such repairs and maintenance will be at the expense of the FRANCHISEE. The COMPANY shall replace the machine if such replacement should be necessary. Such replacement will not affect the terms of the original leasing agreement herein; provided that if the replaced machine is more than 6 years old, the COMPANY may charge the same rental for the new machine as it is then charging for the rental of new machines. The COMPANY will provide such technical advice and instructions as may be necessary for the guidance of authorized local repair sources.

6. The COMPANY may affix on the machine such plates or other marks indicating that the machine is the property of Sight & Sound Education Limited. The FRANCHISEE shall not remove, obliterate, deface or cover up same.

# BEN FRANKLIN
# FRANCHISE AGREEMENT

THIS AGREEMENT, made this_____day of_____ 19___, by and between CITY PRODUCTS CORPORATION, an Ohio corporation, having its principal place of business at 1700 South Wolf Road, Des Plaines, Illinois.

(hereinafter called the "Distributor"), and_____

of_____(hereinafter called the "Owner").

# WITNESSETH:

**W**HEREAS, Distributor is engaged in the business of distributing merchandise to merchants who own and operate retail variety stores, and out of its knowledge and experience gained through many years has developed a merchandising and store operating and service program, known as and designated *The Ben Franklin System*, which it offers to such stores as meet the standards required by Distributor; and

WHEREAS, in connection with such merchandising and store operating and service program, Distributor is the owner of the mark "BEN FRANKLIN" registered in the United States Patent Office and under the laws of various states;

WHEREAS, the Owner desires to avail himself of the advantage of the aforesaid retail system in his store at _____
(STREET)
_____, _____ ,
(CITY)                                    (STATE)
which system consists of a complete retail operating and promotional service and selected basic stock lists of merchandise for Ben Franklin Stores:

NOW, THEREFORE, in consideration of the foregoing and of the mutual covenants and agreements hereinafter contained, the parties hereto agree as follows:

**1** The Distributor agrees to furnish to the Owner for use in his store the merchandising services outlined above known as the Ben Franklin System of Variety type Retail Store Operation. The Owner agrees to receive such services and follow the practices prescribed thereby in the operation of his store as a Ben Franklin Variety type Retail Store to the best of his ability as long as this agreement shall remain in force.

**2** Distributor agrees to furnish the Owner for use in his store basic stock lists of merchandise to be known as the merchandise check list and through supplemental and seasonal check lists to keep it adjusted to conditions, markets and consumer demand. Distributor will also supply general listings of other merchandise which may be desired by the Owner to supplement the basic stock merchandise to be carried by the Owner.

Distributor agrees that said lists at all times during the term of this agreement will be sufficiently complete in its judgment for the successful operation of a modern efficient Ben Franklin Retail Store as contemplated by this agreement. Prices, terms of payment and delivery shall be those quoted by the Distributor from time to time in accordance with its current practices to like stores and the credit standing of the Owner, as to which the Distributor shall be the sole judge.

Owner agrees to purchase merchandise of the type and quality offered by Distributor from time to time pursuant to the aforesaid Ben Franklin Retail System.

**3** The Distributor agrees to furnish to the Owner the retail merchandising, operating and promotional services composed of the instructions, aids, materials, and personal services furnished by the Distributor to all Ben Franklin Stores Franchise holders of the class of the Owner herein. Such instructions, aids, materials, and personal services, and the charges therefor, and the extent to which the name "Ben Franklin Stores" may and shall be used by the Owner herein, are set forth and described in substance in Schedule A, attached hereto, which by reference thereto is hereby made a part of this agreement. The said service, and each part thereof and charge therefor, except the extent to which the Owner may and shall use said name "Ben Franklin Stores," may be altered or modified by the Distributor from time to time, in its discretion, to meet changes in conditions affecting the operation of Ben Franklin type Retail Stores, but no such change or modification shall impose any substantially greater financial burden upon the Owner than may be reasonably contemplated at the date hereof, without the Owner's express consent.

The extent to which the name "Ben Franklin Stores" may be used by the Owner, as set forth in Schedule A, shall not be altered or changed during the term of this agreement, or any renewal term, except as provided in said Schedule A, or by mutual agreement of the parties hereto. All of the literature and materials furnished to the Owner by the Distributor in connection with said merchandising services shall be and remain at all times the property of the Distributor, and shall be returned to the Distributor by the Owner within 30 days after termination of this agreement.

**4** The Distributor agrees, to the extent specified in Schedule A, that the Owner shall have the right to conduct and advertise the Owner's retail store referred to under the name of "Ben Franklin Stores," and the Owner agrees that he shall conduct and advertise his store under said name, and that he shall not use such name in any way, or to any extent, not so specified in Schedule A.

**5** The Owner agrees that so far as practicable his store will be arranged, and his merchandise laid out and displayed in conformity to the standard plans for Ben Franklin Stores and that he will not materially change the physical layout or arrangement without written approval of Distributor.

Owner agrees to a complete relay of the merchandise display and layout, at any time after the first year of the term of this franchise, if the need for such relay is so determined by the Distributor. Distributor agrees to furnish the necessary Store Layout Specialist to plan and supervise this relay work. Owner agrees to reimburse Distributor for these specialized services in accordance with Schedule A, paragraph 4.

**6** Owner agrees to use the standard Ben Franklin accounting records, or records providing similar information, as approved by Distributor.

    a. Where a store becomes newly franchised hereunder, the Owner hereby covenants and agrees to immediately execute the Distributor's regular form contract for the Ben Franklin Mail Accounting Program.

    b. If this franchise is issued to an Owner of an existing Ben Franklin Store and if Owner is not currently using the Ben Franklin Mail Accounting Program, Owner hereby covenants and agrees to furnish Distributor on or before the 20th day of each month, the total gross sales for the preceding month during each year of the term of this franchise. Owner further covenants and agrees to furnish Distributor each month, the amount of his ending inventory at sell, if available.

**7** It is mutually understood and agreed that the Owner is not the Agent of Distributor for any purpose, and that Owner retains full responsibility for the financing, management and operation of the Owner's store. Owner acknowledges that he may have been given or seen sales forecasts and other projections provided by the Distributor or its employees, either referring to the location covered by this franchise or otherwise, but the Owner hereby stipulates and agrees that neither such materials nor any statement made by the Distributor or any employee thereof is intended to be or shall be deemed to be a representation, warranty, guaranty or indemnity of any nature, regardless of by whom or how asserted, and the Owner agrees that the Distributor shall not be responsible for the results obtained in the operation of said store or liabilities incurred thereby.

**8** The Ben Franklin Stores standard sign, and all other signs, insignia, etc. (not including other store fixtures, equipment, and supplies not bearing the name "Ben Franklin Stores" or otherwise exclusively related to the Ben Franklin System of Variety type Retail Store Operation), if the Owner shall have acquired title thereto, shall immediately upon the termination of this agreement, by lapse of time or otherwise, become the sole and exclusive property of the Distributor, and the Distributor agrees to pay the Owner therefor the cost thereof, less depreciation at the rate of ten per cent (10%) per annum, in case of said standard sign; and at the rate of twenty per cent (20%) per annum in the case of all such other signs, insignia, etc.

**9** Upon termination of this agreement, whether by lapse of time or otherwise, the Owner agrees that he will promptly remove the Ben Franklin Stores standard sign from said store, and will promptly discontinue the use of all other signs, insignia, etc., relating to or in any way connected with the Ben Franklin System of Variety type Retail Store Operation and that he will within thirty (30) days after such termination return to the Distributor said standard sign and other signs, insignia, etc. (upon payment or tender of payment by the Distributor to the Owner of the depreciated cost thereof as provided in Paragraph 8 hereof), together with all promotional literature, materials, manuals of instruction, Ben Franklin Merchandise Check list, and other literature or materials which may have been delivered to him by the Distributor pursuant to this agreement, all at his own cost and expense.

If owner shall fail or refuse to deliver to Distributor the said standard sign and all other signs and insignia bearing the mark "BEN FRANKLIN" Owner agrees that from and after the date of termination of this Franchise Agreement and until Owner shall so deliver said signs and insignia, that he will pay to Distributor, as rent for the use of the said sign and as a fee for the continued use of the mark and all insignia relating thereto, a monthly rent in the amount of Five Hundred Dollars, payable on the first day of each and every month. In addition to the right to collect the rental herein stipulated during such continued use of the sign and the mark "BEN FRANKLIN," Distributor shall have the right, with or without process of law, to remove and repossess said standard sign and other signs, insignia, etc., and said promotional literature, materials, manuals of instruction, Ben Franklin Merchandise Check List, and other literature or materials delivered to the Owner by the Distributor pursuant to this agreement, and the Distributor shall have the right to enter upon and have free access to the premises of the Owner, with or without process of law, for the purposes aforesaid, and the Owner agrees that he will pay, promptly on demand, all costs and expenses, including reasonable attorney's fees, suffered or incurred by the Distributor in exercising or enforcing any of its rights aforesaid.

**10** The Owner further agrees that upon termination of this agreement, whether by lapse of time or otherwise, he will not thereafter use the name "Ben Franklin Stores," or any similar name or names, on his store or in his advertising, or on any merchandise or otherwise or will not in any wise infringe upon or attempt to appropriate Distributor's right, title and interest under the registered mark "BEN FRANKLIN."

**11** The term of this agreement shall be for a period of five (5) years and _____ months, beginning _____ , 19_____ and ending December 31,

19 _____ , subject, nevertheless, to termination upon the following conditions: (a) Either party may at the end of any full calendar year terminate this agreement by giving notice to the other party not less than sixty (60) days before the end of any such full calendar year, and in the event of any such termination by Distributor, Distributor shall not have an option to purchase as hereinafter provided in paragraph 12. (b) Distributor may, at its option, cancel and terminate this franchise at any time upon thirty (30) days' notice if Owner shall become delinquent in the payment of any indebtedness due to Distributor on any account including, without limiting the foregoing, the franchise fee provided for in Schedule A. (c) Distributor may, at its option, cancel and terminate this franchise at any time upon thirty (30) days' notice if Owner shall move its operations under this franchise to any other physical location than that under which he commenced operation under this franchise. (d) This agreement shall terminate automatically if the Owner shall at any time sell or liquidate the Store, or if he shall die.

**12** In the event this agreement is terminated upon any of the conditions in paragraph 11 hereof, with the single exception of termination by Distributor under sub-paragraph (a) of Paragraph 11 at the end of any full calendar year, the Distributor shall have the option, within one hundred twenty (120) days from and after the effective date of such termination or notice thereof to Distributor, whichever is later, to purchase the assets of the Owner's store (including the unexpired term of any lease on the premises in which said business may then be conducted at no additional rent) upon the payment of a price to be computed as follows: (a) Merchandise available through the Ben Franklin System at cost or market price, whichever is lower as determined by physical inventory. Any remaining merchandise not identified with the Ben Franklin System shall be purchased at a negotiated price. (b) Fixtures and equipment at original cost, less ten percent (10%) depreciation per annum from the date of purchase, provided, however, that if under this formula fixtures would be depreciated below fifty percent (50%) of original cost, Distributor and Owner or Owner's personal representative, shall agree upon the fair value for such fixtures and equipment which fair value shall not exceed 50% of original cost.

However, it is agreed that if the heirs of the Owner, upon the death of the Owner, shall be qualified and desire to continue the operation of the business under and pursuant to a similar agreement, and shall within one hundred and twenty (120) days after the death of the Owner enter into such an agreement with Distributor for a period of not less than five (5) years, then Distributor shall not have the option to purchase hereunder.

**13** For and in consideration of the services to be rendered by Distributor hereunder, Owner agrees to pay the fees specified on Schedule A attached hereto and the Distributor agrees to make available to the Owner a specific allowance or discount as specified on attached Schedule A in the amounts and for the period designated.

**14** Any notice required to be given hereunder shall be given in writing and shall be served by depositing the same in the United States Post Office in a sealed envelope, postage prepaid, addressed, in the case of

the Distributor, to the Distributor at _____

_____

and in the case of the Owner, to the Owner at _____

_____ ,

to be sent by certified mail, and any such notice shall be deemed to have been served at the time the same was deposited in the United States Post Office as aforesaid.

**15** This agreement shall be construed in accordance with and governed by the laws of the state in which the franchised store is located. Any provisions of this agreement prohibited by the law of any state shall, as to said state, be ineffective to the extent of such prohibition without invalidating the remaining provisions of this agreement.

**16** This agreement and all rights hereunder apply only to the retail variety operation in the store building in which the Owner commenced business under this franchise, and not to any retail operation in any other store building whatsoever. This agreement shall inure to the benefit of and be binding upon the successors and assigns of the Distributor, but shall be personal to the Owner, and neither this agreement, nor any right or privilege hereunder, shall be assignable or transferable by voluntary or involuntary action of the Owner or by operation of law.

The execution of this instrument by City Products Corporation shall be binding on said Corporation when it is accomplished by the manual signing hereof by a Vice-President and the Secretary or an Assistant Secretary of City Products Corporation; or by affixing hereto, by any mechanical device, of a facsimile signature purporting to be that of a Vice-President of City Products Corporation and the manual signing hereof by the Secretary or an Assistant Secretary of City Products Corporation; or by the affixing hereto, by any mechanical device, of facsimile signatures purporting to be those of a Vice-President and the Secretary or an Assistant Secretary of City Products Corporation and the manual signing hereof in the place below provided by a person duly authorized by the Board of Directors of City Products Corporation.

IN WITNESS WHEREOF, this Franchise has been duly executed, under seal, on the day and year first above written.

CITY PRODUCTS CORPORATION

ATTEST:_____     By_____
         *Assistant Secretary*                              *Vice-President*

COUNTERSIGNED:_____

### FOR EXECUTION BY INDIVIDUAL OR PARTNERSHIP:

Witness to Signature of Owner:

_____     _____(SEAL)

_____     _____(SEAL)

### FOR EXECUTION BY CORPORATE OWNER:

_____
                                     *Name of Corporation*

ATTEST: _____     By _____
(Affix Corporate Seal)  *Secretary*                        *President*

# SCHEDULE A

Attached to and by reference made a part of Ben Franklin Franchise Agreement
dated_____between City Products Corporation
and_____ .

 **USE OF NAME "BEN FRANKLIN"**

(a) Outside sign.

As long as Owner's store shall conform to standard specifications for store front and physical appearance established by Distributor, Owner's store sign shall appear as either:

BEN FRANKLIN

or

5-10 BEN FRANKLIN 5-10

Owner shall at all times disclose his own name and proprietorship by appropriate means approved by Distributor.

Owner shall not change or replace the outside sign without the written approval of the Distributor.

Owner shall maintain, repair or replace outside sign, as deemed adequate for the location, by the Distributor, in the manner and at the time designated by the Distributor.

(b) Interior advertising and displays.

Owner shall display cards, price ticket forms and all other material supplied by the Distributor bearing the name "Ben Franklin Stores."

(c) All other advertising and promotion.

Unless otherwise specifically permitted or prescribed by Distributor in individual instances, Owner shall use all other advertising and promotional material to the same extent and in the same manner as prescribed in subparagraph (a).

RETAIL MERCHANDISING SERVICE TO BE FURNISHED

The retail merchandising service to be furnished by the distributor to the owner currently includes the following:

a. *A Complete Warehouse Service*—one source for all merchandise necessary to operate a store with supplementary factory listings on important lines.

b. *Basic and Seasonal Check Lists* which are also complete merchandise listings and merchandise stock control records . . . with store size classifications on most recommended items.

c. *Detailed Procedures for Operating a Ben Franklin Store*—explanation of field tested methods and systems developed for efficient store operation.

d. *Accounting Manual and Accounting Forms,* comprising a simplified retail accounting system for merchandise and operating records required by variety stores.

e. *Planned Program*—A Monthly Program of Store Management Plans, Promotions, and Displays. Includes standard counter layouts, seasonal features, signs, guidance for sales people—keyed to 6-months promotional calendar.

f. *Sale Plans*—completely coordinated store-wide promotions for major selling seasons. Professional display material, colorful circulars, ad mats included.

g. *Syndicate Merchandise Service*—provides automatic shipments of new goods in trial quantities with reordering information—one of several methods of getting new goods and promotional items to Ben Franklin Stores quickly.

h. *Services of a Retail Operating Man* to explain and interpret all phases of the Ben Franklin program.

i. *Poster Service*—provides chain store type of display material . . . colorful posters, banners, and signs for seasonal events and scheduled promotions—coordinated with Planning Calendar and Planning Profits.

Note: A separate charge will be made for printed forms, supplies, merchandise, and other items furnished to the Owner in paragraphs "d", "f", "g", and "i".

**3**

### DISTRIBUTOR STORE COOPERATIVE DISCOUNTS

(a) Distributor will give Owner a special Distributor Store Cooperative Discount, to be payable within ninety (90) days after the end of each calendar year of operation hereunder or upon the date of termination of this franchise (as soon as computation thereof may be made by Distributor), for Owner's purchases (excepting franchise fees or services) during a calendar year, in accordance with the following schedule:

2.0% discount on purchases from Distributor in excess of $10,000 up to $20,000,

2.5% discount on purchases from Distributor in excess of $20,000 up to $35,000,

3.0% discount on purchases from Distributor in excess of $35,000 up to $55,000,

3.5% discount on purchases from Distributor in excess of $55,000 up to $80,000,

4.0% discount on purchases from Distributor in excess of $80,000.

(b) In the event Owner's new store is opened on or before March 31 of a calendar year, credit shall be given on purchases from the Distributor made on or after November 1 of the preceding year.

(c) Should Owner qualify for this franchise by purchasing the assets of an existing store, whether the store is owned by Distributor or not, no Cooperative Discount shall be paid on any purchase of existing assets or previous purchases made by Seller.

### PERSONAL SERVICES TO BE FURNISHED

(a) The Distributor's Retail Operating man will call at reasonable intervals to advise the Owner in the professional application of the Ben Franklin program covering operating, merchandising, promotional and record keeping systems. The services of such Retail Operating man will be rendered at such time or times as shall be considered necessary and appropriate in the sole judgment of the Distributor.

(b) Individual consultation may be given either by mail or personally at the offices of the Distributor, on any special problems relating to the operation of the Owner's store on which the Owner desires the advice of the Distributor.

(c) The Distributor maintains a trained staff of Store Layout Specialists, Accounting Specialists, and Lease and Location Specialists, whose services are available to the Owner, upon request, at rates to be mutually agreed upon.

**5**

For all franchise benefits enumerated in this Schedule or the Franchise Agreement of which it is a part (except any special service provided pursuant to sub-paragraph (c) of this Paragraph 4 of Schedule A and except the separate sub-paragraphs noted in Paragraph 2 of Schedule A), the Owner agrees to pay an annual fee of $          , payable in equal monthly installments, during the term of the franchise to which this Schedule A is attached, beginning on the first day of the month nearest the opening day of business or on the first day of the term of this franchise for a store in operation.

GBS FORM 1062    REV. 7/79

# AREA DIRECTOR AGREEMENT

This Agreement, made this _____ day of _____ , 19___, by and between GENERAL BUSINESS SERVICES, INC., a corporation formed and operating under the laws of Maryland, having its principal place of business at 51 Monroe Street, Rockville, Maryland 20850, hereinafter referred to as "GBS" and _____

_____

residing at _____

hereinafter referred to as "Area Director" for Area No. _____ ;

*WITNESSETH:*

WHEREAS, GBS has acquired unique experience, special skills, technique and knowledge in the development and provision of recordkeeping forms, income tax service, data processing, business counseling and related programs (hereinafter referred to as "The GBS Services") and has devised a standard, unique and uniform system, more fully described in GBS confidential Operations Manual for the establishment, operation, and development of distinctive distributorships for The GBS Services not previously known to Area Director, which system is identified by the service mark "GBS," the trade name "General Business Services," and other trade names and/or proprietary marks including but not limited to "General Business Systems"; "General Tax Service"; "General System Sales"; and "Data Business Services"; and

WHEREAS, GBS has duly registered the service mark "GBS" in the principal register of the United States Patent Office under Certificate Number 761750 which, together with other service marks and/or trade names, identifies the services provided by GBS and thus GBS has the sole and exclusive right to the goodwill connected with the registered service mark and other service marks and trade names used in connection with providing such services; and

WHEREAS, all of the foregoing have distinctive and valuable significance to the public, and Area Director recognizing same desires to make use of and enjoy the commercial benefits by being appointed one such licensee,

NOW THEREFORE, THE PARTIES MUTUALLY AGREE AS FOLLOWS:

## I. Appointment

**A. Grant** — GBS grants Area Director the right, license, and franchise to use the Proprietary Marks and to be identified as a member of the GBS field organization in connection with the operation of a business providing The GBS Services for as long as this Agreement is in force and effect. GBS hereby assigns Area Director the Primary Area of Promotional Responsibility (hereinafter referred to as the "Area") described in Addendum #1.

**B. Fee** — In consideration for said grant, Area Director shall complete payment to GBS at Rockville, Maryland, within ten (10) days after execution of this Agreement by GBS, a fee totaling Fifteen Thousand Dollars ($15,000.00).

**C. Term** — The term of this Agreement and subsequent renewal agreements shall each be for a period of five (5) years. The Area Director, providing the conditions of this and subsequent renewal agreements are fulfilled, shall be granted a renewal agreement for each succeeding five (5) year period on the terms and conditions then being offered all new and renewing Area Directors. The renewal fee shall be three per cent (3%) of the initial appointment fee than being charged newly appointed Area Directors.

**D. Exclusive** — GBS agrees not to enfranchise any additional Area Directors in the Area during the first two years of this Agreement. If, thereafter, Area Director at any time maintains less than thirty (30) registered clients within the Area, GBS reserves the right to enfranchise additional Area Directors in the Area. The Area Director acknowledges and GBS confirms that as of the date of this Agreement those persons listed in Addendum #2 are enfranchised by GBS in the Area.

## II. Initial Training and Support

**A. Training Institute** — GBS shall make available to Area Director and Area Director shall attend and successfully complete the GBS Basic and Advanced Training Institutes, within the first year of this Agreement. Travel, training, meals and lodging will be arranged and paid by GBS.

**B. Field Training** — GBS shall provide four (4) days of field training for Area Director at no additional expense to Area Director.

**C. Initial Operating Supplies and Service Contracts** — GBS shall prescribe and recommend initial Operating Supplies and initial Service Contracts for commencing the franchise business. The initial Operating Supplies will be provided by GBS without additional cost and the initial Service Contracts will be provided by GBS for purchase by Area Director.

**D. Insurance** — Area Director will be eligible to enroll in a group term life insurance plan providing Fifteen Thousand Dollars ($15,000) coverage on Area Director's life with an additional Fifteen Thousand Dollars ($15,000) coverage for accidental death or dismemberment. Coverage will be effective upon receipt by GBS of a completed, signed enrollment card, but not earlier than 12:01 AM on the first day of the calendar month in which the Basic Training Institute is attended. Eligibility for enrollment will expire thirty (30) days after the first day of attendance at the GBS Basic Training Institute. GBS shall pay the premium for the first six (6) months of coverage.

## III. Continuing Support Services

**A. Materials, Supplies and Support Services** — GBS shall develop and make available to Area Director those materials, supplies and support services deemed necessary by GBS for proper operation by Area Director. The availability and price of each will be published in the confidential Operations Manual with a thirty (30) day advance notice of any price change.

**B. Confidential Operations Manual** —

1. GBS shall provide Area Director with a confidential Operations Manual which remains the sole property of GBS.

2. In order to protect the reputation and goodwill of GBS and to maintain the uniform standards of operation thereunder, Area Director shall conduct the GBS franchised business in accordance with GBS' confidential Operations Manual which will not at any time conflict or be inconsistent with this Agreement.

3. In order that Area Director may benefit from new knowledge gained by GBS as to sales, marketing and operational techniques, GBS may, from time to time, revise the contents of said Manual. Area Director shall at all times ensure that Area Director's copy of said Manual is maintained on a current basis and shall not reproduce, in whole or in part, its contents or otherwise make it available to any unauthorized person.

**C. Tax Advisory Service** — GBS shall maintain a Tax Advisory Service to answer income tax inquiries from all registered Clients and other customers of the Area Director as prescribed by GBS.

**D. Return Preparation Service** — GBS shall maintain a Return Preparation Service for the preparation of all income tax returns for registered Clients and other customers of Area Director as prescribed by GBS, who submit information for this purpose in accordance with established GBS policies and procedures. Any claim for payment made by Clients or customers covered by GBS' Guarantee of Accuracy shall be the responsibility of GBS.

**. E. Tax Bulletin Service** — GBS shall prepare and distribute a tax bulletin to all registered Clients and other customers of Area Director as prescribed by GBS.

**F. Training** — The Regional Director or a trainer approved by GBS shall be assigned to provide training, consultation and guidance to Area Director. Training seminars for personal professional development shall be conducted periodically and Area Director will be entitled to attend all such seminars within a given region.

**G. Lending Library Service** — GBS shall make available to Area Director, for his personal professional development, a Lending Library Service containing publications and recordings deemed by GBS to be of benefit to all Area Directors.

**H. Promotional Efforts** — GBS shall engage in promotional efforts which it deems to be beneficial to all Area and Associate Directors nationally.

**I. Monthly Support Fee** — In consideration for providing continuing support services and for the right to use the operating system and Proprietary Marks of GBS, Area Director agrees to pay GBS, on or before the tenth (10th) day of each month, so long as this Agreement shall be in effect, a sum equal to five percent (5%) of the Area Director's gross receipts for the preceding calendar month beginning with the calendar month following attendance at the Basic Training Institute. The minimum payment each month shall be Fifty Dollars ($50.00). "Gross receipts" shall mean the total dollar aggregate of monies received for all services sold or performed by Area Director in the operation of this franchise. Upon request Area Director agrees to provide information on sales and receipts and to give GBS access to all books of account and records as required. An annual reconciliation of monthly gross receipts and support fee payments will be provided to GBS by Area Director upon request.

## IV. Proprietary Marks

**A. Use** — It is understood that the license granted herein to use GBS' Proprietary Marks in connection with the franchised business includes the mark "GBS" and such other trademarks, service marks and trade names of GBS as GBS may from time to time indicate in the confidential Operations Manual, but no other marks of GBS now existing or to be developed or acquired by GBS, and that such license applies only to the operation of a business providing The GBS Service.

**B. Ownership** — Area Director acknowledges GBS' claim to the exclusive right to the Proprietary Marks, in connection with said business and services to which they are applied by GBS and its other franchisees, and expressly covenants that during the term of this Agreement and after expiration or termination hereof, Area Director shall not directly or indirectly contest or aid in contesting the validity of ownership of said Proprietary Marks, or take any action whatsoever in derogation of GBS' claimed rights therein.

**C. Claims** — Area Director shall promptly notify GBS of any claim, demand, or suit based upon or arising from, or of any attempt by any other person, firm, or corporation to use, the Proprietary Marks licensed hereunder, or any colorable variation thereof, in which GBS has a proprietary interest. Area Director agrees also to promptly notify GBS of any litigation instituted by any person, firm, corporation or governmental agency against GBS or Area Director involving GBS' Proprietary Marks. In the event GBS undertakes the defense or prosecution of any litigation relating to the Proprietary Marks licensed hereunder, Area Director agrees to execute any and all documents and do such acts and things as may, in the opinion of counsel for GBS, be necessary to carry out such defense or prosecution.

**D. Other Grants** — Area Director understands and agrees that except as is provided in Paragraph I.D. hereof, Area Director's license under said Proprietary Marks is non-exclusive and that GBS, in its sole discretion, has the right to grant other licenses in, to and under such Proprietary Marks, in addition to those licenses already granted, and to develop and license other marks in conjunction with systems other than The GBS Services, on any terms and conditions GBS deems advisable.

**E. Value** — It is expressly recognized that any and all goodwill associated with and identified by said Proprietary Marks inures directly and exclusively to the benefit of GBS and is the property of GBS, and that, on the expiration or termination of this Agreement, no monetary amount shall be assigned as attributable to any goodwill associated with Area Director's activities as a licensee under said Proprietary Marks.

**F. Obligations** — Area Director shall not use any Proprietary Marks of GBS as part of Area Director's corporate name or name of any other business. Area Director shall not make purchases or perform any other activity or incur any obligation or indebtedness in such a way as to in any way obligate GBS for said acts.

**G. Compliance** — In order to preserve the validity and integrity of the Proprietary Marks licensed herein and to assure that Area Director is properly employing the same in the operation of Area Director's business, GBS or its agents shall at all reasonable times have the right to inspect Area Director's operation. Area Director shall cooperate with GBS' representative in such inspection and render such assistance to him as he may reasonably request.

## V. Independent Contractor

**A. Status** – This Agreement does not constitute Area Director an agent, legal representative, joint venturer, partner, employee or servant of GBS for any purpose whatsoever; and it is deemed understood between the parties that Area Director shall be an independent contractor and is in no way authorized to make any contract, agreement, warranty or representation on behalf of GBS, or to create any obligation expressed or implied on behalf of GBS beyond the regular sale of The GBS Services.

**B. Liability** – Under no circumstances shall GBS be liable for any act, omission, debt or other obligation of Area Director. Area Director shall indemnify and hold GBS harmless against any such claim and the cost of defending against such claims arising directly or indirectly in connection with Area Director's operation of the franchised business.

**C. Registration** – Area Director shall promptly comply with all federal, state and local laws and regulations and shall obtain as required any and all permits, certificates or licenses necessary for the full and proper conduct of this GBS franchise.

## VI. Standards of Quality and Performance

**A. Maintaning** – Area Director recognizes it is essential to the proper marketing of The GBS Services and to the preservation and promotion of its reputation and acceptance by the public at large that uniform standards of quality be maintained. Area Director agrees, as part of the consideration for this Agreement, that Area Director shall at all times sell, promote and offer for sale to the public only those products and services designated by GBS, unless prior written consent of GBS has been obtained. GBS agrees to approve any such requests unless in the opinion of GBS the proposed products or services would tend to confuse the public or harm the reputation of GBS.

**B. Modification of System** – Area Director recognizes and agrees that from time to time hereafter GBS may change or modify the system presently identified by the service mark "GBS," including the adoption and use of new or modified trade names, trademarks, service marks or copyrighted materials and that Area Director will use any such changes in said system, including new or modified trade names, trademarks, service marks or copyrighted materials as if they were part of this Agreement at the time of execution.

**C. Advertising Supplies** – Area Director shall actively promote the sale of The GBS Services in the Area through use of promotional materials and techniques including but not limited to direct mail, media advertising and telephone (both classified and alphabetical directory) listings. Area Director may, in the preparation, printing or production of advertising and promotional materials, purchase from any source, provided the copy of such advertising shall first be approved in writing by GBS, which approval shall not unreasonably be withheld.

**D. Operational Standards** – Area Director understands and acknowledges that each and every detail of The GBS Services is important to GBS, to Area Director, and to other licensed GBS franchisees, in order to develop and maintain uniformity of facilities and services and hence to enhance the reputation, trade demand and goodwill of GBS. Area Director accordingly covenants:

1. To operate under, advertise and promote the trade name "General Business Services" unless otherwise directed by GBS;

2. To conduct business only under said Proprietary Marks in accordance with operational standards established by GBS, as set forth in the confidential Operations Manual; and to ensure that The GBS Services provided by Area Director meet GBS' quality standards, by notifying GBS in writing of any proposed deviation;

3. To represent to the public only that Area Director is a business counselor, and at no time represent that Area Director is an accountant, tax expert, or computer specialist;

4. To ensure that The GBS Services sold to Clients and customers as being performed by GBS are in fact done by GBS; and to refrain from preparing, changing or amending, or accepting the responsibility for preparing, changing or amending any income tax returns without first obtaining the express written consent of GBS; and in the event GBS is required to make any payment on its Guarantee of Accuracy, Area Director agrees to reimburse GBS for all such payment if he is in violation of this provision in any respect – this in addition to any other rights GBS may have;

5. To register with appropriate governmental authorities and to obtain a telephone listing as "General Business Services" in the Area or as otherwise directed. Such name registrations including telephone numbers will automatically become the property of and revert to GBS upon expiration or termination of this Agreement and Area Director will cause any such transfer to be made not later than date of expiration or termination. Area Director agrees to file with the appropriate telephone company at the time the telephone listing is obtained a written authorization on forms provided by GBS, authorizing and directing the telephone company to take such action as GBS may direct with regard to such listing in the event GBS should notify the telephone company that this Agreement has expired or terminated.

6. To register with GBS as Clients all persons, firms or organizations purchasing a Basic GBS Service Contract and to report to GBS as required all customers purchasing any other of The GBS Services from Area Director. Such registration and reporting to be made in accordance with established procedure but not later than seven (7) days after date of sale.

## VII. Transfer Rights

### A. Transfer and Resale Privileges –

1. Area Director may at any time sell or transfer the rights under this Agreement provided the provisions of this Agreement and the established procedures for such transfer applicable to all Area Directors are fully complied with.

2. GBS agrees to assist Area Director in finding a purchaser, upon written request of Area Director, at any price specified, provided Area Director is not in default of any provision of this Agreement. GBS shall be entitled to a fee if advertising is requested by Area Director and placed by GBS.

3. Area Director shall not, by operation of law or otherwise, sell, assign, transfer, convey, give away, or encumber, any interest in the franchise granted by this Agreement, nor permit same without GBS' prior written consent. Any purported assignment not having such consent shall be null and void and shall constitute a material default hereunder.

4. If a proposed transfer would have the effect of transferring the franchise license herein to a person other than the original signatory to the Agreement, it is mutually agreed that the transferee will execute the Agreement then being offered all new Area Directors and GBS will be paid the appointment fee then applicable for a new Area Director. Payment of such fee to GBS shall not be required if the transfer is to a corporation wholly owned by the Area Director and such transfer is made with the express written consent of GBS and is in accordance with established policies and procedures.

**B. In the event of Area Director's death**  — The legal representatives of said individual shall, within sixty (60) days of death, advise GBS the name of the person who will continue to operate the franchise, which right shall be automatically granted without any fee, provided the person named to continue operations is currently a GBS franchisee in good standing who acknowledges in writing to GBS acceptance of such responsibility. Such act will in no way prejudice options for resale at a later date. If such legal representatives fail to comply with this provision, then all rights licensed to Area Director under this Agreement shall terminate forthwith and automatically revert to GBS.

**C. In the event of Area Director's incapacity**  — Area Director or legal representative shall immediately advise GBS the name of the person who will continue to operate the franchise, which right shall be automatically granted without any fee, provided the person named to continue operations is currently a GBS franchise in good standing who acknowledges in writing to GBS acceptance of such responsibility. If Area Director fails because of his incapacity or otherwise, to name such a person, GBS shall have the right to appoint an Acting Area Director of its own choosing to operate the franchise and service Area Director's Clients and customers in such manner, to such extent and under such terms and conditions as GBS, in its sole discretion, may deem reasonable and necessary, until such time as Area Director's capacity to operate the franchise and service Clients and customers is restored, or until the expiration or termination of this Agreement, whichever first occurs. Such act will in no way prejudice options for resale at a later date. In the event a dispute should arise as to the capability or incapability of Area Director to operate the franchise, Area Director agrees to accept the opinion of a qualified physician, psychiatrist or other appropriate person selected solely by GBS.

## VIII. Termination

**A. Basis** — Except for purposes of resale or transfer as provided in Paragraph VII, this Agreement may be terminated only by Area Director or by GBS as provided below:

1. By Area Director — Area Director may terminate this Agreement at any time by notifying GBS in writing, at least ninety (90) days prior to the proposed terminal date, of Area Director's intent to cancel this Agreement. Area Director assumes responsibility for complete payment and discharge, on or before the terminal date, of all obligations, both to GBS and to other parties, incurred in the operation of this franchise.

2. By GBS — GBS may terminate this Agreement if Area Director has failed to make timely payment of any monies owing to GBS or has violated a provision of this Agreement and has been notified in writing of such default, and has failed to remedy such default within thirty (30) days of the giving of such notice. Also, if Area Director is convicted of a felony, becomes insolvent or makes an assignment of his assets for the benefit of creditors, or if the interest of Area Director should be sold or execution or by other legal process, or if Area Director shall file a voluntary petition in bankruptcy, or if an involuntary petition in bankruptcy or for receivership be instituted against the Area Director and the same be not dismissed within thirty (30) days of the filing thereof, or Area Director be adjudged bankrupt, or if proceedings for composition with creditors under any state or federal law should be instituted by or against Area Director, then and in any of said events this Agreement shall immediately cease and terminate at the option of GBS with the same force and effect as though the date of the occurrence of said event was the day herein fixed for the expiration of this Agreement.

**B. Procedures** — Upon expiration or termination of this Agreement, Area Director shall immediately cease to be a licensed GBS Area Director and:

1. Shall promptly pay all sums owing to GBS, said sums to include all damages, costs and expenses, including reasonable attorneys' fees, incurred by GBS by reason of default by Area Director;

2. Shall pay to GBS all damages, costs and expenses, including reasonable attorneys' fees, incurred by GBS subsequent to the termination of the Agreement as herein provided in obtaining injunctive relief for the enforcement of this Agreement.

3. Shall immediately cease to use, by advertising or in any manner whatsoever, any methods associated with the name "GBS" or "General Business Services" or similar names confusing to the public, or any forms, manuals, slogans, signs, marks, symbols, or devices used in connection with the operation of a GBS franchise;

4. Shall immediately turn over to GBS all manuals, Client and customer lists, instructions, and similar material (all of which are knowledged to be GBS property) and shall retain no copy or record of any of the foregoing, excepting only Area Director's copy of this Agreement and any documents which Area Director reasonably needs for compliance with any provision of law.

5. Shall not interfere with the transfer of GBS Clients or customers in the Area to another Area or Associate Director designated by GBS, and shall relinquish any and all rights and interests Area Director may have in such Clients or customers to GBS or its designate.

6. Shall promptly return the confidential GBS Operations Manual to GBS.

## IX. Covenants

**A. In-Term and Post-Term** — Area Director covenants that, except as otherwise approved in writing by GBS, during the term of this Agreement and for a period of one (1) year after expiration or termination of this Agreement, regardless of the cause of termination, Area Director shall not:

1. Divert or attempt to divert any business of, or any former or existing Clients or customers of, the business licensed hereunder to any competitor, by direct or indirect inducement or otherwise.

2. Employ or seek to employ any person who is employed by GBS or by any other Associate Director, Area Director, or Regional Director, or to otherwise directly or indirectly induce such person to leave his or her employment thereat.

3. Either directly or indirectly, for himself, or on behalf of or in conjunction with any other person, persons, partnership or corporation, own, maintain, or engage in, any business the same as or similar to the licensed business within the Area; provided, however, that this provision shall not apply to the ownership or operation by Area Director of additional GBS franchises, or to the ownership for investment purposes only of less than five per cent (5%) of the outstanding securities of any corporation whose securities are publicly held and traded.

**B. Confidential Information** – Area Director shall not during the term of this Agreement and any extension or renewal hereof or thereafter, regardless of the cause of termination, communicate or divulge to, or use for the benefit of, any person, persons, partnership, association or corporation any confidential information or know-how concerning the methods of operating the business licensed hereunder which may be communicated to Area Director, or of which Area Director may be apprised, by virtue of Area Director's operation under the terms of this Agreement.

**C. Interpretation** – Each of the covenants contained in this Paragraph shall be construed as severable and independent and shall be interpreted and applied consistent with the requirements of reasonableness and equity. Area Director expressly agrees to be bound by any covenant, as though contained in and made a part of this Agreement, resulting from striking from any of the foregoing covenants any portion or portions which may deem to be unreasonable or unenforceable.

**D. Liquidated Damages** – In the event a violation by Area Director of any of the provisions of this paragraph resulting in damages to GBS, Area Director agrees to pay GBS as liquidated damages and not as a penalty the sum of Ten Thousand Dollars ($10,000.00) in addition to other rights and remedies available to GBS. This amount is mutually agreed to be an equitable settlement should any competition be evident, and is established in lieu of ascertaining a specific damage claim.

## X. Contract Administration

**A. Applicable Law** – This Agreement, after review by Area Director, was accepted in the State of Maryland, and shall be interpreted and construed under the laws thereof, which laws shall prevail in the event of any conflict of laws.

**B. Notice** – Any notices required to be given hereunder may be given in writing by personal delivery or by certified or registered mail directed to GBS or to Area Director at their respective last known addresses. Notice by mail shall be deemed received on the fifth (5th) business day following the date same was deposited in the mail.

**C. Severability** – Each paragraph, term, covenant and/or provision of this Agreement shall be considered severable, and if, for any reason, a provision herein is determined to be invalid and contrary to, or in conflict with, any existing or future law or regulation of a court or agency having valid jurisdiction, such shall not impair the operation or affect the remaining paragraphs, terms, covenants and/or provisions of this Agreement, and the latter will continue to be given full force and effect and bind the parties hereto; and said invalid provisions shall be deemed not to be a part of this Agreement.

**D. Waiver** – Failure of either party at any time to require performance by the other party of any provision hereof shall not be deemed a continuing waiver of that provision or a waiver of any other provision of this Agreement whether or not of the same or similar nature.

**E. Entire Agreement** – This Agreement constitutes the entire, full and complete agreements, understandings, representations, conditions and covenants by and between the parties hereto. Neither party shall be liable for any representation made unless expressly set forth herein, and this Agreement may not be modified or amended except in writing signed by both of the parties hereto.

**F. Arbitration** – Except for monies due or violation of Paragraph IX above, any controversy or claim arising out of or relating to this contract, or the breach thereof, shall be settled by arbitration in accordance with the Rules of the American Arbitration Association, and judgment upon the award rendered by the Arbitrator(s) may be entered in any Court having jurisdiction thereof.

**G. Remedies** – No right or remedy herein conferred upon or reserved to GBS is exclusive of any other right or remedy herein or by law or equity provided or permitted but each shall be cumulative of every other right or remedy.

**H. Disclaimer** – Area Director acknowledges that Area Director has conducted an independent investigation of the GBS program and recognizes that the business venture contemplated by this Agreement involves business risks and will be largely dependent upon the ability of Area Director as an independent businessman. GBS expressly disclaims the making of, and Area Director acknowledges that Area Director has not received, any warranty or guaranty, express or implied, as to the potential volume, profits or success of the business venture contemplated by this Agreement.

IN WITNESS WHEREOF, the parties hereto have duly executed, sealed and delivered this Agreement in duplicate the day and year first above written.

**AREA DIRECTOR**                    **GENERAL BUSINESS SERVICES, INC.**

_____        by _____

## ADDENDUM #1 – PRIMARY AREA OF PROMOTIONAL RESPONSIBILITY

Identified as Area No. _____ and described as follows:

## ADDENDUM #2 – EXISTING FRANCHISEES IN AREA OF PROMOTIONAL RESPONSIBILITY

# INTERNATIONAL FRANCHISING

# 18

Throughout this book we have discussed the elements of successful franchising on a local, state, and nationwide level within the United States. As we conclude our text, it's timely to take a look at the possibilities offered by an international franchise program.

Approached correctly, overseas franchising can pay huge dividends and result in an enduringly profitable program. Approached haphazardly, it can lead to false optimism, wasted effort, lost capital, and ultimate failure.

## COMMON MISTAKES TO AVOID

There are a number of "wrong ways" to undertake overseas expansion trying to equate overseas franchisees with American franchisees; it cannot be done. People and attitudes are significantly different in other countries. Rather than trying to mold them to your program, it is usually necessary to mold your program to them. European businesspeople, for example, operate at a much slower pace than their hyperactive American counterparts. It is exceedingly important that you win their trust and confidence.

## CHARACTERISTICS OF THE EUROPEAN FRANCHISEE

Here are some salient facts to consider about the average European prospective franchisee:

1. They want you, as the franchisor, to "get involved." Ideally, they prefer a program wherein you are effectively a partner. Their rationale is this: *"If you think your program is good, fine—however, let's see you share both the risk **and** the benefits with me."*

2. They do not mind paying royalties (particularly when related to achievable earnings). Usually, in fact, they are accustomed to paying larger royalties than we are, here in the United States.

3. They will resent and resist paying substantial front-load franchise fees. This resistance has probably led to the growth of a number of vertical-type fran-

chised operations overseas, enabling the franchisor to achieve the desired earnings from products thereby minimizing needed franchise fees. One hamburger franchise, for example, has been spectacularly successful, with over 500 franchised operations. The so-called front money and royalty are minimal. However, because the overseas entrepreneurs were in the meat-packing business, they were able to achieve their adequate collateral earnings from product sales while offering their franchisees a price comparable to that offered on the market.

4. There is a European trend for franchisors to tie-in with existing related operations, rather than follow the route of recruiting individual franchisees on a one-by-one basis. These existing businesses are generally those that seek diversification. Let's look at a few examples:

   • A European department-store chain committed itself as a franchisee for a franchised quick-copy business, acquiring seven units as a first phase.

   • Another department store committed itself to the establishment of 40 franchised units in the fast-food field.

   • One franchisor was highly successful in selling drain- and sewer-cleaning franchises to plumbers and other related businesses.

   • An organization called "Sight and Sound" licenses equipment that teaches touch-typing in ten one-hour lessons through an electronic system. Now operating in some 24 countries, at the outset, it franchised newspaper offices which, in turn, conducted schools that were advertised to the public via the respective papers.

5. Large overseas supplier organizations often show interest in becoming the equivalent of a master franchisee and acquiring franchise rights to a large area or even one or more countries. It offers potential for other U.S. franchisors seeking to go overseas. Thus they may avail themselves of local expertise, facilities, and supply sources simultaneously—in addition to an already established operational organization with expert personnel in a related field. For example, a grocery-type franchise business may want to consider a large grocery wholesaler as a master franchisee.

6. European franchisees have a great respect for USA know-how. It's their feeling that whatever comes from this country may possibly represent the ultimate in marketing accomplishment, but they'll lean on *you* to prove out the success in *their* instance. They are accustomed to their own pace and their own attitudes. You can't effect cultural changes, so you must build around them. One U.S.-initiated, car-rental franchise, for example, required several modifications until the organization reached the point at which it became "tuned in" to the franchisee. By adapting to the franchisee, rather than struggling to have the franchisee adapt to the program, handsome dividends were achieved.

7. Overseas franchisees move slowly, and are ordinarily less money-motivated than those in the United States. Other outstanding qualities offset this. They will work hard for less money. Labor and other operational costs are frequently lower than in the States. Yet in many cases the charges for the

product or service are comparable to U.S. prices, thus giving the American franchisor a potentially higher margin of profit.

8. There is a marked difference overseas in sites and structures. There are very few drive-in sites available; hence a U.S. drive-in operation often must adapt to a store-front operation overseas. You will find, however, that this is not a serious handicap. The typical European is accustomed to doing a lot of walking and doesn't expect or even desire the drive-in convenience that Americans demand. Many ride bicycles and motorbikes. It's quaint but customary to see elderly women—literally by the dozens—riding their bicycles to the market. Business executives do likewise: The president of one large French investment firm travels a number of miles to and from work every day on his motorbike, zig-zagging in and out among traffic complete with a helmet, goggles. . . and attache case!

9. The facades of stores and other structures are generally different from designs we're accustomed to here at home. Old buildings and other structures are the accepted norm, in fact, many zoning regulations restrict drastic modernization. Signs are subdued. Hence it may behoove you to accept a "reblended image" of your own structure in conformance to a particular country. One successful franchised hamburger operation resembles a "pub" in England and a *bierstube* in Germany. Another fast-food operation came in from the States and failed to research the proper image for its products and structure. Reports indicate that this franchisor lost over $200,000 in its prototype operation.

10. Financing is all-important overseas. There is little highly speculative venture capital as we know it in the States. There are, however, "merchant" banks and bankers who may finance desirable concepts or proven ventures. There are also independent individual and group investors. In most instances, however, you will have to *prove* your earnings and the viability of your operation before you can expect to receive financing. If you are franchising through an existing respected operation (such as a department store), frequently you can obtain almost unlimited credit from banks because of the status and repute of the existing franchisee. Here it clearly becomes a matter of the tail wagging the dog.

11. The varying legalities from country to country tend to be complex. The English code regulates the United Kingdom, the Napoleonic code governs France, and Italy has its own complex codes. It is important to enlist the aid of competent native legal counsel. European laws frequently do not resemble ours. Often, for example, stockholders cannot shield themselves behind the corporate organization in the event of bankruptcy.

12. When you are selling franchises, you'll find that typical Europeans are slow in making decisions. You have to recognize that their "I am interested" is merely polite conversation and does not necessarily mean "Yes." Even when they say "Yes," it may only mean "Maybe." They will not be pushed into buying; you must adjust to longer sales-closing intervals than you've experienced in the States. In many instances, bargaining is *expected* as a normal prerogative, and Europeans tend to reject the first price arbitrarily.

13. Possibly even more damaging than litigation is the almost spontaneous public indignation generated in the event a franchise operation is deemed to "do wrong" by the franchisee. It is not unusual for a local newspaper to do its own in-depth investigation and feature a full-page expose of the allegedly errant franchise operation. Word-of-mouth exposure is another factor, and it's amazing how fast and far it can travel. Once an operation is stigmatized it can never restore itself to status quo.

14. European tastes and attitudes are different from ours. The food products that win favor in the States may prove unpalatable overseas. You will want to research carefully and orient your product. Europeans drink warm beer, for example, and rarely serve water. When they do, they don't add ice.

On the other hand, one American franchise openly flouted all these traditions. Using the unlikely name of "The Great American Disaster," it sold hamburgers for the fantastic price of $1.25 (at that time approximately three times the normal price of a hamburger) each and served water with ice. Not only did the name and price differ from the usual, but so did the taste—it was a uniquely American departure from the customary bland taste of similar products. Yet the operation was almost immediately successful, with customers actually queuing up outside the store. The question is *Why?* It's like the story of the bumble bee: Anatomically, it *can't possibly* fly. Yet it does!

## RECOMMENDED STEPS FOR ENTERING THE INTERNATIONAL MARKET—A REVIEW

1. Carefully assess the feasibility of your product or your service for the particular countries you plan to enter. It is essential to conduct a thorough on-the-spot market-research program in each of these countries.

2. Determine the necessary program modifications to adjust your product or service to each country.

3. Assess your ability to deliver the needed products or equipment at a competitive economically viable price. Determine which type of overseas suppliers can be obtained and under what conditions?

4. Determine your financing channels. What type of financing and what sources? At what point can you resort to Eurodollars?

5. Plan competent overseas representation to implement your program.

6. Phase-in one or two countries at a time. Don't try to digest the entire hemisphere in one gulp. There's enough potential and enough to do, just working one country at a time. Take care not to overextend yourself.

## SOME SCHOLARLY DOCUMENTATION— THE DE PAUL UNIVERSITY STUDY

A study of the status and potential of international franchising was conducted some years ago by the Department of Marketing at De Paul University, Chicago. It was concluded that franchising, by definition, is a form of licensing, and, by implication, is a means of knowledge transfer. As such, it was considered a legitimate area for research. These scholars then embarked upon a study of international franchising by United States firms that encompassed the entire scope of operations, from the initial decision to expand abroad to the impact of their franchising on the local cultural setting.

The study concentrated on seventeen United-States firms operating abroad. Included were two firms in automotive products and services, two in business aids and services, four fast-food restaurants, two hotel/motel chains, two automobile and truck-rental companies, one laundry and drycleaning service, three home-improvement, maintenance and cleaning services, and one beverage/soft-drink operation. All represented some type of extension of multinational corporate operations.

The study recommends that before a company undertakes a foreign marketing strategy, it examine the characteristics of the market based on geography, demographic and cultural characteristics, level of socioeconomic development, and political climate.

One approach is to consider each country as a separate market and to develop separate marketing policies and strategies for each individual country. Another is to identify countries having similar characteristics and construct marketing programs for each *group* of countries. A third approach is to view the entire world as a single market in which consumers everywhere have the same or similar characteristics.

The third approach was followed by one firm in the study, but the rest of the companies embraced the first strategy, under which the international market was regarded as a series of homogeneous national markets. This separate-market approach is rooted in the practical consideration of the cultural and sub-cultural differences among nations, including lifestyles and standards of living.

In support of this approach it was illustrated that a company offering home-improvement, maintenance and cleaning services markets its products in France through personal selling and house calls by company salespeople. In Germany, however, the same services are sold through plumbers' shops, because the German consumer traditionally purchases all household water equipment and plumbing fixtures through a plumber. Neither does the German consumer react favorably to house calls or door-to-door solicitations. German families maintain personal relationships with their plumbers, whom they regard as skilled craftspeople and individuals to be trusted. On the other hand, in France, maintenance service is expected as a free and natural extension of the product purchase.

The study advised that companies contemplating expansion into foreign markets by means of the franchising techniques should, first, consider the market from two viewpoints: (1) *characteristics of the host country,* and (2) *consumer characteristics* of that marketing area.

1. **Characteristics of the host country.** Here it was recommended that market analysis consider the following areas for study:

a ) *Characteristics of physical geography.* This includes the geographic location, the size of the country, land formations and attributes of the terrain, the presence of rivers and bodies of water, plus climatic conditions.

b) *Demographic population characteristics.* These relate to the size and composition of the population and include age distribution, education, class structure, and the ethnic composition of the society.

c) *Level of socio-economic development.* This is measurable in a number of ways depending upon criteria relevant to the firm, such as Gross National

Product per capita, number of automobiles in the population, and disposable income per capita. The assumption here is that the level of a country's economic development greatly influences the level of consumption of both industrial and consumer goods and services; thus it is an index of the readiness of the society to accept the franchising concept.

d) *Urban configuration.* This is evaluated in terms of the number, size, and distribution of cities throughout the country, and includes a city's internal organization, development, and complexity. The spatial and economic relationships between industrial, commercial, and residential sectors affect the locations and therefore affect the prospect of success for a franchise.

e) *Language.* The linguistic affiliation of the host country influences the market.

f) *Cultural characteristics and patterns.* These pervade every aspect of individual and organizational behavior. They influence attitudes, values, and beliefs, the ownership and use of material possessions, and how people use space.

g) *Political factors.* These may influence or place constraints upon both consumption and the company's local operations. Both cultural and political factors greatly influence the type and intensity of franchise promotion.

h) *Economic and legal constraints.* These include various forms of governmental involvement in the economic sphere, and thereby greatly influence the nature and extent of demand for a firm's products and services. Aside from the economic constraints on consumption, legal regulations may affect the amount of ownership, site location selection, the treatment and compensation of employees, retail prices, the source of products, the type and amount of advertising used, the degree of trademark protection, and the repatriation of profits.

i) *Market conditions.* Included in this sphere are such things as the sophistication of the marketplace, business attitudes and practices, the state and level of technology, and the stage of product life cycle domestically and internationally.

j) *Development of communications media.* Demographic variables in the population affect this characteristic, which involves the types and availability of printed media, the literacy of the people, the sophistication and availability of the electronic media, and the ownership of radio and television sets. Essentially, the development of the communications media must be related to the compatibility of the franchisor's offering.

k) *Product-bound culture and lifestyle characteristics.* Those cultural values and elements of lifestyle that affect attitudes towards specific products must be considered. They affect the demand and consumption of the product or service, the acceptance of the brand name or trademark, plus acceptance of the fact that the product and the concept originate in the United States. Ultimately these things lead to acceptance or rejection of the franchising concept. Initially, introduction into the host country often makes the acceptance of the franchise concept as important—if not *more* important—than selling the new product or service. When evaluating a foreign market, the firm must consider the value the local people place upon knowledge and the acquisition of new knowledge or ideas. It must be determined whether or not local culture or lifestyle characteristics will present barriers to franchising and demand the types of goods and services offered.

2. **Consumer Characteristics.** This examination should retrace the previous general and specific country characteristics. It is a second level of analysis based on real and observable national differences. Conducted carefully, it should help determine how to service the market with a minimum of tactical errors.

The study indicates that the extent of market research required, as well as the number of items and variables which must be considered, are greater for foreign markets than for the United States. Most franchisors who were surveyed used their local franchisee as a source of marketing information and local problem-solver. It is felt that the local franchisee can supply maximum information concerning the most appropriate and effective media use, consumer tastes and preferences, local products, parts sources, channels of distribution, and site selection.

The study reiterates the fact that foreign-market success depends more upon how the franchisor's goods and services are promoted within the context of the local market than upon the actual nature of those goods and services.

Most firms alter their overseas advertising to fit the local market. The only country where U.S. advertising can be used without modification is Japan, where American television commercials are actually shown unchanged except for voice dubbing! Even printed advertising is used in Japan with little or no format change—only the language is different.

In other countries, however, ad creation and cooperative advertising with franchisees are tailored to the local market. The franchisor sends his ad package abroad; then, through consultation with the local ad agency or franchisee, advertisements are created specifically for the local market. In most cases American franchisors prefer printed rather than electronic media when advertising abroad, because radio and television there are not as sophisticated as they are here. Despite problems with some newspapers and magazines, franchisors continue to use them as the best alternative for local advertising. Wherever possible, advertising is done in city and regional newspapers.

Alternatives to mass-media advertising include couponing, direct-mail, brochures, door-to-door leaflet distribution, and point-of-purchase display. Most of these techniques are used more extensively abroad than in the United States.

In closing, a word of caution seems in order. As domestic markets approach the point of diminishing returns for certain firms, overseas expansion becomes an irresistible boardroom pressure. You are urged to proceed thoughtfully and cautiously. Before your company implements the foreign-market-expansion policy decision, you must study, research, and observe. It is essential to "taste," "feel," and "smell" these local foreign markets *before* you commit your dollars!

## DATE DUE

| | |
|---|---|
| 4 14 '83 | |
| 5. 12. '83 | |
| 6. 09. 83 | |
| returned 7/14 | |
| 10 01 '86 | |
| 2. 25. '87 | |
| | |
| 8 25 '87 | |
| ILL 8295398 | |
| | |
| | |
| | |
| | |
| | |
| | |
| | |

BRODART, INC.    Cat. No. 23-221